Justice
Oliver Wendell Holmes

II

THE PROVING YEARS
1870–1882

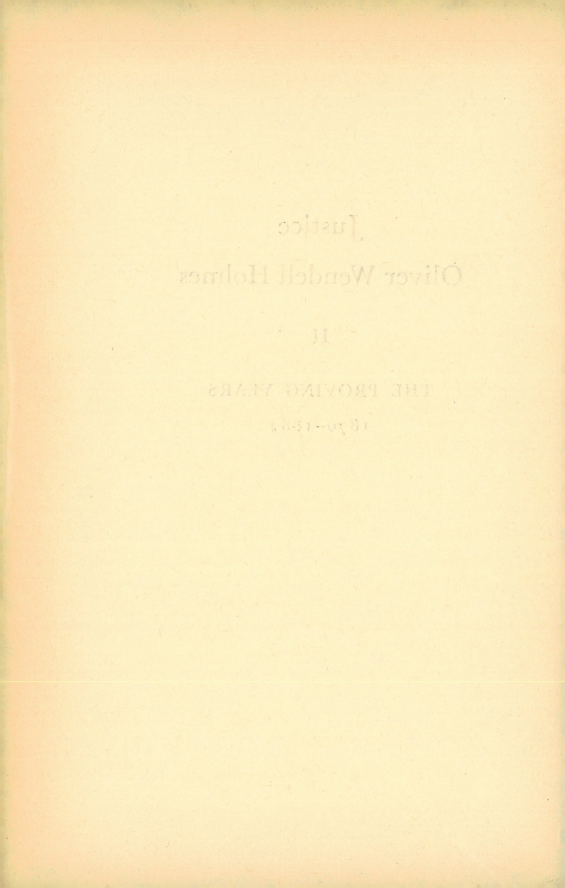

Holmes at the age of thirty-one
(1872)

Justice
Oliver Wendell Holmes

THE PROVING YEARS
1870–1882

By

Mark DeWolfe Howe

II

1 9 6 3

THE BELKNAP PRESS OF

HARVARD UNIVERSITY PRESS

Cambridge, Massachusetts

Distributed in Great Britain by
OXFORD UNIVERSITY PRESS, LONDON

Library of Congress Catalog Card Number 63–10867
Printed in the United States of America

Foreword

Thomas Beven in the preface to his *Principles of the Law of Negligence* quoted a reflection ascribed to Sir Roger L'Estrange: "Most Prefaces are effectually apologies, and neither the Book nor the Author one jot the better for them. If the book be good, it will not need an apology; if bad, it will not bear one; for where a man thinks by calling himself noddy in the epistle to atone for showing himself to be one in the text, he does, with respect to the dignity of an author, but bind up two fools in one cover." These cautionary words restrain me from giving an extensive account of my effort in this second volume of my biography of Holmes. It may nonetheless be appropriate for me to say a few preliminary words.

The short span of twelve years traversed in this volume was, in many senses, an uneventful period in the life of Holmes. The story which I tell is not built upon the chronicles of war, nor is it drawn from the records of public affairs. It is the account of a young man's progress towards intellectual accomplishment. Because Holmes had chosen to work his way towards that goal by the pathway of the law, I have felt compelled to follow the route of Holmes's choosing, though some readers may find it is a little dusty. A short cut might have led me through clearer air to the same crossing. It seemed to me, however, that the way towards understanding of Holmes must be that which he selected for his own achievement.

Once more, as in my first volume, I must express especial gratitude for grants from the Jacob Brenner Memorial Foundation and the Philadelphia Community Foundation, Inc. Through their kindness, stimulated by the enthusiasm of Arthur W. A. Cowan, Esquire, of the Philadelphia bar, a leave of absence from teaching facilitated the completion of this volume.

M. DeW. H.

Cambridge, Massachusetts
9 November 1962

CONTENTS

ILLUSTRATIONS

Justice
Oliver Wendell Holmes

II

THE PROVING YEARS
1870–1882

ABBREVIATIONS AND SHORT TITLES

CL   Holmes, *The Common Law* (Boston, 1881)

CLP   Holmes, *Collected Legal Papers* (New York, 1920)

HLL   *Holmes-Laski Letters* (2 vols., Cambridge, Mass., 1953)

HLS   Harvard Law School

HPL   *Holmes-Pollock Letters* (2 vols., Cambridge, Mass., 1941)

LC   Library of Congress

OS   *The Occasional Speeches of Justice Oliver Wendell Holmes* (Cambridge, Massachusetts, 1962)

Commentaries James Kent, *Commentaries on American Law*, 12th Edition, edited by O. W. Holmes, Jr. (4 vols., Boston, 1873)

Shaping Years Mark DeWolfe Howe, *Justice Oliver Wendell Holmes: The Shaping Years, 1841–1870* (Cambridge, Massachusetts, 1957)

I

The Stars and the Plough

On March 8, 1870, Oliver Wendell Holmes, Jr., counselor-at-law, reached the age of twenty-nine. The searing experience of war lay six years behind him, and in the intervening stretch of time he had worked his way through varying temptations of interest and inclination to the crucial resolve that he would seek for eminence not in letters or philosophy but in law. That decision, of course, was but the starting point for choice. The calling of a lawyer may be that of advocate, counselor, scholar, teacher, man of affairs. If a contemporary observer did not look beyond the fact that Holmes had committed himself to the profession of the law it would have seemed quite possible that the gifted young man might find each path towards eminence equally appealing. Yet there were already signs that his hopes for accomplishment were turning him down that pathway of the law which promised an ending in the neighborhood of philosophy. His friendships and enthusiasms outside the profession (and within it as well) indicated that he would not be content with the worldly ways of the pedestrian. Surely it was evident to those who knew him best that he would not voluntarily take that turning which would bring him the easy successes of respectable Boston—the achievements, for instance, of a staid trustee—or choose the harder course, through politics, towards power. For Holmes already had shown himself to be by temperament an intellectual, bearing that special stamp which Dr. Holmes considered to mark the Brahmin caste of New England.

1

Justice Oliver Wendell Holmes

There are races of scholars among us, in which aptitude for learning, and all [its] marks . . . are congenital and hereditary. Their
names are always on some college catalogue or other. They break out
every generation or two in some learned labor which calls them up
after they seem to have died out. At last some newer name takes their
place, it may be,—but you inquire a little and you find it is the blood of
the Edwardses or the Chauncys or the Ellerys or some of the old historic scholars, disguised under the altered name of a female descendant.[1]

Though the genealogist may not be able to trace the inheritance of
the younger Holmes back to the headwaters of New England learning there can be no question, I think, but that the young lawyer's
affiliations of mind and sympathy had early shown themselves to
be more with the Brahmins than with the merchants of New England.

In the April evenings of 1897—more than twenty-five years
after Holmes had chosen the path of the law as the roadway to
achievement—he and his wife read aloud Nansen's recently published story of his arctic journey across the polar ice. It would be
easy to see this episode in reading as the touching effort of two
middle-aged Bostonians to escape in imagination beyond the
placid waters of the Back Bay and above the gentle slope of Beacon Hill to a more exciting world of challenge and of danger. On
the face of things it would seem unlikely that either of the readers,
seated in the tranquil security of Beacon Street, could find in the
pages of their lives events or aspirations related to those recounted
in *Farthest North*. Of course there were moral and scientific—even
philosophical—lessons to be learned from Nansen's story, and
Holmes was not slow to indicate that some of these he had learned.
Within a month of his reading of Nansen he used the example of
the explorer's fortitude to sustain the skeptical thesis that there
may be "no true measure of men except the total of human energy
which they embody—counting everything, with due allowance for

[1] From *Elsie Venner*, in *The Complete Writings of Oliver Wendell Holmes*
(Boston, 1900), V, 4.

quality, from Nansen's power to digest blubber or to resist cold, up to his courage, or to Wordsworth's power to express the unutterable, or to Kant's speculative reach." [2] A few weeks later, in a brief Commencement address at Brown University, Holmes made it clear that he had read the story of heroism not only as a general lesson in moral philosophy but as a parable which bespoke the longing and the discipline from which he had built his own achievement. He took that ceremonial occasion to report to the young men who were about to start on their journey from the University something of his own experiences, "and to give a hint of what is to be expected on the way." The images by which he brightened the story of his own professional life were taken from Nansen's world of exploration.

My way has been by the ocean of the Law . . . There were few of the charts and lights for which one longed when I began. One found oneself plunged in a thick fog of details — in a black and frozen night, in which were no flowers, no spring, no easy joys. Voices of authority warned that in the crush of that ice any craft might sink . . . One saw that artists and poets shrank from it as from an alien world. One doubted oneself how it could be worthy of the interest of an intelligent mind. And yet one said to oneself, law is human—it is a part of man, and of one world with all the rest. There must be a drift, if one will go prepared and have patience, which will bring one out to daylight and a worthy end. You have all read or heard the story of Nansen and see the parallel which I use. Most men of the college-bred type in some form or other have to go through that experience of sailing for the ice and letting themselves be frozen in. [3]

It was in the concluding portion of his reflections on his own career that Holmes gave us the outline of its structure. He spoke of its earliest beginnings—of "the first stage, [in which] one has companions" and in which, if he sticks to it,

2 "George Otis Shattuck," *The Occasional Speeches of Justice Oliver Wendell Holmes* (Cambridge, Mass., 1962), 95.

3 "Commencement Address—Brown University, June 17, 1897," *Occasional Speeches* (hereafter *OS*), 97–98; Holmes *Collected Legal Papers* (New York, 1920), 164–165.

3

he finds at last that there is a drift as was foretold. When he has found that he has learned the first part of his lesson, that one is safe in trusting to courage and to time. But he has not yet learned all. So far his trials have been those of his companions. But if he is a man of high ambitions he must leave even his fellow-adventurers and go forth into a deeper solitude and greater trials. He must start for the pole. In plain words he must face the loneliness of original work. No one can cut out new paths in company. He does that alone.[4]

If it is fair, as I believe it is, to read this passage as the rough tracing of the course which Holmes's professional life had followed, it is appropriate to look upon the period with which this volume is concerned as the second stage in exploration. In his very first years at the bar Holmes had enjoyed the companionship of questing friends—some of them, like John C. Gray and John C. Ropes, also lawyers; others, like William James and Chauncey Wright, philosophers. In their company he had come to believe that the drift of a lawyer's accomplishment need not be towards the traditional successes of the profession, but could be towards a larger achievement. In 1870, or thereabouts, he made what was perhaps the most important decision of his professional life, the decision to leave his fellow adventurers and go forth into "a deeper solitude" than he had yet known. It was to be the solitude of the thinker.

It may seem that this translation of an orator's rhetoric into a speaker's self-revelation is a distorting conversion of fancy into fact. There is much evidence, however, to support the conviction that for ten years or more, beginning in 1870, Holmes sought to lead that dedicated life of thought of which he spoke when he addressed the graduating class at Brown and of which, in somewhat less personal terms he also spoke in 1886 when addressing students at Harvard College.

Only when you have worked alone—when you have felt around you a black gulf of solitude more isolating than that which surrounds the dying man, and in hope and in despair have trusted to your own unshaken will—then only will you have achieved. Thus only can you

4 *Id.*

4

gain the secret isolated joy of the thinker, who knows that, a hundred years after he is dead and forgotten, men who never heard of him will be moving to the measure of his thought—the subtle rapture of a postponed power, which the world knows not because it has no external trappings, but which to his prophetic vision is more real than that which commands an army.[5]

Throughout 1872, while Holmes was living in his father's household, first as a bachelor and after June as husband of Fanny Dixwell, the last of Dr. Holmes's Breakfast Table series, *The Poet at the Breakfast Table,* was appearing in the pages of the *Atlantic Monthly.* A central character in that series was the young Astronomer: "a strange unearthly being; lonely, dwelling far apart from the thoughts and cares of the planet on which he lives,—an enthusiast who gives his life to knowledge . . ."[6] The Astronomer, most conveniently for the Doctor's purposes, was secretly a poet. Among his efforts in reflective verse were lines on fame, lines which repudiated "the stained laurel such as heroes wear," and praised, instead, the sense

> That in the unshaped ages, buried deep
> In the dark mines of unaccomplished time
> Yet to be stamped with morning's royal die
> And coined in golden days,—in those dim years
> I shall be reckoned with the undying dead,
> My name emblazoned on the fiery arch,
> Unfading till the stars themselves shall fade.[7]

The young Astronomer's poetic hopes are so like the young Holmes's dream of postponed power that we may accept, without serious doubt, the suggestion of a discerning biographer of Doctor Holmes that he modeled his Astronomer's character on that of his eldest child.[8] The Astronomer had insisted that "the noblest service comes from nameless hands" and had asked a series of hopeful questions:

[5] "The Profession of the Law," *OS,* 30–31.
[6] *Complete Writings,* III, 59.
[7] *Id.,* 144–145.
[8] Eleanor M. Tilton, *Amiable Autocrat: A Biography of Dr. Oliver Wendell Holmes* (New York, 1947), 309–310.

Who found the seeds of fire and made them shoot,
Fed by his breath, in buds and flowers of flame?
Who forged in roaring flames the ponderous stone
And shaped the moulded metal to his need?
Who gave the dragging car its rolling wheel,
And tamed the steed that whirls it circling round?
All these have left their work and not their names,—
Why should I murmur at a fate like theirs? [9]

When his turn came to speak of similar problems, Holmes asked similar questions. "Who invented the wheel, or ships, or the city, or contracts? Who first used a future tense or spoke of conscience or the freedom of the will?" Like his father's Astronomer, Holmes found final satisfaction in the thought that "even in matters of general import we owe vastly more to the forgotten than to the remembered." [10]

Doctor Holmes wrote not only of the Astronomer's ambitions and his solitude but of his almost studied search for heartlessness. Early installments of *The Poet at the Breakfast Table,* written before Holmes's engagement to Fanny Dixwell was announced, introduced the figure of Scheherazade—or, more simply, the Young Girl—to whose tender devotion the Astronomer for many months preserved a cold indifference. When Doctor Holmes reproached the Astronomer for his prolonged failure to warm his hands "just for a little while in a human consciousness" was he not, perhaps, scolding his son for his apparent indifference to the affection of Fanny Dixwell? [11] Was not the Doctor expressing some of that same disapprobation of his son's postponement of true engagement which was implied in the comment of a young friend both of Holmes and of Fanny Dixwell, when she heard of their forthcoming marriage: "O.W.H. has gone up in my opinion most amazingly since [the engagement] came out. I have always liked him very much but never quite believed in his disinterestedness even in his affections—and I feel quite ashamed now I think I have not appreciated him better. I think she is just the wife for him & I can

9 *Complete Writings,* III, 146.
10 "Anonymity and Achievement," *OS,* 59, 60.
11 *Complete Writings,* III, 141.

quite conceive of their being happy 'ever after.' " [12] Ten years earlier, the Doctor had felt no hesitation in giving the American public a full account of his hunt after the Captain. Was he not once more inviting his readers to look upon the disguised figure of his son and to share with a father the hope that the lonely thinker would come to see the living world around him, "to feel the breath of a young girl against his cheek . . . But our young man seems farther away from life than any student whose head is bent downwards over his books." [13] "If he would only fall in love with her, seize upon her wandering affections and fancies as the Romans seized the Sabine virgins, lift her out of herself and her listless and weary drudgeries . . . dear me, dear me—if, if, if— . . . I am afraid all this may never be. I fear that he is too much given to lonely study, to self-companionship, to all sorts of questionings, to looking at life as at a solemn show where he is only a spectator." [14]

By the time that these paternal hopes and fears were published in the *Atlantic Monthly*, the engagement and marriage of Holmes and Fanny Dixwell had occurred. On March 11, 1872, the Doctor had written to a friend telling him that in two days the engagement of his son was "to come out." He went on to say that he and Mrs. Holmes "both knew her well and love her much. She is a most superior lady in every respect, and the attachment rivals that of Edward in duration and constancy. They did not see their way to marriage and consequently have not called themselves engaged until quite recently, though it was plain enough that they were entirely devoted to each other." [15] On the same day, the younger Holmes wrote to Mrs. Kennedy, his post-Antietam hostess in Hagerstown, Maryland, announcing his engagement and stating that his fiancée had been "for many years my most intimate friend." [16]

Do these contemporary accounts of the devoted and prolonged

[12] Rose Hooper (later Mrs. Gordon Bowles) to Eleanor Shattuck Whiteside, March 17, 1872 (Shattuck Papers, Massachusetts Historical Society).

[13] *Complete Writings*, III, 142.

[14] *Id.*, 238.

[15] To "Dear Charles" (Harvard Law School, hereafter HLS). Holmes's younger brother, Edward, had married Henrietta Wigglesworth in October 1871.

[16] See *Maryland Historical Magazine*, 33:121 (1938).

intimacy of Holmes and Fanny Dixwell suggest that it is a distortion to read some of Doctor Holmes's comments on the chilled intellectualism of the Astronomer as sermons to his son? To exaggerate the similarities between portrait and subject would, of course, misrepresent the nature of Doctor Holmes's effort. Yet it well may be that even after Holmes and Fanny Dixwell were married Dr. Holmes thought that his son should change his old habits of intellectual ambition for the more human ways of sympathy. One may fairly wonder whether, when Fanny joined the Doctor's household on Beacon Street, she did not do so with a clear understanding that her husband's dedication would be no different from that of the young man who had been her most intimate friend. Already he had set forth on his lonely voyage of ambition, and it seems likely that it was understood by his wife that he would not permit the conventional burdens of marriage to distract him from his search for the goals of achievement which he had already chosen for himself.[17] It was an article of his faith, furthermore, "that if a man was to do anything he must do it before 40." [18] This

[17] Among the avoidable burdens, there is some reason to believe that Holmes counted children. It seems not unlikely that it was by his decision that no children were born of the marriage. Writing to Lewis Einstein on August 31, 1928, Holmes recounted an anecdote which he had often told to others: "Once at dinner in England Sir Fitzroy Kelly on hearing that we had no children said 'Le bon temps viendra.' " To that recollection of a trivial incident Holmes added a significant gloss: "But I am so far abnormal that I am glad that I have [no children]. It might be said that to have them is part of the manifest destiny of man, as of other creatures, and that he should accept his destiny as he accepts his destiny to strive—but the latter he can't help—and part of his destiny is to choose." (Autograph letter, Library of Congress, hereafter LC. Copy at HLS.) There was another time described by Judge Learned Hand: "We were sitting together in the library some time after his wife's death. I do not know how I ventured on so intimate a subject, but in some way the question did come up, and I said to him: 'Mr. Justice have you ever been sorry that you never had any children?' He said nothing; he did not look at me, he waited for a perceptible time and then said very quietly (still not looking at me): 'This is not the kind of world I want to bring anyone else into.' " (Autograph letter and memorandum to the author, April 29, 1959, HLS.)

[18] Holmes to Mrs. Charles S. Hamlin, Oct. 12, 1930 (copy, HLS). See also *Holmes-Laski Letters* (Cambridge, Mass., 1953), I, 793; Felix Frankfurter, "Oliver Wendell Holmes, 1841–1935," *Dictionary of American Biography;* reprinted in Frankfurter, *Mr. Justice Holmes and the Supreme Court* (Cambridge, 1961), 12. A more aphoristic version of the same belief has been ascribed to Holmes: "If you

fervent sense of urgency deeply colored the nine years which spanned the interval between his marriage and the given deadline for achievement. It is hard to believe that Fanny Dixwell did not realize that, at least for those years, his striving would be far more for an accomplishment of a public mind than for an achievement of a private devotion. The devotion, doubtless, was true and strong but it was not to be permitted to soften his resolution that he would establish his eminence in the world of intellect before ten years had passed.

The marriage service of the nominally Unitarian couple was, surprisingly, Episcopalian and was performed in Christ Church in Cambridge by Phillips Brooks on June 17, 1872.[19] No records seem to survive which indicate that there was even a wedding journey for the young couple. Two days before his marriage Holmes was reading Heineccius, *Recitationes in elementa juris civilis,* and three weeks after the event he had finished Kant's *Éléments métaphysiques de la doctrine du droit* and had completed the writing of his second major essay on classification of the law.[20] Between these two works the only volume included in his reading list was Rhoda Broughton's *"Goodbye, Sweetheart!"*—a volume fitting in its sentiment, if not in its title, to mark the beginning of a marriage. Yet the young Holmes, married, remained in mind, if not in heart, the young Astronomer. Rhoda Broughton quickly gave way to Kant, to Bentham, and to Fustel de Coulanges.[21]

The weight of professional commitments which Holmes had assumed by the time of his marriage in 1872 was very great. Prac-

---

haven't cut your name on the door of fame by the time you've reached 40, you might just as well put up your jackknife" (Harvey C. Lehman, *Age and Achievement,* Princeton, 1953, 186) .

[19] Unhappily I have not been able to find any friend's account of the wedding. On July 5, 1872, Henry James, Jr., writing to his parents, said: "Father's account of Wendell Holmes's marriage was interesting, but we would fain have known how Miss Dixwell looked" (letter in Houghton Library) . The letter of Henry James, Sr., has not been located.

[20] "The Arrangement of the Law—Privity," *American Law Review,* 7:46 (October 1872) ; reprinted, *Harvard Law Review,* 44:738 (March 1931) .

[21] See Eleanor Little, "The Early Reading of Justice Oliver Wendell Holmes," *Harvard Library Bulletin,* 8:163, 184–185 (Spring, 1954) .

ticing law in association with his younger brother,[22] occasionally joining Mr. Shattuck in court proceedings,[23] editing the *American Law Review* with Arthur G. Sedgwick, lecturing at Harvard College, and preparing in four volumes the 12th edition of Kent's *Commentaries on American Law,* were the demanding responsibilities which he carried—most of them at the same time—between 1870 and 1873.[24] The burden of merely administrative obligation must have been very heavy. While it was borne by one whose intellectual conscience required familiarity with current learning in many fields of knowledge, and whose ambition set creative achievement as its goal, it is not surprising that his friends found that his "pallid face, and this fearful grip upon his work, [made] him a melancholy sight." [25] Marriage, it seems clear, did not significantly change the way of life which Holmes had chosen. There are no indications that his wife allowed herself to want it otherwise. Her dedication from the very first to the very last was to his welfare, therefore to his aspiration. For at least the first ten years of their marriage the story of their life was, in its essentials, the story of his striving for and achievement of intellectual eminence.

The decision which Holmes had made in 1869 to involve himself deeply in the preparation of a new edition of Kent's *Commen-*

[22] Edward Jackson Holmes, following his graduation from the Harvard Law School in 1869, had gone to Washington as secretary to Senator Sumner. He returned to Boston in March 1871, and shared offices at 7 Pemberton Square with his brother and another young practitioner, Isaac Taylor Hoague. Edward Holmes's classmate, Edward Jackson Lowell, stated that the Holmes brothers, though they had shared an office from 1871 to 1873, were not in partnership (*Class of 1867, Secretary's Report No. 8,* Boston, 1887, 19).

[23] See *Young v. City of Boston,* 104 Mass. 95 (1870); *The Becherdass Ambaidass,* 1 Lowell 569 (1871). The Harvard Law School's copy of the plaintiff's brief in the *Young* case has interlineations in Holmes's hand and the Court's docket of cases, evidently that of Mr. Justice Gray, indicates that Holmes argued the case before the full Court on March 18, 1870. The position argued by Holmes was sustained. *The Becherdass Ambaidass,* which was won by Shattuck and Holmes, was commented on in the *American Law Review,* 6:74, 743 (1871).

[24] See Howe, *Justice Oliver Wendell Holmes: The Shaping Years* (Cambridge, Mass., 1957), 273.

[25] These were the comments of Mrs. Henry James to her son Henry in 1873 (Ralph Barton Perry, *The Thought and Character of William James,* Boston, 1935, I, 519).

taries may seem surprising. The editor of another man's work may prove his industry and his intelligence; he is unlikely to reveal his own inspiration and his own creativeness. Holmes surely realized that the editorial challenge confronting him would do little to test his constructive capacities or to establish his reputation as an originator. It would, however, do two things. It would force him to make a comprehensive survey of the law—to continue, as it were, his legal education—and it would give him the opportunity, at least on occasion, to suggest by critical annotation of the almost sacred text that new perspectives of learning and philosophy might broaden understanding of law. Kent's earlier editors had, to borrow Carlyle's image, edited the *Commentaries* "as you edit bricks, —by tilting the wagon." Like good and reliable wagoners they had dumped the recent cases in sprawling heaps at the bottom of each page. There they lay, awaiting the builder's hand. Surely Holmes did not become the editor of the 12th edition to prove his skill as wagoner. His finished work, in any case, proved that his gifts of analysis and synthesis, his reach of learning and imagination, were far more impressive than those of a mere journeyman editor.

At the outset of Holmes's involvement in the preparation of a new edition, it seems that his contemplated services were to be of an entirely commonplace sort. James Kent, the Chancellor's grandson, had approached James Bradley Thayer seeking to secure him as editor of the 12th edition. Thayer, busy in practice, was evidently unwilling to assume unassisted responsibility. As the arrangements went forward it was anticipated by Kent and Thayer that the editorial work would be jointly done by Thayer and Holmes. In November of 1869 Thayer had asked Holmes to try his hand at the preparation of the sort of annotations which would be appropriate to a new edition. Early in December Holmes had turned over to Thayer suggested notes to Kent's discussion of easements. On the 10th of that month he sent Thayer some general reflections on the task that lay ahead.

First and above all I esteem it necessary that we should be at liberty to rewrite so far as time allows and we think best, all below the line of original notes.[26] My only fear is that it will prove impossible to do this thoroughly in the time allowed. But so far as we can we must, if we want to do something better than slopwork with which I for one would not associate my name . . . Secondly, although I agree that as you say continence is a great virtue, I cannot but think that if time allows it is desirable that the notes should be somewhat full on points which are the present fighting grounds of the law . . . The apprehension that most haunts me is as to the time allowed. I hate to leave a subject until I feel a certain confidence that I am on the right track at least. You know that I have devoted all my afternoons and a large part of my mornings to the work for the last three weeks or more—and I have hardly been able to attain the necessary pace. If as I hope my business increases it will be still harder. I should like therefore to feel that in a question between time and thoroughness I was to go for the latter so far as I could afford it. The plan which I have laid out is to do the work thoroughly at the first going over and when I am through to put on the finish from the late Digests.[27]

Among the papers of James Bradley Thayer is a copy, in his hand, of a letter addressed to James Kent and bearing the date "Dec. 1869." It seems probable that the original was sent after Thayer had received Holmes's note of the 10th, for it repeated most of Holmes's expressions of preference for thoroughness to punctuality. The letter from Thayer opened with a specific promise:

With the cooperation of Mr. Holmes I undertake to edit a new edition of Kent's Commentaries, which is to be ready to go to press in two years from Dec. 1, 1869. I understand that you wish me to consider myself responsible for the undertaking and I do so. But at the same time it is to be understood that Mr. Holmes is associated with me and that our names are to appear jointly as editors in the preface,—which I am to write if I desire to. But our names are not to appear on the title page . . . As your name is to appear on the title page you reserve the right of passing finally on the work which we shall furnish.

[26] This suggestion, which was followed, meant the retention of all of Chancellor Kent's annotations, without change, and the elimination of virtually all notes of subsequent editors.

[27] To J. B. Thayer, Dec. 10, 1869 (HLS).

Thayer then went on to request that Kent should allow the editors "some grace" should they be unable, "with all reasonable diligence" to have the 12th edition ready in two years. "Mr. Holmes who will have the laboring oar is getting together the material & getting it into shape has already found that the work is going to require pretty close application . . ." Thayer then reiterated the understanding that the editors were to receive $3000 in quarterly payments as compensation for their work.[28]

When the promised edition of the *Commentaries* was published in 1873 the title page carried this entry: "Twelfth Edition, Edited by O. W. Holmes, Jr." The closing paragraph of the Preface, signed by Holmes, expressed the editor's gratitude to his "friend, James B. Thayer, Esq., upon whom has rested the whole responsibility for my work to the owners of the copyright." Holmes went on to say that Thayer had "read all that I have written, and has given it the great benefit of his scholarly and intelligent criticism." Title page and Preface thus indicate that matters had not gone forward as the parties to the arrangement of 1869 had planned that they should.[29] The cooperating participant who was to have the laboring oar had become the editor; Thayer, who had undertaken "to edit a new edition" of the Commentaries, was thanked by the younger man for his scholarly and intelligent criticism. The name of James Kent the younger did not appear on the title page.

In 1882, when Holmes relinquished his professorship at the Harvard Law School, James Bradley Thayer put in his personal memorandum book an embittered account of Holmes's conduct at that time.[30] The memorandum concluded with the following reflection: "My experience with him in editing Kent, which I had been willing to forget, comes all back again & assures me that this

[28] Thayer Papers, HLS.

[29] The contract for publication of the 12th edition by Little, Brown does not, apparently, survive. A "contract card" indicates that the ultimate agreement was signed on February 16, 1871. This suggests the possibility that the arrangements outlined in Thayer's letter of December 1869 were superseded by a subsequent contract.

[30] See *Shaping Years*, 282.

conduct is characteristic,—that he is, with all his attractive qualities & his solid merits, wanting sadly in the noblest region of human character,—selfish, vain, thoughtless of others." [31] Beyond this biting reflection on Holmes's conduct with respect to the editing of Kent, little survives to reveal the basis of Thayer's resentment. In letters written to Thayer when the 12th edition was published, the Chancellor's grandson said that he was "much provoked" that Thayer was not in the first place. "I wanted your *name* and you should have had the reward." When Thayer gave some explanatory word, no copy of which survives, Kent replied: "You are a saint; I am an ordinary mortal." [32]

Some further light is cast on the issue by letters which John Norton Pomeroy wrote to Holmes early in 1874 in connection with a review of the Holmes edition of Kent which he had prepared for *The Nation*. When Pomeroy's enthusiastic notice reached *The Nation*, Arthur G. Sedgwick, Holmes's associate as coeditor of the *American Law Review*, who had recently moved to New York and the editorial board of *The Nation*, suggested to Pomeroy that his review was defective in its failure to refer to Thayer's part in preparing the new Kent. Pomeroy reported to Holmes that he had replied to Sedgwick that the preface "had very fully acknowledged" Mr. Thayer's connection with the work, and, further, that he had been told by Holmes "that Mr. Thayer had been employed by the owners of the copy right & had in turn employed [Holmes]—and as such private matters had no place in a review of the book, I really did not know what to say about Mr. Thayer except some general sort of puff which I thought would be unwished for by Mr. Thayer himself." [33] In the end, however, Pomeroy had complied with Sedgwick's request and had added a brief paragraph making "due acknowledgment of Mr. Thayer's services." [34]

[31] Memorandum Book D., 143–144 (HLS).

[32] James Kent to J. B. Thayer, Dec. 16 and 17, 1873 (HLS).

[33] Pomeroy to Holmes, Feb. 9, 1874 (HLS).

[34] Pomeroy to Holmes, Feb. 15, 1874 (HLS). When the review appeared in the issue of February 12 (18:110), Pomeroy was shocked to find that though the new paragraph was printed, much of the review as he had submitted it, with its commendations of Holmes's work, had been omitted (*Id.*).

From such a scanty record as the few surviving documents provide, it would not be appropriate to draw final conclusions concerning the conduct of Holmes in relationship to Thayer. It seems not unlikely that Holmes seized the opportunity which had come to him to prove his competence and in doing so was not as sensitive to the interests of Thayer as he might have been. He transformed a joint venture in scholarship into an individual achievement and publicly took credit for the accomplishment. A person of more delicate modesty—James Bradley Thayer, for example— would perhaps have thought it better in such circumstances to let credit for individual achievement be shared with one who was nominally a partner in the enterprise. In his first years of aspiration and ambition Holmes was not such a man. The contemplated partnership had not materialized. Holmes had done much more than pull the laboring oar; he had prepared the 12th edition. In July of 1872, less than one month after his marriage, Holmes wrote to Thayer of his continued work on the *Commentaries*.

I have finished my notes . . . on Vols 1 & 2 and on Vol. 3 except the chapter on Insurance which I have begun, find easy, and expect to get through rapidly. I consider that the fourth volume will need comparatively few notes and have devoted my energies especially to the second and third, on which the law has grown immensely. I am expecting to go to press now very shortly . . . I have acted on the desire expressed by Mr. Kent . . . that the time necessary for thorough work should be taken rather than hasten it to its disadvantage, as would have been necessary to finish the notes in two years. I hope the results will not disappoint him. It has been at considerable pecuniary sacrifice that I have done as I have.[35]

There is absolutely no reason to doubt that the 12th edition of Kent was wholly the work of Holmes and that its relatively rapid completion had foreclosed, for him, opportunities in practice similar to those which had come to Thayer and which he had not re-

[35] Copy of letter from Holmes to Thayer, July 15, 1872 (HLS). The handwritten copy, which is among Thayer's papers, carries a notation that the original was sent on to Mr. Kent. It was not until the spring of 1873 that Holmes finally completed work on the 12th edition (letter to T. M. Cooley, April 16, 1873; copy at HLS).

jected.[36] If there was any fault in Holmes's conduct it was nothing more than his unwillingness to hide the light which he had lit and sustained under the bushel which conventional modesty made available.

Holmes's labor to produce the 12th edition of Kent was evidently not inspired by deep admiration for the Chancellor's renowned *Commentaries*. After working on the new edition for two years and a half Holmes said that "I . . . have to keep a civil tongue in my head while I am his valet—but his arrangement is chaotic—he has no general ideas, except wrong ones—and his treatment of special topics is often confused to the last degree. Still," he acknowledged, "he has merits and there is lots of law in his book if you can only find it." [37] The editors who had kept the *Commentaries* alive after the Chancellor's death had not improved the work by their willingness laboriously to assemble "a chaos of cases . . . which lie in a tangled mass across the current of the text, and too often obstruct where they should enlarge." [38] The earlier editors performed their services with respect and piety, proceeding on the comfortable assumption that the eighteenth century's concepts embodied in the Chancellor's text could usefully be kept afloat on a sea of nineteenth-century citations.

To assert that Kent's *Commentaries* were built upon the presuppositions of the eighteenth century is not to say that the Chancellor's learning was that of the antiquarian or that he was unaware of the new demands which another century and another land were making on the principles and traditions of the common law. The *Commentaries* would not have become, as they had become, an indispensable element in the law library of the American practitioner if Kent had spoken with a purely English accent of problems transmitted unaltered from a British past. The book was,

[36] It was not until 1873 that Thayer gave up practice to become Royall Professor at the Harvard Law School.

[37] Holmes to J. N. Pomeroy, May 22, 1872 (copy, HLS).

[38] This was Holmes's comment on earlier editions. It is found in his unsigned review of the 10th edition of Story on Equity, *Am. L. Rev.*, 5:115 (October 1870). Holmes identified himself as author of the review in his copy of the volume, now at the Library of Congress.

however, an expression of the eighteenth century's view, in its conception of what were the questions to which a thoughtful bar and a learned bench should direct their attention. Chancellor Kent, like Blackstone before him, was concerned with what Sir Frederick Pollock called practical or empirical jurisprudence,[39]—with an explication, rather than with an analysis, of the legal concepts of Anglo-American law. Because Kent believed that familiarity with history would add grace to comprehension, he affixed historical embroidery to the tapestry. His jurisprudence did not, however, by that incidental effort in refinement become historical in nature. Though the Chancellor paid sincere respect to Roman law and found it appropriate to devote a chapter to a summary view of its history and its substance, that excursion did not involve a deep commitment to comparative jurisprudence.[40]

To say that Kent showed small concern with the analysis, history, or comparison of legal concepts is to suggest that he was either unaware of or unsympathetic to those tendencies in jurisprudence which were to dominate nineteenth-century thought. He made it abundantly clear that he distrusted such analytic and scientific efforts as Bentham had stimulated.[41] His loyalty was to the elegant order which Blackstone had discovered in the common law. He explicitly indicated distaste for the "new historical school of the civil law [which] has been instituted in Germany" and which was represented by Hugo, Savigny, Eichorn, and Niebuhr. Though "they have undoubtedly enriched the science with acute and searching criticism, and enlarged and philosophical views," Kent could not but be "of opinion (though with much deference) that the importance of the new Germanic school, as contradistinguished from that of the old professors, is greatly exaggerated . . ." [42] The calling of the lawyer is practical, not speculative. The American bench and bar should not, accordingly,

39 "The Methods of Jurisprudence," *Oxford Lectures and Other Discourses* (London, 1890) , 9.

40 Lecture XXIII, "Of The Civil Law," *Commentaries*, I, *515.

41 See the letter of Kent to Edward Livingston, March 13, 1826, *American Jurist*, 16:370 (1837) .

42 *Commentaries*, I, *545, note (b) .

trouble their minds with efforts to analyze the concept of possession, to justify the imposition of liability on a master for acts done by his servant, to discover a basic principle of liability in tort, or to trace rules of testate and intestate succession to their sources. The Anglo-American jurist fulfills his highest responsibility when he explains to lawyers and judges how they may apply the concepts which a benevolent tradition has bequeathed to them.

There can be little doubt that most American lawyers and judges throughout the first half of the nineteenth century saw the problems of jurisprudence as Kent saw them. Those who rejected his conservatism and repudiated his answers did not commonly intimate that he had asked the wrong questions. If English lawyers were slow to see the importance of Austin's analytic efforts or to appreciate the significance of Henry Maine's studies in comparative law, and to feel the repercussions of the continental struggles between the historical and rationalist schools of legal philosophy, it is surely not surprising that the American bar remained, for the most part, satisfied with traditional inquiries and traditional methods. Holmes, of course, was not entirely alone in his recognition that the time for exploration had come. In the Boston community John C. Gray and Nicholas St. John Green, to name but two lawyers, were in their varying ways showing an awareness that questions of a different order from those which Kent and his generation had asked were awaiting consideration. A few American writers and scholars of an older generation—notably William G. Hammond and John Norton Pomeroy—had already begun to broaden the horizons of legal inquiry. Yet it is not surprising that when Holmes set forth on his quest for understanding he saw his mission as an engagement with loneliness.

For a nineteenth-century philosopher and prophet, turned editor, to suggest with a civil tongue that the eighteenth century's presuppositions on which Kent had built his *Commentaries* were inadequate and misleading was a demanding effort in self-control. Probably the average practitioner, using Holmes's edition for his daily professional purposes, saw little beyond the civility and industry with which the editor had fulfilled his responsibility. Much of the annotation was of the sort conventional in the literature of the law, and sought to achieve no more ambitious end than that of providing a serviceable and discriminating compendium of relevant decisions and statutes. Those readers who looked more carefully at Holmes's total achievement, however, were quickly able to see that the editor had a mind of his own, and that the mind was moving with those currents of thought and scholarship which were setting against the traditional streams of doctrine. Holmes's civility cautioned him to editorial silence when Kent, writing of the natural-law foundations of the absolute, individual right of property, used the Book of Genesis as the conclusive refutation of the radical suggestion that communal preceded individual rights of property.[43] Holmes was able, however, at a later point in his annotations, to present a condensed summary of recent learning with respect to village communities in primitive societies, the Germanic, Roman, and Greek origins of property in land, the history of the manorial system in England, descent in Aryan tribes and under the classical law of Rome, and alienation *inter vivos* in Roman and English law.[44] The presentation made it entirely clear that the editor was unwilling to let Biblical authority foreclose or conclude historical inquiry. Surely few practitioners followed the leads which Holmes provided them in this essay into the writings of Nasse, Laveleye, Maine, and Freeman. But such an expedition in scholarship was necessary to make even the casual reader see that Holmes was building his views of history and his philosophy of law on foundations wholly different from those which had satisfied Chancellor Kent.

Though Holmes did not scorn the menial task of assembling relevant cases and statutes, he saw that employment as but a necessary step towards the higher end of building a legal structure which would have an ordered design. The anonymous reviewer in the Boston *Daily Advertiser* (obviously one who knew Holmes personally) perceptively described Holmes's purpose and enthusiastically praised his achievement. "His endeavor . . . is to see and

43 *Id.*, II, *319, note (c) .
44 *Id.*, IV, *441, note 1.

make others see in the law a symmetrical, consistent, intelligible science, not a fagot of independent rules and more or less general principles." The reviewer suggested that Holmes's

tastes and habit of mind have fitted him well for his undertaking. He is a *legal scholar,* a rare spectacle among our active and busy people. He has a natural aptitude for study and research, for the patient collecting and sifting of abundant material. The establishment of a fundamental principle is his especial delight. The tracing of a subtle thread of theory fascinates him. One would conceive from the style of many of his notes that the writings of the metaphysicians had had no small share and influence in his mental training.[45]

John C. Gray's younger brother, Russell Gray, reviewing the Holmes edition anonymously in the *North American Review* called attention to Holmes's intellectual affiliations. Since Kent's time

a class of books . . . has come into fashion [and] a new school of writers and thinkers on legal subjects has appeared of late; men who put their trust in Bentham and Austin, who have revived the study of civil law, who have attempted to collect and compare the legal ideas of many nations, ancient and modern, and who aspire to create or contribute to a consistent, rational, and universal system of jurisprudence, which shall be of general, or even universal, application . . . Mr. Holmes, is, we understand, a disciple of this new school (if, indeed, he be not . . . the prophet of one yet newer) [46]

With a combination of admiration and regret, Holmes's reviewers characteristically spoke of the skillful condensation and extreme conciseness of his annotations of the *Commentaries.* Those who admired and regretted clearly had in mind not the notes which contained traditional accumulations of recent cases and statutes but those which were brief yet critical essays in history and jurisprudence. Such an essay is that already mentioned on village communities, descent, and alienation. Among other notes which reviewers referred to were those concerned with vicarious

[45] Boston *Daily Advertiser,* Jan. 2, 1874.
[46] *North American Review,* 118:387–388 (April 1874).

liability, negligence, *ultra vires,* and grain elevators.[47] It is un-questionably true that the note on each of these subjects was so concisely written that it required an imaginative or knowing reader to realize fully that it was built upon extensive knowledge and constructive analysis. Holmes, in other words, was seeking to communicate with men of mature and well furnished minds. Quite probably the succinctness of the annotations was forced upon the editor by a decision of the publisher that the volumes should not in total bulk exceed that of the earlier editions. We know in any case that, with respect to nearly all of the topics dealt with in important and ambitious notes, Holmes wrote more ex-tensively in essays and comments which were published in the *American Law Review* while the 12th edition of the *Commenta-ries* was in process of preparation. It is more through those essays than through the annotations to Kent that one can see the growth of Holmes's fundamental theories of law. Attentive readers of the *Commentaries* could see, from Holmes's numerous references to his own unsigned contributions to the *American Law Review,* that his notes to Kent were frequently abbreviations of analysis and sug-gestion developed more fully elsewhere. They could see, in other words, that this valet of the Chancellor was a master in his own right.

It would be misleading to treat Holmes's edition of the *Com-mentaries* as the work of a speculative jurist and legal historian. Many of the annotations have their strength and their distinction in clarifying analysis. A series of notes on easements—particularly, perhaps, that in which he sought to draw the line between leases, licenses, and easements—was marked by an impressive capacity to systematize confused and chaotic doctrine.[48] His careful note on covenants which run with the land, on which he and others in later years were to build elaborate structures of theory, was an original and penetrating analysis.[49] A master of commercial law

[47] *Commentaries,* II, *260, note 1; *id.,* *561, note 1; *id.,* *300, note 1; *id.,* *590, note 1. Holmes had already written longer reflections on *ultra vires* and grain ele-vators in the *American Law Review,* 5:275 (January 1871) and 6:455 (April 1872).

[48] *Commentaries,* III, *419, note 1.

[49] *Id.,* IV, *480, note 1.

spoke as recently as 1931 of the "astounding clarity . . . and prophetic vision" in Holmes's analysis of warranty in the law of sales. "The law," said Professor Llewellyn, "was uncertain, confused, full of fuddled groping. [Holmes] leaves it with a clearer statement than one will find today." [50] The publication of the 12th edition of Kent made it thoroughly clear to those who examined the book with care that the thirty-two-year-old editor was a lawyer of extraordinary gifts.

As Holmes reached the end of his editorial road he had an air of almost frightening intensity. It was in the spring of 1873 that Mrs. Henry James described the recent occasion on which Holmes had dined with the James family.

His whole life, soul and body, is utterly absorbed in his *last* work upon his Kent. He carries about his manuscript in his green bag and never loses sight of it for a moment. He started to go to Will's room to wash his hands, but came back for his bag, and when we went to dinner, Will said, " Don't you want to take your bag with you? " He said, " Yes, I always do so at home." [51]

The pallor of his face made him a melancholy sight. By the close of the year, however, the strain had been relaxed. On December 3, Mrs. James again wrote to her son Henry, telling him of a call she had just had from "Mrs. Dr. and Mrs. Wendell Holmes." The latter, Mrs. James had not seen since her marriage.

She looks well in health and says Wendell is remarkably well, quite made over by his recreation at Milton last summer . . . Sara Sedgwick said last evening that Fanny Holmes had told her yesterday that Wendell's Book would be out today—and that she talked with great interest about it, and of all the labor it cost *them,* and what a relief it was to *them* to have it off their hands, as if it were a common work. This sounds delightful.[52]

[50] Karl Llewellyn, "What Price Contract? An Essay in Perspective," *Yale Law Journal,* 40:704, 748–749, note 91 [sic] (1931). The passage praised by Llewellyn is in *Commentaries,* II, *479, note 1.

[51] See Perry, *William James,* I, 519.

[52] Autograph letter, Houghton Library.

The entries in Holmes's reading list of 1873 give some indication of the ways in which the association of husband and wife in bringing his four years of labor to a conclusion had been carried on. "March 1: 9½ P.M. *finished 2d vol. of Kent revision.* March 3: Went in with Shattuck and Munroe as partner. Fanny read proof alone—from or before date." [53] On April 16 Holmes said, in a letter to Thomas M. Cooley, that about a month ago he had finished his work of more than three years on the new edition of Kent, that nearly three volumes had then been stereotyped, and that he expected that the printing would be finished by midsummer.[54] It seems likely, in view of Mrs. James's reference to Holmes's "recreation" at Milton in the summer of 1873, that with proofreading largely behind them something like a vacation had marked the virtual end of the long stretch of labor. November still brought in a few last-minute obligations: "Nov. 13 read last proof of table of cases Kent. Nov. 14. Sent last copy of addl cases. Nov. 17 Sent last 3 add. cases—*Finis.*" And then on December 13: *"Kent published —see Nov/69."* [55]

That Holmes saw his partnership with Shattuck and Munroe and his completion of the *Commentaries* as the mark, as it were, of his transition to man's estate is indicated by the fact that in October of 1873 he purchased a summer place at Mattapoisett, a quiet resort on Buzzards Bay made peculiarily attractive to him by the presence there of his senior partner. The property acquired was on the shore and was a tract of some thirty-seven acres, on which was situated a double house. A farming caretaker, after Holmes's purchase, continued for some years to occupy one half, and the Holmeses the other. Later they occupied the whole.[56] There is no indication, however, that before 1875 they did more

53 Little, "Reading," 186.

54 Original letter in the Michigan Historical Collections of the University of Michigan; copy at HLS.

55 Little, "Reading," 186–187.

56 Holmes recited these facts in a letter to Mrs. Charles S. Hamlin dated October 12, 1930 (copy, HLS). The deed of conveyance to Holmes is recorded at the Registry of Deeds in Taunton, Lib. 400, p. 88. In October 1876, the Mattapoisett property was transferred from Holmes to his wife (Lib. 430, p. 27).

than make week-end uses of their new possession. They were, how-ever, freeholders with a footing of their own.

By the time when Holmes completed his editing of the *Com-mentaries* he had already put behind him his lectureships at Har-vard and his coeditorship of the *American Law Review*. The for-mation of the partnership with Shattuck and Munroe signified Holmes's "return to active practice " [57]—a conscious assumption of obligations in practice very different from those which he had car-ried, somewhat casually, while sharing an office with his brother. He had established a reputation as a young lawyer of exceptional intellectual power and learning whose industrious temperament and capacities had set him apart from other gifted contemporaries. It surely was not because of an acquired distaste for the intellec-tual enterprise on which he had embarked some four years earlier that Holmes made his turning towards affairs in March of 1873. Much of his energy, as we shall later see, continued to be given to scholarship while he maintained his partnership with Shattuck and Munroe. The mere fact that he made it his business, almost as soon as that association commenced, to master German so that he would turn to works in the original which, while editing Kent, he had only read in translation, shows that his intellectual energy had not been exhausted. [58]

In a letter written to James Bryce in August 1879 Holmes spoke in revealing terms of the career which he had chosen for himself.

There are so few men . . . who have any kind of idealism in their practice that I cling pretty closely to those who have . . . The men who really care more for a fruitful thought than for a practical success are few everywhere and I doubt if the fellowship is complete anywhere without going beyond national boundaries . . . I wish that the neces-

[57] The phrase was used by Jeremiah Smith writing to Holmes on April 18, 1873, after he heard of the partnership of Shattuck, Holmes & Munroe (HLS).

[58] In a letter to his English friend James Bryce, dated May 17, 1871, Holmes stated explicitly that he could not read German; he did, however, ask Bryce to send him the name of any very important German book (original at the Bodleian Li-brary, Oxford; copy at HLS). Titles of German books in the original language first appear in Holmes's reading list in 1874.

sity of making a living didn't preclude any choice on my part—for I hate business and dislike practice apart from arguing cases—though I have every reason to be thankful for the situation in which I am, given that the above necessity exists. As it is I console myself by studying towards a vanishing point which is the center of perspective in my landscape—but that has to be done at night for the most part and is wearing, and my articles though fragmentary in form and accidental in order are part of what lies as a whole in my mind—my scheme being to analyse what seem to me the fundamental notions and principles of our substantive law, putting them in an order which is a part of or results from the fundamental conceptions.[59]

As already suggested, the careful and attentive reader of Holmes's edition of Kent may find there glimpses of the young man's "vanishing point" and intimations of what he conceived to be the fundamental principles of the common law. The point and the principles may, however, be much more clearly discerned in his earlier lectures and writings. To those first expressions of belief we must, accordingly, direct our attention.

[59] Original at Bodleian Library; copy at HLS.

2

The Constitution and the Judges

*W*hen *Charles William Eliot* turned Harvard over "like
a flapjack," [1] Holmes and Henry Adams found themselves companions in the frying pan. In many ways it was surprising that they
were associated in Harvard's revolution. Neither felt any special
gratitude for the education which Harvard had provided him. Adams' true interest was in contemporary American affairs, yet he
accepted a full-time teaching post to try his cultivated but unpro-
fessional hand as medieval historian. Holmes's true interest was in
jurisprudence and legal history, yet maintaining his law office in
Boston, he undertook the part-time obligation of instructing Harvard juniors in Constitutional Law, a subject so intimately related
to public affairs that its philosophical and historical aspects are
unlikely to lure the scholar who seeks for a scientific jurisprudence. Perhaps the salary of $300 which Holmes received for teach-
ing 158 juniors for two hours a week in the spring term of 1870, or
even the $200 which he was paid in the following year for do-
ing the same course again,[2] was an important consideration in

1 Dr. Holmes to John Lothrop Motley, Dec. 22, 1871: "Our new President,
Eliot, has turned the whole University over like a flapjack. There never was such
a *bouleversement* as that in our Medical Faculty" (J. T. Morse, *Oliver Wendell
Holmes* (Boston, 1896), II, 190).

2 A letter from Eliot to Holmes, written on Friday, February 10, 1871, announced Holmes's appointment as Instructor in the Constitution and the commencement of classes on the following Monday. The President apologized for the
shortness of notice but explained it by saying, "As you know I had supposed that
Mr. Adams was to give the instruction" (HLS).

Holmes's decision to teach the Harvard students a subject in which he had but limited interest. Beyond the financial attraction there probably lay in Holmes's mind, as there clearly did in Adams's, a hope that he might do something to refresh the processes of learning at Harvard. When Holmes wrote to President Eliot accepting the offer which he had received he summarized his understanding of the proposal: "I am to teach the Juniors Constitutional Law from a small text-book—asking questions enough to mark them and telling them such matters as I think likely to be interesting and instructive . . . I am, I suppose, under the control of nobody but yourself." [3] The concluding supposition seems to indicate that Holmes would have been reluctant to join the Harvard faculty if its traditionalists, rather than its reforming president, were to sit in judgment on his achievement.

Though reformation of teaching thus seems to have been one of Holmes's purposes, there is no indication that reformation of scholarship was an objective leading Holmes to accept this first Harvard appointment. By contrast, of course, Henry Adams came to the Harvard faculty a disciple of the new, German school of learning. While Adams's students of medieval history plunged into the *lex salica,* the Anglo-Saxon dooms, McLennan's *Primitive Marriage,* and Maine's *Ancient Law,* Holmes's students of Constitutional Law turned to Joseph Alden's *Science of Government in Connection with American Institutions.* There they found an outline of American constitutional law, drawn with all the innocent piety which a minister of the gospel could bring to his study of government. Dr. Alden prefaced his work with the reassuring word that "though primarily designed as a textbook, the general reader will find every portion of it perfectly intelligible." He opened his work by setting forth some basic principles of political science:

Savages are in all respects inferior to civilized men. They have not those means of guarding the body from disease which civilized men have. Their intellectual, social, and moral powers are very imperfectly developed . . . No man has a right to be a brute, or anything but a

3 To Eliot, Jan. 25, 1870 (Harvard Archives).

man. In order to be a man, he must be a member of society and subject to law.

When Dr. Alden turned from political theory to constitutional law he found the same comfort in platitude which he had discovered in triteness:

If a State were to pass a law altering the terms of an existing contract or agreement between parties, the law would be null and void, because it would be unconstitutional . . . It is desirable that the judges be independent, so that they may not be in danger of being biassed by their interest in the exercise of their official power . . . If the judges make arbitrary decisions, they are liable to impeachment. Haughtiness of manners may not be pleasant, but a judge of haughty manners who decides right, is better than a judge of pleasant manners who decides wrong.[4]

How could a skeptically alert young lawyer put such a book as Alden's in the hands of college students in 1870? In part the answer may be found in the fact that among the most significant changes which Eliot was encouraging in the course of Harvard instruction was the abandonment of the so-called "recitations" of the earlier day and the substitution of lectures with written examinations. If Holmes had been expected to have his class "recite" on some text on constitutional law one may be sure that he would have used another work than Alden's trivial little volume. Surely Holmes realized that Cooley's *Constitutional Limitations* and Pomeroy's *Introduction to Constitutional Law* were books of far more thoughtful and critical maturity than Alden's primer. As it was, however, he was expected to tell his students of such matters as he thought "likely to be interesting and instructive." To put Alden in their hands was to make available to them an annotated edition of the Constitution. However inadequate its annotations might be, Holmes as lecturer, rather than as auditor of recitations, was given the opportunity to stir the interest and stimulate the critical capacities of his students. That he succeeded in doing so is indicated in the report which the Committee to Visit the Aca-

[4] Joseph Alden, *The Science of Government in Connection with American Institutions* (New York, 1867), 10, 12, 142, 176, 177.

demical Department of the University presented to the Board of Overseers in June of 1871. Describing Holmes's course, the Visiting Committee said that the instructor "has been very successful with his pupils . . . and while it is taught as at present [the Committee] have nothing to suggest." [5] Many years later, one who had been a student in Holmes's course in the spring of 1871 remembered "well the ease with which [Holmes] spoke, and the familiarity with which he treated us, so different from the more formal method of the professors of those days." [6]

Surviving copies of the final examination which Holmes gave the students in Constitutional Law do not, to be sure, indicate that instructor or students had traveled far beyond the documentary outskirts of the subject. "What is a bill of rights?" "Define, (1) Treason; (2) *Ex post facto* law; (3) Bill of Attainder; (4) Habeas Corpus, with the provision as to it." "How are the officers of the United States appointed, and how removed?" It would seem that these questions could be satisfactorily answered by a student who had read his Alden with any care. Others, however, indicate that Holmes had made some effort to go beyond text and platitude to questions of theory. "It is said that a law which is in conflict with the Constitution is void. Must not this mean that a law which in the opinion of some person or body is unconstitutional is void? If so, in the opinion of what person or body? Why, and how far is this true?" "Suppose Congress enacts an unconstitutional law, with the assent of the President, and in due form. What is the function of the Supreme Court, and how far does its declaration that the law is void extend in its operation—theoretically and practically?" [7] Few of his examination questions indicate, however, that Holmes had used his opportunity as teacher of constitutional law as the occasion for attempting to recast traditional doctrine.

[5] "Report of the Committee to Visit the Academical Department for the Year Ending, June, 1871," 19 (Harvard Archives).

[6] Remarks of Bishop William Lawrence at exercises at the Harvard Law School receiving the portrait of Holmes by Charles Hopkinson, *Harvard Alumni Bulletin*, 32:747 (March 27, 1930).

[7] These two long questions come, respectively, from the examinations of June 1871 and June 1870.

While Holmes was delivering his first series of lectures on constitutional law in Harvard College he was working on those portions of Kent's *Commentaries* which dealt with the American Constitution. In the annotations there are scarcely any indications that Holmes saw need for building constitutional law upon other philosophical or historical foundations than those which the Chancellor had accepted. Quite probably this acquiescence was the consequence, at least in part, of the fact that Kent's nationalistic views of the American system of government were essentially those which time had validated and which Holmes accepted as given. Perhaps the acquiescence was also due to the fact that there are relatively few aspects of constitutional law in which a "scientific" jurisprudence, whether built on historical or analytical foundations, will give doctrine a shape significantly different from that which was fixed by the eighteenth-century language of the document. Kent, of course, found that language well suited to his thought and could blend the two into periods of resounding comfort. Despite his deeply nationalistic inclinations he could eloquently sing the praises of State power.

Though the national judiciary may be deemed pre-eminent in the weight of its influence, in the authority of its decisions, and in the attraction of their materials, there are abundant considerations to cheer and animate us in the cultivation of our own local law . . . The vast field of the law of property, the very extensive head of equity jurisdiction, and the principal rights and duties which flow from our civil and domestic relations, fall within the control, and we might almost say the exclusive cognizance, of the state governments. We look essentially to the state courts for the protection to all these momentous interests. They touch, in their operation, every chord of human sympathy, and control our best destinies. It is their province to reward and punish. Their blessings and their terrors will accompany us to the fireside, and " be in constant activity before the public eye." [8]

Surely Holmes addressed his Harvard students with another cadence when he discussed these same matters in his classroom. It is

[8] *Commentaries*, I, *445.

unlikely, however, that he saw any reason to bring in question the basic position which Kent, Chief Justice and Chancellor of New York, had made with respect to the ultimate and continuing significance of the State courts in the American scheme of things. It should not be forgotten, furthermore, that Holmes's basic interest was far less in problems of public affairs, policy, and law than it was in the philosophic structure and historic roots of the common law. It is no more surprising, accordingly, that Holmes's expressions of dissatisfaction with Kent's constitutional presuppositions were few, than that he saw no reason to outline a new philosophy of constitutional law when he instructed the Harvard juniors in that subject.

In the fall of 1870 two English visitors came to Boston—James Bryce, Regius Professor of Civil Law at Oxford, and Albert Venn Dicey, London barrister and cousin of Leslie Stephen. Carrying letters of introduction to Holmes they sat in his room overlooking the Charles River and laid the foundations of friendship which was to continue throughout their lives. The visitors, like other compatriots of their time, found it natural to combine extensive learning with an active concern with public affairs. As they talked with Holmes, Bryce was puzzled to find that the young American "cared so comparatively little" for "the ample and stimulating drama" of politics.[9] The bewilderment was not surprising, for would it not seem natural that one who had risked his life to preserve the Union, and who was blessed with the advantages of position and energy, should find the problems involved in the reconstitution of the nation a challenge both to interest and to action? If Henry Adams, teaching medieval history, found that the true center of his concern was the American political scene, how could Holmes, teaching American constitutional law, remain largely indifferent to the public affairs of his times?

Holmes made no response to Bryce's puzzled reflection, but on another occasion, writing to another friend, he revealed his own awareness of the nature of his temperament. "My interest is in

[9] Bryce to Holmes, Sept. 19, 1892 (HLS).

ideas—and the law being the door by which I entered, I stick to that . . . It isn't a matter of the difference between English and American views of politics, etc., but a question of personal aptitudes and preferences, deep in my make-up." [10] To recognize that Holmes had little interest in the public affairs of his times does not mean that questions of public controversy fell outside the realm of his intellectual concern. The lawyer's mode of thought, however, deeply colored that concern. As teacher of constitutional law to Harvard undergraduates, as editor of Kent, and as contributor to the *American Law Review* he was led, at the very beginning of his professional career, to examine a number of the most important public issues of the day. As teacher, editor, and author, however, he made it clear that he was an ally of those who believed that the role of judges is that of resolving questions of public law, not that of settling issues of public policy.

At the very beginning of his career Holmes had published comments on a burning issue of law and politics.[11] In February of 1868 the House of Representatives had voted to impeach President Johnson. The *American Law Review,* in its April issue, printed the Articles of Impeachment and an unsigned analysis of the legal questions which were presented by the proceedings.[12] The analysis was by Holmes. He identified the crucial issues of law and summarized the conflicting arguments on which the prosecutors and the defense might be expected to rely. The analysis was so technical that the matters discussed seemed to have no affiliation with the ghost of Lincoln, the flesh of Andrew Johnson, or the passion of Thaddeus Stevens. If the achievement had more of the quality of an exercise in abstraction than of a contribution to political understanding it was because of Holmes's conviction that when politics makes law its instrument the lawyer's, not the politician's, standard must be used to judge the legitimacy of the enterprise. In view of the spirit with which Holmes carried out his analysis it is not surprising that he found the best possibility of a valid presi-

[10] Holmes to Lady Ellen Askwith, June 28, 1916 (copy, HLS).
[11] *Shaping Years,* 279–280.
[12] 2:547, 560 (April 1868).

dential defense in narrow, statutory, rather than broad, constitutional, grounds.[13]

There was but one question of theory with which Holmes concerned himself in his consideration of the impeachment proceedings. The issue had been much discussed in the press. If President Johnson's conviction that the Tenure of Office Act, with which he had refused to comply, was unconstitutional should be confirmed by a decision of the Supreme Court of the United States, would that adjudication of unconstitutionality give him a defense to the congressional charge that in his refusal to enforce an Act of Congress he had committed an impeachable offense? Recognizing that Mr. Chief Justice Chase in *Mississippi* v. *Johnson* [14] had indicated that the Congress was not bound to respect the Court's determination that a congressional enactment was unconstitutional, Holmes, with some of the simplicity of Dr. Joseph Alden, bluntly asserted that "a law which is unconstitutional is void *ab initio,* and can impose no obligation." [15] He went on to say that were it not for the dictum of the Chief Justice it would seem abundantly clear that "when the Supreme Court of the United States had once declared an act unconstitutional, every department of government was bound to respect their decision." [16] Within two years Holmes evidently came to see that the justification of congressional and presidential respect for the decisions of the Court could not be based on the simple syllogisms which satisfied Dr. Alden. In his annotation of Kent's comforting assertion that "the judicial department of the United States is, in the last resort, the final expositor of the constitution," Holmes, citing the pronouncement of Chase, C.J., added a *caveat:* "But the judicial power seems to be

13 The strongest "legal" defense was, in Holmes's judgment, the contention that since Secretary Stanton had not been reappointed by Lincoln at the beginning of his second term as President, a special proviso in the Tenure of Office Act made Stanton a mere "tenant by sufferance" after one month of Lincoln's second term had expired. Under this proviso it was certainly arguable that Johnson did not violate the Act when, more than a month after the beginning of Lincoln's second term, he removed Stanton from office. See *id.,* at 562–563.

14 4 Wall. 475, 501 (1867).

15 *Am. L. Rev.,* 2:565.

16 *Id.*

limited as against a co-ordinate branch of the government." [17] As teacher of Constitutional Law he instructed the undergraduates that the Supreme Court does not "invalidate" or "annul" an Act of Congress; "it declines to enforce it—which for most purposes does annul it indirectly, but not, I think, in theory. If an impeachment were tried before the Senate I don't see what would bind the Senate to follow the ruling of the Court, except respect, and policy, etc." [18] We do not know what considerations or what influences led Holmes to take a different position in 1871 from that which he had taken three years before. It is significant, however, that he had come to believe that a platitude of American political theory—an unconstitutional statute is a void enactment—should not be taken as a rule of law but as a principle of public policy.

In the spring of 1871 the Congress and the American people were deeply concerned with the efforts of the Ku Klux Klan, through violence and terror, to frustrate reconstruction of the South. It was quite natural that many persons of integrity and good will, stirred to indignation by reports of the defiant lawlessness of the Klan, should support the congressional Radicals in their insistence that national authority should be brought to bear upon the Klan. If the states were incapable of bringing terrorists to trial, was it not clear that the national government should act to protect the life and property of American citizens? Such considerations as these made it relatively easy for the Republicans in Congress to secure the enactment of a tangled and elaborate Force Bill,[19] containing provisions designed to authorize federal action against persons who conspired to deny others their constitutional rights or to deny them equal protection of the laws. The second section of the statute, among its many provisions, authorized the initiation of either civil or criminal proceedings in federal courts when persons acting in concert or combination sought to deny others the equal protection of the laws. The third and fourth sections authorized the President

[17] *Commentaries*, I, *296, note 1.

[18] Holmes stated that this was what he had taught the Harvard undergraduates (letter to Albert J. Beveridge, Jan. 19, 1919; HLS). See also the question from the 1871 examination quoted, *supra*, p. 29.

[19] 17 Stat. 13 (April 20, 1871).

to employ military force, and to suspend the writ of habeas corpus, when unlawful combinations or conspiracies "shall so obstruct or hinder the execution of the laws [of any State] and of the United States as to deprive any portion or class of the people of such State of any rights, privileges, or immunities, or protection, named in the Constitution and secured by this act . . ."

In the pages of *The Nation,* John Norton Pomeroy, speaking as a Northern moderate, presented a series of thoughtful arguments against the constitutionality of the Force Bill.[20] The statute was entitled "An Act to enforce the provisions of the Fourteenth Amendment to the Constitution of the United States, and for other purposes." Pomeroy urged that because the Fourteenth Amendment does nothing more than prohibit state action destructive of constitutional rights, national powers to make the Amendment's prohibitions effective cannot reach the unofficial acts of private persons, whether acting alone or in concert with others. He also insisted that the structure of American federalism would be wholly overturned were Congress empowered to convert private offenses against state law into crimes against the nation. "It is a monstrous perversion of legal language and legal thought to maintain, as this statute does, that any violence or wrong done by private citizens, either singly or in numbers, either with or without concert, can constitute the denial of the equal protection of the laws contemplated by the Fourteenth Amendment."[21]

In view of the arguments which had been made by the proponents of the legislation, Pomeroy's interpretation of the enactment's revolutionary purpose was not surprising. Any person who was informed of the political mood and legislative program of the Radicals would very naturally proceed upon the same assumptions as those which lay behind Pomeroy's protest. Some might share his alarm that the traditions of American federalism were being violated; others might urge that those traditions were no longer entitled to respect. Critics and champions of the statute alike,

20 "The Force Bill," *Nation,* 12:268 (April 20, 1871); "Police Duty," *id.* 284 (April 27, 1871). Pomeroy identified himself as the author of the papers in letters to Holmes dated May 23 and July 9, 1871 (HLS).

21 *Nation,* 12:270.

35

however, seemed quite willing to give the enactment an essentially political interpretation, to judge its spirit and neglect its letter. If such a careful scholar and lawyer as Pomeroy let his reading of the enactment depend on his understanding of the motives of its supporters, surely the same inclination affected the judgment of others.

After the enactment of the Force Bill, Holmes published an unsigned comment on the statute in the *American Law Review*.[22] Expressing admiration for the articles in *The Nation,* Holmes went on to suggest that there was need for greater discrimination in criticism than Pomeroy had shown. Evidently sharing Pomeroy's hostility to revolutionary changes in the federal system, and indicating that he had grave doubts concerning the constitutionality of Section 2 of the statute,[23] he went on to suggest that "some arguments" may be adduced to support the constitutionality of Sections 3 and 4, the sections in which the President was empowered to use military force and to suspend the writ of habeas corpus. He suggested that if one were to disregard the radical pronouncements of the bill's sponsors and look instead to the letter of Sections 3 and 4 as they were enacted, one might see them as the legitimate assertion of the nation's traditional authority. Though it was true that under the statute the President might act when crimes were committed against state law, the statute specifically said that the presidential power should be exercised only when the conduct also involved an obstruction of the law of the United States. Holmes acknowledged that his emphasis would necessitate the giving of another constitutional justification for the statute than that which Congress had specifically given. "But as the section must stand, if at all, not on the fourteenth amendment, but on the authority to enforce the laws of the United States, and as a law is to be construed so as to be constitutional if possible, should not the act be taken as meaning what it says?"[24] The authority of the nation to

---

[22] 5:749 (July 1871).

[23] The Supreme Court of the United States held Section 2 of the statute unconstitutional in *United States v. Harris,* 106 U.S. 629 (1882).

[24] *Am. L. Rev.,* 5:751. In September 1956, when President Eisenhower sent troops into Little Rock, Arkansas, he based his authority to do so in part upon the provisions of Section 3 of the Act of 1871.

assure respect for its laws was neither dependent upon nor weakened by the Fourteenth Amendment, and it seemed clear to Holmes, therefore, that Congress might adopt a statute providing for the exercise of the nation's powers when private action was frustrating the enforcement of federal law.

What did Holmes's effort to find constitutional justification for some of the provisions in the Force Bill signify? Surely it did not reflect sympathy for the resounding humanity of Charles Sumner who, in supporting the bill, had asked for "the centralism of liberty [and] the imperialism of equal rights." [25] Had Holmes felt that sympathy he would not have conceded the validity of Pomeroy's argument against the constitutionality of making private deprivations of secured rights actionable. It may be felt that Holmes's endeavor to justify significant portions of the statute was the quite natural response of a Union veteran to a renewed Southern challenge of national authority. One cannot, of course, be sure that considerations of that sort played no part in Holmes's defense of Sections 3 and 4 of the statute. Yet the explanation seems to lie more in the qualities of his temperament than in the lessons of his experience. In formulating the case in favor of national power he said that the matter of highest importance was that "the act should be discussed in an impartial and professional spirit." [26] That phrase revealed his anxiety that the processes of legal interpretation should be sterilized against political infection. Pomeroy spoke in a mood more characteristically American when he permitted his distrust of the political objectives of the Radicals to lead him to assume that their purpose was written in the letter of all portions of the law which they had enacted. With greater caution Holmes urged lawyers to read the text before them with care and consider the problem of constitutionality as a question of law rather than an issue of political principle. He was suggesting to lawyers that they should judge the 3rd and 4th sections of the statute as the Supreme Court should judge them—as provisions which must be

25 The phrase was quoted by a Boston critic of Pomeroy's position. See *Nation,* 12:274 (April 20, 1871).
26 *Am. L. Rev.,* 5:749.

sustained if a reasonable basis for constitutionality could be dis-covered. He found a basis for presidential power in provisions of the Constitution which had been there from the first, and he thus believed that the aspirations of Radical Republicans had no rele-vance to the question of constitutional law—however much sig-nificance they might have in politics. Pomeroy seemed to have no doubt that legislative action, when inspired by the rashness of revo-lutionaries, may be condemned as unconstitutional. He believed that because the Constitution was law and was designed to safe-guard tradition, judges should condemn the enactments of men who spoke their commands with the voice of radicals. Holmes, by contrast, urged us to disregard the tone of the commander's voice and read the text of his command.

In the summer of 1871 the crisis of reconstruction in North Carolina led Pomeroy and Holmes once more to the friendly ex-pression of differing views. This time the difference concerned po-litical theory more than it did constitutional law. Government by Radical Republicans in North Carolina had brought from the conservatives of the state a demand that the state's constitution of 1868 should be amended. It was clear to all, however, that if the provision in the existing constitution were respected, by which no amendment could be submitted to the people without a three-fifths majority supporting it in the legislature, no changes in the fundamental law could be effected. The conservatives insisted that in a democratic society it is lawful for a majority of the qualified electorate to establish, from time to time, such system of govern-ment as they may prefer, and that restrictions in the existing con-stitution on the mechanics of effecting change were not legally binding on the people. A popular revolution, they urged, is lawful.

In *The Nation* of July 20, 1871, Pomeroy published an un-signed editorial on the issues of political theory thus presented in North Carolina.[27] In his comments on the Force Bill, he had used the standards of conservatism to condemn radical legislation. Now he used the standards of popular sovereignty to sustain a violation

[27] *Nation*, 13:37.

of constitutional limitations. No specific restriction, he asserted, which is "inserted in a State constitution, and attempted to be placed upon the supreme will of the people acting in an orderly manner through the regular and customary legislative means, can be effective; the action of the people in this matter and by these means must be legal and valid and not revolutionary." On this issue a good Austinian, Pomeroy asserted that "sovereignty cannot exist under limitations, nor can its free exercise be controlled." [28]

It was not surprising that some correspondents in *The Nation's* columns protested against the political theory on which Pomeroy founded his defense of the efforts of North Carolina's Democrats to tear down the constitution which the Republicans had erected. The German historian of American institutions, Dr. Hermann von Holst, objected that Pomeroy, in his effort to legitimize a counter-revolution, was disregarding the central principle on which American governments had been established—the principle that constitutional restrictions which the people impose upon themselves must be recognized as binding. Defiance of those restrictions may, *de facto,* bring new forces into power, but to acknowledge that the successful repudiation of constitutional limitations may produce *de jure* government is to sacrifice the rule of law to the tyranny of convenience.[29]

In reviewing the second edition of Cooley's *Treatise on Constitutional Limitations* in the *American Law Review* for October 1871, Holmes took the occasion to comment on the thesis which Pomeroy had outlined and which von Holst had criticized.[30] Judge Cooley's discussion of the problem was not extensive. He seemed, however, to accept the principles of von Holst, rather than those of Pomeroy.

If any attempt [he said] should be made by any portion of the people, however large, to interfere with the regular working of the agencies of government at any time in any other mode than as allowed by existing law, either constitutional or statutory, it would be revolution-

28 *Id.,* 38.
29 *Id.,* 71 (Aug. 3, 1871).
30 6:140.

ary in character, and must be resisted and repressed by the officers who for the time being represent legitimate government.[31]

In his review, Holmes said that he was "inclined" to accept Judge Cooley's formulation of principle. Evidently he did not feel the righteous indignation which led von Holst to protest against the effort to wrap the indecent figure of revolution in the decorous robes of law. As a preliminary to his discussion Holmes emphasized the necessity that we identify the authority which is to decide the question whether a constitution may validly be amended without respecting the preliminaries set forth for its amendment. "We must suppose the question to be argued before a court established under the old constitution, for the obvious reason that the new instrument could hardly be effectively and peaceably assailed except from a *point d'appui* outside of it." [32] Holmes seemed willing to recognize that such a tribunal should acknowledge the theoretical force of Pomeroy's argument that since sovereign power is incapable of limitation "the will of the majority must be obeyed in spite of the trammels which a previous majority has attempted to impose . . ." The imagined court, however, would be unlikely to act upon the basis of political theory alone and might be expected to find such grave difficulties in "attributing a popular act to the people in its sovereign capacity" that it would, in most conceivable circumstances, respect the prior constitutional limitation. The attribution is hampered by tradition if not by law. "Suppose the women, taking advantage of the majority which they are said to have in Massachusetts, should call a convention, and enact a new constitution by a clear majority of adults, but against the will of nearly every man in the Commonwealth: would the men obey it, or the courts regard it? . . . It is true that if the will of the majority is unmistakable, and the majority is strong enough to have a clear power to enforce its will, and intends to do so, the courts must yield, as must everybody else, because the foundation of

[31] Thomas M. Cooley, *A Treatise on the Constitutional Limitations which Rest upon the Legislative Power of the States of the American Union* (Boston, 2d ed., 1871), *598.

[32] *Am. L. Rev.*, 6:140.

sovereignty is power, real or supposed. But so long as there is a reasonable doubt of that power and intent . . . the question is in substance the question of recognition, which so often perplexes foreign governments. Where the sovereign power resides at any time, and what is the sovereign will, are questions of fact. But the old constitution is an admitted expression of the sovereign will, and that assures us that no other is authentic which does not come through certain channels. The courts may properly abide by that until they see that the new manifestation is not only unmistakable, but irresistible." [33]

Though it would seem that Holmes came closer to von Holst's theory of constitutionalism than to Pomeroy's, he showed less concern for theory than did either of the others. He was unwilling to ally himself with von Holst's effort to condemn as simply revolutionary the effective exercise of political power outside the settled channels of command. Yet he would not support Pomeroy's attempt to show that in the American scheme of things the people's will when made effective must be recognized as lawful. In the last analysis, Holmes suggested, the "lawfulness" of action must depend on the decision of the existing courts as to where power is then vested. Their conservatism will rightly tell them that drastic redistributions of power have the burden of proving their irresistible character. Their realism will tell them that when that burden has been sustained a new supremacy, and therefore a new sovereignty, has been established.

Perhaps Pomeroy was justified in saying that Holmes, in imagining the revolutionary convention of Massachusetts women, was not describing a process which Pomeroy would consider lawful.[34] But what Holmes had added to the discussion was significant. By

33 *Id.,* 140–141.
34 Pomeroy to Holmes, Oct. 12, 1871 (HLS). "I spoke of an act having all of the forms of a valid *law,* passed in due form by the existing legislature, followed by the act of the people in electing a convention and by a further act in voting to adopt the work of that convention. All this certainly has the form and semblance of a valid law. The only thing in the way of its validity was a restraining clause in the existing constitution. My argument went to show that such a restraining clause was simply null and void. If I am right here, then we have a perfectly *legal* proceeding."

41

urging that the problems of identifying the sovereign authority and ascertaining its will require the resolution of questions of fact, he brought discussion of the issue down to earth. His willingness to recognize that a court confronted by the sort of issue which Pomeroy had raised might in some circumstances decide it in one way and in different circumstances dispose of it quite otherwise revealed his hesitation to let abstractions either conclude discussion or determine decision. He again showed no inclination to pass judgment on the political merits of the issues which Reconstruction had cast up for resolution.

Two years after Holmes's discussion of these current issues of American constitutional law he commented on a lively issue of English law and politics in terms of basic theory—terms which indicate a point of view of profound importance to his philosophy of law and government. In the fall of 1872 there had been much controversy and consternation in England when leaders of the gas-stokers union, which had gone on strike in London, were sent to jail for one year, convicted of the common-law crime of conspiring to break contracts of employment. In the *Fortnightly Review* for January 1873, its editor, John Morley, expressed the indignation of the liberals:

The five workmen were tried before a judge, who made himself the organ of the class to which he belongs, refused them an extension of time for preparing their defence, fetched out of the old armoury of oppression the notion of conspiracy, made a most unusual and questionable application of it, made a most unexpected and questionable interpretation of a new law, thrust aside a recommendation of the jury, and then passed a sentence so severe that even if every one of his doubtful steps had been as assured as they were all doubtful, it would have been an excess of rigour. As I understand the phrase, this is a piece of iniquity.[35]

In the February issue of the *Fortnightly*, Henry Crompton published a more detailed condemnation of the action of Mr. Justice Brett. His essay bore the title "Class Legislation." The article called attention to the many ways in which the criminal law of Eng-

[35] "The Five Gas-Stokers," *Fortnightly Review*, 13 (N.S.) :138, 140.

land, both in its substance and its procedure, was designed by the rich and used by the government for the oppression of the poor. Crompton put primary emphasis upon the inequality of a rule of law which made servants guilty of a crime when they broke their contracts of employment yet imposed no criminal penalties on masters who, without reason, discharged their employees, or otherwise failed to fulfill their responsibilities as employers. Mr. Crompton showed himself a Spencerian when he rejected the possibility of extending the criminal law to reach the guilty employer: "The true course of progress on these matters is to depend less and less on the power of the state, which has culpably lent itself to the master's side . . . the true policy for the legislature is to abstain from interfering with industrial, as with family life." [36]

To the July issue of the *American Law Review* Holmes contributed an unsigned summary of and comment on the Gas-Stokers case. In his opening reflections on the Crompton thesis he made it clear that he did not question the contention that the English court had applied the law in an abusive and needlessly rigorous way against the defendants. He protested, however, that Crompton's essay contained a number of "unsound notions of law." Holmes read the essay as built upon the false presuppositions of Herbert Spencer that there exists "an identity of interest between the different parts of a community." It was fundamental to Spencer's theory of legislation that

the reaction of legislation is equal to its action. By changing the law, [Spencer] argues, you do not get rid of any burden, but only change the mode of bearing it; and if the change does not make it easier to bear for society, considered as a whole, legislation is inexpedient. This tacit assumption of the solidarity of the interests of society is very common, but seems to us to be false.[37]

It should be particularly noticed that in this passage Holmes did not question the validity of Spencer's insistence that action and reaction resulting from legislation are inevitable and are usually equal. On many later occasions he referred to the common unwill-

[36] *Id.*, 205, 215.
[37] *Am. L. Rev.*, 7:583 (April 1873) ; *Harv. L. Rev.*, 44:795.

ingness of reformers to recognize the fact, as he saw it, that all that legislation can accomplish is a shifting of burdens from the shoulders of one group to the shoulders of another.[38] To that extent Holmes was a faithful follower of Herbert Spencer. His protest was against the view that because this is a law of social force the state should exercise its legislative power with an extremely cautious and reluctant hand. In Holmes's opinion, Spencer and his disciples had forgotten the law of nature taught by Darwin—the law that makes struggle for survival and advantage "the law of human existence." Not only are human beings engaged in constant battle with the organic and inorganic forces seeking their destruction, but "the struggle does not stop in the ascending scale with the monkeys, but is equally the law of human existence . . . It is mitigated by sympathy, prudence, and all the social and moral qualities. But in the last resort a man rightly prefers his own interest to that of his neighbors." [39]

Holmes's demand, in effect, was that we recognize that the Darwinian view of nature compels an adjustment in traditional theories of law and of sovereignty.

All that can be expected from modern improvements is that legislation should easily and quickly, yet not too quickly, modify itself in accordance with the will of the *de facto* supreme power in the commu-

[38] In two letters to Felix Frankfurter, Holmes reiterated his thesis that most legislation achieves little more than the redistribution of discomfort. "You know that I am rather sceptical and still, as when editor of the Am. L. Rev., regard most statutes that are called 'good' as simply shifting the place where the rub or strain comes. They are especially praised when the bill to be paid in detrimental reactions is concealed by the fact that the reactions are interstitial and hard to be detected" (March 24, 1914; HLS). "I like to see someone insist on the fact that the march of life means a rub somewhere. As they used to say about saddles in the army—one strained the man, another galled the horse" (Sept. 5, 1916; HLS). See also his statement to Harold Laski: "I think . . . that every mitigation of the lot of any body of men has to be paid for by some other or the same body of men" (*Holmes-Laski Letters*, I, 207). See also *id.*, 272. "I always say that I regard legislation like buying a ticket to the theatre. If you are sure you want to go to the show and have the money to pay for it there is an end of the matter. I may think you foolish to want to go, but that has nothing to do with my duty" (to Franklin Ford, April 6, 1911; HLS).

[39] *Am. L. Rev.*, 7:583; *Harv. L. Rev.*, 44:795.

nity, and that the spread of an educated sympathy should reduce the sacrifice of minorities to a minimum. But whatever body may possess the supreme power for a moment is certain to have interests inconsistent with others which have competed unsuccessfully. The more powerful interests must be more or less reflected in legislation; which, like every other device of man or beast, must tend in the long run to aid the survival of the fittest. The objection to class legislation is not that it favors a class, but either that it fails to benefit the legislators, or that it is dangerous to them because a competing class had gained in power, or that it transcends the limits of self-preference which are imposed by sympathy.[40]

Holmes then suggested that the prosecution of the gas-stokers should be condemned, if at all, on the second ground—that it was initiated and carried through by those who were unaware that the *de facto* power of labor had reached such proportions that the erstwhile ruling classes must recognize that their own power was no longer supreme.

A notable aspect of this passage is its implicit qualification—perhaps rejection—of the Austinian concept of sovereignty. Holmes, who never formulated either a political or legal theory of sovereignty, in this brief comment, however, made it clear that he was anxious to look beyond the concept of a theoretically "sovereign state" to those forces which actually determine the incidence of public power and authority. The "legislators," in Holmes's mind, were not the members of Parliament or the English judges who enforced the Statutes of the Realm and the common law of England. They were the persons and classes whose actual, *de facto* power was so real that the Parliament and the Courts felt a political obligation to give effect to their wishes. As his earlier discussions of the issue of the lawfulness of a departure from constitutional procedures had indicated, he saw that the ultimate issue of where sovereignty resides turns upon the answer to a question of fact. The lawmakers, whether they be judges or members of a legislature, must always seek to calculate the existing allocation of power and, having made their calculation, give effect as law, to the

40 *Id.*, 583–584.

demands of that group which, as survivor in the Darwinian struggle, has proven itself to be the fittest. Sympathy and the moral virtues may lead either the dominant group or the judges to alleviate the tyranny of power. To the extent that those forces operate, and to the extent that an equilibrium of competing demands exists effectively within a society, law will temper its triumph with moderation.

In this succinct analysis of law there surely is implied a repudiation of the natural-law tradition. Furthermore, there is nothing to suggest that Holmes believed with Kant, Spencer, or Mill that the ultimate objective of the legal system must be the safeguarding of each man's freedom to do what he wills, so long as he does not infringe the equal freedom of other men. Does this mean that Holmes's theory of law, as outlined in his comment on the Gas-Stokers case, was thoroughly Hobbesian and deeply infected with the concept that might makes right? [41] To the extent that Holmes was tying the laws of man to the Darwinian law of nature one may fairly assert that he made tooth and claw more significant than heart and soul.[42] It seems vastly important, however, to notice that he did not say anything in his comment to suggest that he favored an absolute authority—an unquestionable might—in the authority of the State. The State's responsibility is not that of carrying out the will of an identifiable monarch or parliament or judge. It is to recognize the existing distribution of power and to respect it as the prevailing force, making due allowance for the demands of sym-

[41] Writing to Bryce on September 17, 1919, Holmes acknowledged that he came "devilish near to believing that might makes right" (Bodleian Library; copy HLS).

[42] Holmes evidently felt some concern that he did not bear in his heart sufficient affection for the human race. "I revere the people who seem to live in an atmosphere of moral exaltation, but I can't believe that mankind has changed much in the last 50 years, and while I often feel like a worm when I read of men whose dominant motive is love for their kind, I console myself by thinking that most of the great work done in the world comes from a different type" (to Lewis Einstein, Jan. 15, 1915; LC; copy, HLS). He had earlier expressed the same concern to the same correspondent: "I reproach myself a little . . . for not loving my fellowmen in general enough. I console myself by thinking that if one does one's job as well as one can one achieves practical altruism and that it doesn't matter so much how one feels about it—but still it makes me uneasy—just as I say I don't believe in Hell but am afraid of it" (July 17, 1909; LC; copy, HLS).

pathy, morality, and the shifting equilibrium between those forces which are in the ascendant and those which are in process of decline and defeat.

The comment on the Gas-Stokers case not only casts light on what Holmes had in mind when he discussed the issue of the "lawfulness" of an unconstitutional adoption of a new state constitution in North Carolina. It gave him the opportunity to bring in question the basic dogma of utilitarian jurisprudence—the dogma, that is, that the crucial test of every act of the legislature is whether it promotes the greatest good of the greatest number:

> Why should the greatest number be preferred? Why not the greatest good of the most intelligent and most highly developed? The greatest good of a minority of our generation may be the greatest good of the greatest number in the long run. But if the welfare of all future ages is to be considered, legislation may as well be abandoned for the present. If the welfare of the living majority is paramount, it can only be on the ground that the majority have the power in their hands. The fact is that legislation in this country, as well as elsewhere, is empirical. It is necessarily made a means by which a body, having the power, put burdens which are disagreeable to them on the shoulders of somebody else. Communism would no more get rid of the difficulty than any other system, unless it limited or put a stop to the propagation of the species. And it may be doubted whether that solution would not be as disagreeable as any other.[43]

In the course of this volume we shall see Holmes often reasserting and redefining these principles of political and legal theory. First enunciated with clarity in 1873, they cast light not only on the foundations which lay behind his discussions of constitutional law as youthful lecturer, editor, and commentator, but, more significantly, indicate the nature of his early dissatisfaction with the utilitarian and non-Darwinian foundations of Austin's jurisprudence and his growing skepticism concerning the ethics of utilitarianism. Though his comments on the Gas-Stokers case were published before he had read James FitzJames Stephen's *Liberty, Equality, Fraternity*—that muscular attack on the sentimental-

43 *Am. L. Rev.*, 7:583; *Harv. L. Rev.*, 44:795.

ity, as it seemed to Stephen, of Mill's essay on Liberty—it is surely evident that much of the spirit which moved Stephen to criticize Mill also moved Holmes to insist that a theory of politics and a theory of legislation which disregarded the Darwinian theory of evolution was necessarily inadequate.[44]

One phrase in Holmes's comment on Crompton's protest against class legislation deserves particular attention. "In the last resort," he said, "a man rightly prefers his own interest to that of his neighbors." The word in this sentence which shocks the liberal mind into resentful attention is, of course, the word "rightly." It implies the same things which were suggested some ten years later in his lectures on *The Common Law* when he asserted that it seemed to him clear that "the *ultima ratio,* not only *regum,* but of private persons, is force, and at the bottom of all private relations, however tempered by sympathy and all the social feelings, is a justifiable self-preference." [45] In what sense, one is compelled to ask, did Holmes mean that a man "rightly" prefers his own interest to that of his neighbors and "justifiably" seeks his own advantage? Is it not clear that in the Gas-Stokers comment, at least, Holmes, speaking as Darwinian (or, perhaps more accurately, as Malthusian) , was speaking of a "rightness" established not by a law of morality but by a law of nature which demands that each organism seek its own survival? In both passages he acknowledged that this law of nature was qualified by sympathy—a sense which deserves from society and from the individual a respectful if undefined degree of recognition. Holmes, however, was unwilling to pass judgment on a law of nature, and therefore dignified the instinct for self-preference by speaking of its "rightfulness." As a "devout Malthusian," [46] he accepted not only the master's theories of population but shared his belief that "to the apparently narrow principle of self-interest which prompts each individual to exert himself in bettering his condition, we are indebted for all the noblest exertions of the human genius, for everything that dis-

44 Holmes read *Liberty, Equality, Fraternity* (London, 1873) in the summer of 1873.

45 *The Common Law* (1881) , 44.

46 *Holmes-Laski Letters* (hereafter *HLL*) , I, 658.

tinguishes the civilized from the savage state." [47] Like Malthus, Holmes recognized that benevolence and sympathy are admirable qualities alleviating the brutality of the struggle for existence. Yet no man should be ashamed of making his own interest his first pursuit. "Abolition of self love I think undescribable rot. As I have often observed, nature makes self love an instrument of altruism and martyrdom, but the self lover is not required to know it, although more intelligent if [he] does." [48]

For a parenthetical moment one cannot resist the temptation of asking an unanswerable question. Did Holmes's intellectual acceptance of the Darwinian hypothesis contribute to his personal scheme of life, or did the temperament of an ambitious man grasp eagerly at a view of nature which would dignify a trait of character? Doubtless a quality of temperament made the Darwinian hypothesis sympathetic, yet it seems to me that Holmes, in the conduct of his life, was ruled more by intellectual conviction than he was by the drive of an instinct for achievement. Had his temperament rather than his mind made triumph the goal of effort, he would have been more likely to seek the conventional success of power—riches, office, command. Instead, like his father's Astronomer, his aspiration was for intellectual eminence. The Darwinian view persuaded him that for that goal to be achieved an almost ruthless dedication of effort was required. Those minds which are fittest to survive must prove their strength. Holmes was resolved that for him the proving must occur before he was forty years of age. At least in the years of proving, an "educated sympathy" should not be permitted to interrupt the drive for supremacy.

This reading of Holmes's purpose and decision makes him, of course, a calculator of action and a planner of accomplishment. It is the reading which led William James to speak of Holmes's ef-

47 T. R. Malthus, *Principles of Population* (London, 8th ed., 1878), 480.
48 To Mrs. Charles P. Curtis, Feb. 27, 1921 (HLS). Two days before he wrote those words Holmes expressed the same thought in another letter: "It makes me tired to read of the mellifluous days when it is to be all SERVICE—and love of our neighbor and I know not what. There shall be one Philistine, egotist, unaltruistical desirer to do his damnedest, and believer that self, not brother, was the primary care entrusted to him, while this old soldier lives" (*HLL*, I, 315).

49

fort to gouge from life a deep and self-beneficial groove.[49] If it does not find gentleness and sympathy as qualities which played their part in making him what he was, one must also recognize that had he nurtured those qualities, his accomplishment might well not have been what it was. It must also be remembered that the goals which he had chosen were not those to which the prevailing values of America gave significant respect. If his character was scarred by the zeal of his resolve to achieve eminence, the brand of intellectual eminence he sought set him apart from the self-seekers who, not only surviving but ruling as the fittest, could see their personal victory as the fulfillment of Darwin's law of nature. It is the special nature of Holmes's aspiration, coupled with the fact that when he had proved his capacities he allowed sympathy to play a larger part in his life than he had permitted it to when he was gaining his end, which leads me to believe that Holmes's planning of achievement was more the result of an intellectual decision to test himself in the Darwinian struggle than of a temperamental inclination to seek a personal victory. Yet it must be remembered that Holmes himself spoke with some shame of the fact that when he was concerned with human affairs he could not help "feeling in a personal way and wanting to beat the whole crowd—thinking about my work as *my* work which I hope may be useful." [50]

During the period of Holmes's association with the *American Law Review,* the Supreme Court of the United States, in a series of fluctuating opinions, passed upon the constitutionality of the statutes in which Congress had endeavored to make greenbacks legal tender for pre-existing debts. In 1870 a majority of the Court determined that the legislation was unconstitutional.[51] In the April issue of the *Review,* John C. Ropes published an unsigned and devastating criticism of the Court's decision.[52] He was principally concerned with the fact that the Chief Justice, speaking for a majority, had built his opinion on the dangerous assumption that

[49] *Shaping Years,* 282.
[50] Letter to Clara Sherwood Stevens, Sept. 8, 1906, quoted in *id.,* 283.
[51] *Hepburn* v. *Griswold,* 8 Wall. 603 (1870).
[52] *Am. L. Rev.,* 4:604. Ropes is identified as the author in John C. Gray's set of the *American Law Review* (HLS). Gray added a footnote (p. 607) to Ropes's paper.

the Court is empowered to decide whether or not a means which Congress has chosen for exercising a granted power is either necessary or proper for achieving the end in view. Both the Chief Justice, writing for a majority, and Justice Miller, in dissent, seemed to take it for granted that the Court may settle the question of the legality of a Congressional measure by conducting an "historical and political inquiry into the *actual net benefit or injury* resulting to the country" from the questioned measure. "We are sure that we speak the mind of most of the profession, when we say that all this examination of history and forming of conclusions was entirely outside of the duty of the Court." [53]

Ropes went on to suggest that there was one argument of some force which the majority had chosen not to make in support of its decision—an argument which Ropes believed to be invalid but which he considered much more persuasive than any the Chief Justice had used. The Court had conceded that Congress had the power of issuing a paper currency. Ropes suggested that this concession need not have been made.

It is certainly a fair question, whether Congress, having express grants of power to coin money, to borrow that money, and to fill its coffers by taxation with that money, has any further financial powers: whether the power to emit bills of credit as currency is not a different sort of thing altogether; and whether it is not reasonable to suppose that the express grants of coining, borrowing, and taxing, exhaust the financial powers of Congress on the subject of the currency.[54]

Had the Court denied the existence of a congressional power to issue paper currency it might never have reached the question of whether it was necessary or proper to render that currency legal tender. Condemnation of the Legal Tender Acts on such grounds as these would, in Ropes's judgment, have been mistaken, but the mistake would not involve the abuse of judicial power which characterized the opinions as they were delivered.

There is no doubt that Holmes concurred in Ropes's views

[53] *Id.*, 607.
[54] *Id.*, 612.

concerning the Court's discussion of the necessary and proper clause of the Constitution. A few years later he wrote that the opinions of the Justices in *Hepburn* v. *Griswold* "presented the curious spectacle of the Supreme Court reversing the decision of Congress on a point of political economy." [55] Despite his dissatisfaction with the ground of decision in the Hepburn case, in 1870 he wrote a letter to the *Review* indicating that he did not believe that Congress had the power to make paper currency legal tender. The argument against constitutionality as he there formulated it, though not wholly unrelated to that which Ropes had outlined in the concluding portion of his comment on *Hepburn* v. *Griswold,* had a different emphasis from that which Ropes had given it.

It is hard to understand [wrote Holmes], when a power *is* expressly given, which does not come up to a required height, how this express power can be enlarged as an incident to some other express power. The power to "coin money" means, I take it . . . (1) to strike off metallic medals (*coin*), and (2) to make those medals legal tender (*money*). I cannot, therefore, see how the right to make paper legal tender can be claimed for Congress when the Constitution virtually contains the words "Congress shall have power to make metals legal tender." It is to be remembered that those who deny the power have only to maintain that it is not granted by implication. They are not called on to find a constitutional prohibition.[56]

A few months after Holmes's letter appeared in the *American Law Review,* a new majority of the Supreme Court overruled the decision in *Hepburn* v. *Griswold.*[57] Now it was decided that the Legal Tender Acts were valid. Stephen J. Field, who had been with the earlier majority, wrote a vigorous dissent which was based in part on the logic of Holmes's letter to the *American Law Review.*[58] There is nothing to tell us whether Field had seen Holmes's communication and was persuaded by it, but Holmes evidently liked to believe that his letter had been of some influ-

[55] Review of *The Legal Tender Cases of 1871* in *Am. L. Rev.,* 7:146.
[56] *Am. L. Rev.,* 4:768 (July 1870).
[57] *The Legal Tender Cases,* 12 Wall. 457 (1871).
[58] *Id.,* 649–650.

ence. After the Field opinion was published, Holmes, in reviewing an unofficial edition of *The Legal Tender Cases of 1871,* quoted his own words as correspondent in the earlier issue of the *Review,* and went on to point out that Justice Field had restated the argument "in explicit language." [59] He added the comment that the Justices who spoke for the majority were not, in his opinion, successful in overthrowing the argument. Returning to the same problem in his annotations to Kent's *Commentaries,* Holmes again restated his position and emphasized Field's concurrence in his thesis.[60]

In these expressions of opinion with respect to the Court's decision in the Legal Tender cases, Holmes followed a syllogistic course of argument to condemn an act of Congress as unconstitutional. There is no reason to believe that he chose that form of reasoning because it led him to a conclusion which his own theory of political economy favored. It would seem that the choice of method was the consequence of his conviction that the lawyer's opinion, and *a fortiori* the judge's decision, on a question of law should be based upon "legal" reasoning. He shared the conviction of Ropes that the Court's initial condemnation of the congressional statute on the ground that experience had shown its folly was wholly unjustified. So far as one can see, however, at this time he felt no appreciable reluctance to have an act of Congress fall before the impact of a syllogism. Is it fair to ask whether Holmes had yet come to recognize the validity of his own later and most famous aphorism: "The life of the law has not been logic: it has been experience"? [61] Perhaps one may best deal with that question by remembering that in the first years of his career Holmes's concern was not with the life but with the structure of the law—with its analysis rather than its history.

In 1887, James Bradley Thayer, Holmes's former employer, published an article in the *Harvard Law Review* in which he considered at length the question whether Congress has constitutional

---

[59] *Am. L. Rev.,* 7:146.
[60] *Commentaries,* I, *254, note 1, *314, note 1.
[61] *The Common Law* (hereafter *CL*) , 1.

power to make paper good tender in payment of debts.[62] The Court had recently reaffirmed, with new vigor, the majority's decision in favor of congressional power.[63] The distinguished historian George Bancroft had published an impassioned attack on the Court's latest decision,[64] and Thayer, aroused by Bancroft's misconceptions, sought to identify and expose them. Thayer's insistence that the scope of judicial power in the resolution of constitutional questions must be narrowly confined led him, of course, to share the opinions which Ropes had already expressed in his comments on *Hepburn* v. *Griswold*. In his essay, however, Thayer went into other aspects of the constitutional issues involved in the legal-tender legislation and decisions. Identifying Holmes as the author of the letter of 1870 and the book review of 1871 which had appeared in the *American Law Review,* he gave special attention to the argument for unconstitutionality which Daniel Webster had suggested, Holmes had formulated, and Field had utilized, and asserted that Holmes's reasoning seemed to him "obviously defective." [65] The first error, according to Thayer, was in the major premise of his syllogism. Holmes's textual argument had taken the following form. In Article I, Section 8, Congress is empowered "to coin money." This power he had described as the power "to strike off metallic medals (coins) and to make these medals legal tender (money). If the Constitution says expressly that Congress shall have power to make metal legal tender, how can it be taken by implication that Congress shall have power to make paper legal tender?" [66] Thayer called attention to the fact that Holmes had imported into the text of the Constitution an explicitness which was not there, and had then built his argument upon the imported explicitness. If Holmes had taken the constitutional text as he had

---

62 *Harv. L. Rev.,* 1:73 (May 16, 1887), reprinted in Thayer, *Legal Essays* (Boston, 1908), 60.

63 *Juilliard* v. *Greenman,* 110 U.S. 421 (1884).

64 *A Plea for the Constitution of the United States of America* (New York, 1886).

65 *Harv. L. Rev.,* 1:83; *Legal Essays,* 73. Thayer also referred to Holmes's reiteration of his argument in his edition of Kent's *Commentaries,* I, *254, note 1.

66 *Commentaries, id.*

found it, his argument would have to take another form: "(a) Congress has an express power to coin money; (b) in that, is implied a power to make it legal tender; and (c) this implied power excludes an implied power to make anything else legal tender. That argument is not a strong one." [67]

It would seem that Thayer's analysis of the fault in Holmes's syllogism is accurate. It has been stated that in later years Holmes acknowledged the fact.[68] Perhaps when that acknowledgment occurred he had come to believe that syllogistic reasoning, however acute, should not play a dominant role in the resolution of constitutional issues. Whether the acknowledgment was of logical error or of a too narrow perspective of judgment, it seems clear that for Holmes the concession of fault implied a recognition that the questioned enactment was valid. By contrast, one may feel sure that if Stephen J. Field had been persuaded that there was a fallacy in the syllogism which he and Holmes had used to establish the unconstitutionality of the legal tender legislation he would have continued, with no less ardor, to insist that the legislation was invalid. With Field, the logic of a lawyer was the instrument of a statesman, a means for achieving ends that he considered essential for the welfare of the nation. If, in a particular instance, logic should fail to do appropriate service, theories of political economy and constitutional government disguised as principles of jurisprudence would have been called upon to achieve the desired end. For Holmes, however, the concession that condemnation of the statutes could not be based on a syllogism was usually coupled with an acknowledgment that they were valid. This tendency, first shown in 1870, reflected something more significant than a lawyer's instinctive confidence in logic. It revealed an aspect of a

67 *Harv. L. Rev.*, 1:84; *Legal Essays*, 74.

68 Charles Fairman, *Mr. Justice Miller and the Supreme Court, 1862–1890* (Cambridge, Mass., 1939) , 160, footnote 34. Mr. Fairman tells me that Mr. Justice Holmes in conversation told him in 1929 that Thayer seemed to have had "the better of the argument." A letter from Holmes to Thayer written after Thayer, in his *Cases on Constitutional Law* (Boston, 1898) , II, 2269, had repeated his criticism of Holmes's logic, did not admit defeat or error (Holmes to Thayer, Dec. 11, 1898; HLS) .

conviction already emphasized—an inclination to insist that so long as the American alchemy converted great political issues into questions of law their resolution must be found in legal rather than political reasoning. This attitude, though it initially led Holmes to condemn the Legal Tender Acts as unconstitutional, also led him to join Ropes and Thayer in their disapproval of the increasing tendency of judges to let their views of political economy determine their decisions on questions of law.

In October 1870, Charles Francis Adams, Jr., published an anonymous comment on a recent decision of the Supreme Court of Michigan in which Judge Cooley, speaking for a majority of the Court, had held that municipal taxation for the aid of railroad corporations, being for a private purpose, was unconstitutional.[69] Adams' criticism made it clear that another alert intelligence had come to accept the principles which Ropes had outlined in the pages of the *Review* and which Thayer was later to reassert and redefine. The question before the Michigan court, said Adams, was "simply a question of law with which neither the lessons of experience, no matter how bitter, nor considerations of expediency, no matter how strongly entertained, have any connection." [70] It was peculiarly disturbing to Adams that a judge as wise as Cooley had permitted his economic and political views to make him an ally of those American judges who were showing an increasing willingness to exercise from the bench powers which were vested in other agencies of government.

In his notice of Cooley's *Constitutional Limitations,* to which reference had already been made, Holmes called attention to the somewhat inconsistent position which Cooley the commentator and Cooley the judge had taken on the problem of supporting "private" enterprise with public funds. Though Holmes did not then indicate explicitly whether his sympathies were with the commentator or the judge, a few years later, in his annotations of Kent, he made it clear that he indorsed the views which Adams

[69] *Am. L. Rev.,* 5:148 (October 1870), commenting on *People* v. *Township of Salem,* 20 Mich. 452, 470 (1870). Adams is identified as author of the comment in Holmes's copy of the *American Law Review* (LC).

[70] *Id.,* 149.

had so vigorously expressed in discussing *People* v. *Salem*.[71] In review and annotation, however, Holmes touched on issues which neither Ropes nor Adams had discussed.

In his review of Cooley, Holmes called attention to the sleight-of-mind by which judges transformed questions of policy into questions of law. Courts and lawyers had come with increasing frequency to assume—perhaps to pretend—that they were dealing with an issue of constitutional law, rather than an issue of political policy, when they set limits to the police power. Holmes, expressing gratitude for Cooley's "instructive" discussion of the matter, went on to ask a question which he was often to repeat in later days. Was not the phrase "police power" perhaps "invented to cover certain acts of the legislature which are seen to be unconstitutional, but which are believed to be necessary . . ."?[72] If written by von Holst, such reflections as these could properly be taken as a condemnation of those judges who permit the law of the Constitution to be overridden by a popular notion of necessity. Written by Holmes, however, the words have a very different significance. In his controversy with Pomeroy concerning popular sovereignty, as in his later comments on the Gas-Stokers case, Holmes acknowledged that judges, recognizing the realities of popular power, may properly bow to the necessities of the occasion and treat the commands of an effective majority as law. The "apologetics of the police power" are more than a convenience;[73] they provide a serviceable formula for the legitimation of the irresistible demands of the dominant forces in society. When judges resist that

[71] "It has been said that whether the object for which property is taken or a tax imposed is a public use must be determined by the judiciary . . . But it has also been laid down, and it would seem to be the better doctrine, that on such questions the discretion of the legislature cannot be controlled by the courts, except, perhaps, where its action is clearly evasive or where there is a palpable usurpation of authority . . . [N]ote to *People* v. *Salem*, 5 *Am. L. Rev.*, 148 *et seq.*" *Commentaries*, II, *340, note 1.

[72] *Am. L. Rev.*, 6:141–142. It should be pointed out, perhaps, that Holmes gave credit to Mr. Justice Christiancy for an earlier formulation of this reflection. See *People* v. *Jackson & Michigan Plank Road Co.*, 9 Mich. 285, 307 (1861).

[73] In *Kansas Southern Railway* v. *Kaw Valley District*, 233 U.S. 75, 79 (1914), Holmes spoke of "the convenient apologetics of the police power."

demand and convert their own predilections into constitutional dogma they achieve—if they do not consciously seek—a supremacy inappropriate in a society which respects the Darwinian hypothesis.

It may be urged that Holmes violated his own principle that courts should so read a constitution as to permit the dominant interests to have their way when he formulated his syllogistic criticism of *Hepburn* v. *Griswold*. Though it may well be that in his discussion of that case he overlooked the relevance of the standards of judicial humility which he, Ropes, Thayer, and Adams had all in varying ways enunciated, it is well to remember that Holmes's discussion of the police power was principally directed to the interpretation of state constitutions by state judges. In the 1870's the Supreme Court of the United States had not yet begun to use the due process clauses of the 5th and 14th Amendments as barriers to substantive power. When Holmes criticized the Supreme Court for permitting Congress to make paper legal tender, he doubtless brought to the problem his strong feeling that problems of national power were very different from problems of state power. It was still the presupposition of most of his generation that when the action of the government of the United States is questioned the challenge must be sustained unless the government can show a constitutional provision clearly authorizing the action which has been taken. The power of the states is essentially different. Those who deny a state's authority must show that the constitution of the state or nation explicitly prohibits action. The prevailing concept of federalism, in other words, may explain in part the contrasting views of Holmes with respect to the Legal Tender Cases and his contemporaneous attitude towards the apologetics of the police power. The nation's powers may be limited by a syllogism implicit in the constitutional text; nothing but an explicit prohibition confines the authority of the states to let *de facto* power have its way.

Separated in time by a span of some seven years from his lectures on the Constitution, it is not, perhaps, permissible to assume that Holmes's comments on *Munn* v. *Illinois,* published in 1878, represent doctrine which he outlined to his students. Yet his reflections on the Granger Cases seem to bespeak attitudes which had governed his thought in the earlier period and which were to persist for a lifetime. In *Munn* v. *Illinois* the Supreme Court, with Justices Field and Strong dissenting, had sustained the power of Illinois to regulate the rates charged in the grain elevators of Chicago. Holmes's unsigned review of the volume of the Reports in which the case was published was concerned almost wholly with that decision.[74] After stating that discussion in the majority opinion "leaves something to be desired," Holmes went on to suggestive commentary.

It is very true that "the police power" is open to the suspicion of being a convenient phrase to cover acts which cannot be justified by the letter of the Constitution, but which are nevertheless deemed necessary. It is also true that the exercises of this power with which we are most familiar are such as are mentioned by Mr. Justice Field, in his dissenting opinion . . . But legislation as to prices has been common to all periods of the English law; and, even if it were hitherto unheard of, the circumstances to which this legislation applies are at least equally new. A hundred years ago, one could hardly use his land so as to injure another except by creating a nuisance. But things have grown more complex. The relations between property owners are not only those of mere contiguity: they are organic. Cities are grown up whose existence depends upon the railroad, and the products of millions of acres have to pass through the elevators of Chicago. If you cut the motor nerve, you paralyze the hand. If the railroads and elevators have a constitutional right to charge what they please, it is just as truly a right to destroy the property of others as a right to make noxious vapors would be. In such cases, it is immaterial that there is no statutory monopoly, so long as there is actual power on one side and actual dependence on the other. It was objected that the question what was a reasonable charge, was a judicial question. But the legislature did not attempt to say what should be charged: it only fixed a limit, and there was nothing to show that this was not considerably higher than the reasonable charge. If the court had been able to see that this was a mere cover for confiscation, it would have had a wholly different ques-

[74] "*United States Reports, Supreme Court.* Vol. 94," *Am. L. Rev.*, 12:354 (January 1878). The review is identified as Holmes's in a letter he wrote to Franklin Ford, May 29, 1907 (HLS).

tion before it. Of course, the question may be raised where to draw the line; but no experienced lawyer is disturbed by that, for he is well aware that the best-settled legal distinctions illustrate the Darwinian hypothesis no less than the diversities of species.

In what I have said I have indicated that Holmes was not, in his early years, a great innovator of doctrine. As lecturer and critic he expressed views which were shared by vigorous and perceptive contemporaries at the Boston bar. Some of his convictions may have been derived from those associates. It would seem, however, that a deeper influence on the development of his constitutional philosophy was a framework of legal and social theory. It was not because Holmes had interests and convictions relating to public affairs that he felt called upon to touch upon constitutional issues. He turned to those issues because they were a necessary, if subordinate, part of a total view of law. It was the chance of opportunity, not priority of concern, that led Holmes in his first lectureship and in his work on the first volume of Kent to consider constitutional law. One might even say that it was also chance and not priority of interest which led him, in 1902, to shift the center of his official life from the administration of justice under a common-law system to that of enforcing the Constitution of the United States. In any case we must turn from his first considerations of constitutional principle to his earliest inquiries into the nature and history of law.

3

Law's Philosophic Order

On April 28, 1871, the President and Fellows of Harvard College appointed Holmes "University Lecturer on Jurisprudence" for the next academic year. It would, doubtless, have been discouraging for those who were named to university lectureships in 1871 had they realized that President Eliot was contemporaneously reporting to the governing authorities of the university that the nine-year-old experiment in higher education had "failed hopelessly, and in an unexpectedly short time." [1] The dream of those who had encouraged these lectureships for college graduates was that a Graduate School of Arts and Sciences might grow out of them. Few enrollments and diminishing interest in the experiment had quickly made it clear that the lectureships would not be the beginning of a new era in higher education. Though President Eliot acknowledged his disappointment, he emphasized one advantage which the effort had brought to the university. Students enrolled in the schools of Law, Divinity, and Medicine had found the University Lectures an important supplement to the professional courses offered by the faculties of their schools. Acclaiming this by-product of the experiment, the President and Fellows in the spring of 1872 re-employed a number of the university lecturers under new titles. Among the men thus retained was Holmes. During 1872–73, he filled the post of Lecturer in Jurisprudence in the Harvard Law School.

[1] *Annual Report of the President of Harvard College, 1871–1872* (Cambridge, 1873), 13.

It is not unlikely that the initial suggestion that Holmes might become University Lecturer on Jurisprudence came to President Eliot from friends at the Boston bar who knew Holmes to be the author of an anonymous essay, "Codes, and the Arrangement of the Law," in the *American Law Review* for October 1870.[2] A critic in the *Albany Law Journal,* to be sure, had said of the essay that it was "about as vague, indefinite, and unsatisfactory as we ever care to read," [3] an opinion which was shared by the Commissioners to Revise the Statutes of the State of Iowa who wrote scornfully of "the elaborate theories which have been devised out of their own consciousness or borrowed from foreign jurisprudence, by recent writers on jurisprudence." [4] John Norton Pomeroy, however, had probably accurately represented academic and scholarly opinion when, writing a long letter to Holmes, he expressed the greatest admiration for his essay and indicated that though practitioners might not appreciate what Holmes had done for them "it is doing them a real kindness to startle them with ideas above and beyond their common experience." [5]

In this first of his systematic essays on law Holmes was concerned with two problems—the one practical, the other theoretical. In 1870 English and American lawyers were still discussing the merits of Bentham's insistence that codification of the law was

[2] *Am. L. Rev.,* 5:1; *Harv. L. Rev.,* 44:725 (March 1931) .

[3] *Albany Law Journal,* 2:323 (Oct. 15, 1870) . Cf. the far more favorable comment in *Law Magazine and Review,* 1 (N.S.):1098 (December 1872) .

[4] In an unsigned review of *The Code of Iowa* and other volumes, *Am. L. Rev.,* 7:318 (January 1873) ; *Harv. L. Rev.,* 44:792, Holmes indicated that he took the disparaging comment of the Commissioners to be applicable to his essay.

[5] Feb. 6, 1871 (HLS) . The fact that in 1897 Sir Frederick Pollock and other leading English lawyers organized the *Encyclopedia of the Laws of England* upon the arrangement which Holmes had outlined in the first of his major essays indicates that the effort had something more than theoretical significance. See *Holmes-Pollock Letters,* I, 71–72. The indebtedness which Pollock expressed in his General Introduction to the *Encyclopedia* (I, 7, footnote 2) was for suggestions with respect to a suitable arrangement of the law which Holmes made in three of his early essays: "Codes, and the Arrangement of the Law," *supra,* note 2; "Misunderstandings of the Civil Law," *Am. L. Rev.,* 6:37 (October 1871) ; *Harv. L. Rev.,* 44:759; "The Arrangement of the Law—Privity," *Am. L. Rev.,* 7:46 (October 1872) ; *Harv. L. Rev.,* 44:738.

a first necessity for the regeneration of society and its legal institutions. In England, as in New York and other states of the Union, the disciples of Bentham had not wholly lost their fervor. In his comments on the hopes of the Benthamites, Holmes here, as in other later reflections on the movement for codification,[6] revealed the gravest distrust of its presuppositions. Since "law is not a science, but is essentially empirical," the common law's reluctance to put its trust in "any faculty of generalization, however brilliant" is profoundly wise.[7] It is the merit of the common law, he said, "that it decides the case first and determines the principle afterwards."[8]

It may seem surprising that one who thus praised the pragmatism of the common law and justified his opposition to the movement for codification by the principles of empiricism should couple the praise and the opposition with a plea for a philosophical arrangement of the *corpus juris.* Many lawyers shared the conviction of Holmes's *Albany* reviewer and the Iowa Commissioners that if scientific order were brought to the common law its common sense would be fatally infected by speculative theory, its practicality be seriously jeopardized by dogmatic logic. There was still some sympathy for the "old-fashioned English lawyer's idea" that "a satisfactory body of law was a chaos with a full index."[9] Lawyers of that stamp were not seriously troubled by the fact that such order and shape as could be discovered in the common law had been born of outmoded and discarded forms of action. They somehow found it easier to let the ghosts of trover, detinue, case,

6 See review of *The Code of Iowa, supra,* note 4.

7 *Am. L. Rev.,* 5:1, 4. The contrast between science and empiricism may seem surprising in one whose philosophical loyalties were dedicated to the empiricism of science (see *Shaping Years,* 257–258, 270–272). It seems clear that in 1870 Holmes used the word "science" in the sense that he gave it in 1899 when he rejected the notion that "the true science of the law . . . consist[s] mainly in a theological working out of dogma or a logical development as in mathematics" ("Law in Science and Science in Law," *Collected Legal Papers,* 225).

8 *Am. L. Rev.,* 5:1.

9 The phrase was Thomas Erskine Holland's and was quoted by Holmes in his unsigned review of Holland's *Essays upon the Form of the Law,* in *Am. L. Rev.,* 5:114 (October 1870).

and trespass keep the legal mansion tidy than to rearrange its apartments on a "scientific" or utilitarian basis. Holmes not only protested against this stubborn fidelity to tradition [10] but complained of another class of textwriters, those who aim at a commercial market by building their classifications of law around facts "of dramatic instead of . . . legal significance." An author of a treatise on law who "takes such subjects as railroads or telegraphs, or, going a step further, as mercantile law, or shipping, or medical jurisprudence, thinks he is doing a very practical thing." In fact the exaggeration of the legally irrelevant element accentuates the difficulties of comprehension and breeds disorder in the study and practice of law. "The methods which are commonly called practical are in truth the most unpractical and destructive of sound legal thinking." [11] And "the end of all classification should be to make the law *knowable;* and . . . the system best accomplishes that purpose which proceeds from the most general conception to the most specific proposition or exception in the order of logical subordination." [12]

Holmes went so far in his desire to start afresh that in 1871 he suggested—as if he were adding a footnote to his first essay—that it was exceedingly doubtful if there was any logical or analytic justification for publishing textbooks on the law of torts. Tradition said that such books should deal with the wrongs remedied by

[10] In the closing paragraph of an unsigned review of Townshend's edition of the New York Code of Procedure, (the rest of the review having been written by A. G. Sedgwick), Holmes made it clear that he thought that the preservation of the common-law forms of action was most unfortunate. "If those forms had been based upon a comprehensive survey of the field of rights and duties, so that they embodied in a practical shape a classification of the law, with a form of action to correspond to every substantial duty, the question would be other than it is. But they are in fact so arbitrary in character, and owe their origin to such purely historical causes, that nothing keeps them but our respect for the sources of our jurisprudence" (*Am. L. Rev.*, 5:359 (January 1871). See also his review of Dicey on *Parties to an Action, id.,* 534 (April 1871); *Harv. L. Rev.*, 44:786.

[11] Review of the *Code of Iowa, supra,* note 4. See also Holmes's unsigned review of the second edition of Shearman and Redfield on *Negligence,* in *Am. L. Rev.,* 5:343 (January 1871).

[12] "The Arrangement of the Law—Privity," *Am. L. Rev.,* 7:46, 47 note (October 1872).

the actions of trespass, trespass on the case, and trover. It seemed to Holmes that this forced into an artificial association concepts which had no close philosophic relationship with each other and excluded others which analytically were closely affiliated. He recognized that it would require a lawyer possessed not only of exceptional philosophical capacity, but blessed with a self-sacrificing willingness to defy the given classification of the market-place, to undertake the preparation of a textbook which would bring together the wrongs which philosophically should be brought together and discard, for other texts, those which fell within the boundaries of a different category of order. He suggested that his friend Nicholas St. John Green, then teaching Torts at Harvard, might be such a man.[13]

Bentham's energy had set in motion two separate yet related endeavors. The one was essentially practical seeking drastic reform of procedure in the courts of common law and equity. The other was philosophical and asked for a system of law designed by reason for the achieving of defined ends. The first movement towards practical reform had achieved notable successes both in England and the United States by the 1870's. The intricacies of procedure no longer ruled the administration of justice with that proud insolence which had outraged Bentham. The elimination of artificiality meant, however, the casting aside of the one element which had provided a degree of order in the English legal system. While the forms of action prevailed it was possible for lawyers, though doubtless impossible for philosophers, to see structure in the English legal system. The common-law practitioner saw no need for a theory of liability in tort when he knew the scope of the action on the case and the reach of an action of trespass. He did not have to formulate a theory of possession when he knew that a possessor (whoever he might be) could find suitable remedies in the arsenal of the common law to protect his interest (whatever it was) from injury by another. The common law, in other words, had not felt the need for a philosophical classification of its elements while it

---

13 Unsigned review of an abridgement of Addison on *Torts, Am. L. Rev.,* 5:340–341 (January 1871).

had a procedural scaffolding from which the practitioner could pursue his disorderly calling. As the reformers pulled down the scaffolding, the need for carrying forward Bentham's second endeavor—the philosophical—became imperative. By mid-century the time had come for English and American lawyers to offer an arrangement of the law possessing a rational and philosophic strength wholly lacking in the dissolving procedural order of the earlier day.

Even before the reformers had begun effectively to remove the old scaffolding, John Austin had responded to Bentham's call for a new jurisprudence. If his audience at London University did not fully realize what the lecturer's painful efforts signified, the next generation, deprived by the procedural reformers of the traditional scaffolding, saw Austin's achievement as profoundly important. What Austin offered was something of much more practical importance than a mere theory of sovereignty. He had sought to define the province of jurisprudence and to discover and classify the essential concepts within the provincial boundaries. Austin had prepared his mind for jurisprudence on the Continent and had brought back to London a greater understanding of the structure of the Roman law than most English lawyers possessed. His compatriots, hungry for an ordering philosophy, were not so hampered by parochialism as to deny the possibility that Roman wisdom and civilian learning might usefully be brought to bear upon the common law inheritance. What was more natural in mid-century than that English and American jurists, having been deprived of the old procedural order, should see in the elaborate elegance of the Roman law the philosophic structure so badly needed in the Anglo-American legal system? [14] Few Englishmen of the 1860's

[14] It would be misleading, of course, to hold Austin exclusively or even primarily responsible for the mid-century revival of English interest in Roman law. One could refer to many jurists other than James Bryce who were actively seeking to persuade English lawyers that there was much to be learned from the study of Roman law, but Bryce's name deserves special emphasis because of his intimacy with Holmes. See his *Academical Study of the Civil Law* (London, 1871) and Holmes's review of the pamphlet in *Am. L. Rev.*, 5:715 (July 1871).

were troubled by the fact that Austin had built his jurisprudence in the pre-Darwinian age and that he tended, accordingly, to look upon the legal order as a scheme fixed for all times and all places by the categories of reason. Yet the time of philosophy and the time of law were both ripe for the reception of continental order.

In this intellectual setting it was quite natural that Holmes should make his first effort in jurisprudence that of offering an acceptable classification of the law. Some twenty years after the publication of his "Codes, and the Arrangement of the Law," Holmes's friend John C. Gray, speaking as historian of legal philosophy, asserted that until the publication of Maine's *Early History of Institutions* in 1874, Anglo-American jurists, recognizing Austin as their philosophical sovereign, had been absorbed in the effort to discover an analytically acceptable classification of the law.[15] The character of Holmes's first effort in jurisprudence surely bore out his friend's thesis. In 1870 Holmes's endeavor was purely analytic, and the framework of his inquiry was that into which Austin had forced the problems of jurisprudence.

When Holmes published the essay on Codes and Arrangement it is clear that he saw his most significant and original contribution to analytical theory the suggestion that classification should be built upon a schedule of duties rather than a structure of rights.[16] Though, as we shall see, the essay contained a few critical

15 "Some Definitions and Questions in Jurisprudence," *Harv. L. Rev.*, 6:22 (April 15, 1892).

16 Shortly after the essay was published Holmes was distressed to learn that what he had supposed to be his wholly original suggestion that classification should be based upon duties instead of rights had been made by others. In reading Shadworth Hodgson's *Theory of Practice* in July 1872, he found Hodgson acclaiming Auguste Comte for the suggestion that "law should be approached and its object-matter arranged from the point of view of duties, and not from that of rights . . . To take rights and not the corresponding duties as the ultimate phenomena of law, is to stop short of a complete analysis and to make 'entities of abstractions.'" Holmes called attention to the originating priority of Comte and Hodgson in his essay on privity, *Am. L. Rev.*, 7:46. In Holmes's own copy of his essay on Codes and Arrangement a marginal reference to Hodgson's book is supplemented by the comment that he had not seen the work until after his own essay was in print. In his own bound volume of the *American Law Review* for 1870–1871, now at the Library

comments on Austin's philosophy of law, this insistence that "logically and chronologically" [17] duties precede rights seems to have
been derived from the most fundamental of Austin's theses—the
proposition that every law is, ultimately, identifiable as the command of the sovereign. Surely the immediate legal product of an
authoritative command is the duty of obedience. The existence of
that obligation may incidentally give rise to rights in third persons, but there is much force in Holmes's contention that while
laws are looked upon as commands, duties rather than rights
should, logically, be made the basic elements in a scheme of classification.

It was not until near the end of the essay that Holmes sought
to clarify the concept which he proposed to make fundamental in
the suggested scheme of classification. "A duty, strictly so called,
is only created by commands which may be broken at the expense
of incurring a penalty. That which the law directly compels, although it may onerously affect an individual, cannot be said to
impose a duty upon him." [18] Holmes was willing to concede that
while rights are made the fundamental elements in a system of
classification there is no need to distinguish between a plaintiff's
enforceable claim to damages from a neighbor who, by maintaining a nuisance, has done injury to the plaintiff, and the plaintiff's
right to call upon the sheriff to abate the nuisance by his official
action. On account of "the practical cohesion of the conception
property" [19] we need not, while we classify law on the basis of
rights, pay attention to the distinction between the true duty—
to respect possession—and the quasi duty which finds its sanction
in the sheriff's abatement of the nuisance. In Holmes's scheme,
however, the distinction must be recognized, though it meant the
exclusion of the subject matter of "sanctioning rights" which had
played such an important part in Austin's classification of law.

---

of Congress, there is a further comment on this matter in Holmes's hand: "My coincidence is so striking that it is proper to say that the book [presumably Hodgson's] was received at the Athenaeum (where I first saw it) Aug. 24/70 at which
time this was in print. I had noted the idea in the flyleaf of Austin long before, and
never saw the passage in Comte."

[17] *Am. L. Rev.*, 5:3.   [18] *Id.*, 12.   [19] *Id.*

In 1870 Holmes was evidently quite willing to accept the Austinian thesis that a duty may always be found when a penalty—such as liability for damages, fine, or imprisonment—has been prescribed. He did not, accordingly, question the orthodox view that one who enters into a binding contract and, by that commitment, subjects himself to liability in damages for non-performance may properly be said to owe a duty of performance. The entire scheme of classification which Holmes outlined in "Codes and Arrangement" and developed in further detail in the subsequent essays on "Privity" and on "The Theory of Torts" was built upon this Austinian theory of duty. As we shall see, before that series of essays was completed Holmes had come to question the philosophic validity of Austin's concept of duty and offered a new concept in substitution. The fact that he continued to refine his scheme of classification in the Austinian terms of duty makes it peculiarly difficult to understand his final position. Perhaps something like comprehension can be achieved, however, if one recognizes that between 1870 and 1873 the center of his interest shifted from the analytical problems of classification to the historical problems of explanation. During that period of shifting concern he did not wholly abandon his effort to present a classification of law which would be useful to students and practitioners. When he was concerned with that task he continued to use the Austinian concept of duty, believing, evidently, that for the practitioner's purpose it was adequate. His recognition that it was philosophically questionable made it easy for him, however, to turn from the relatively sterile occupation of classifying artificial concepts to the study of the processes of growth and adaptation of legal institutions. To understand the changing nature of his interest it will, perhaps, be helpful first to follow the course of his development as critic of Austin and then to trace the development of his increasing concern with problems of legal history.

Though Holmes, as we have seen, was initially satisfied to accept Austin's concept of duty, he did, in his first essay, question other basic elements in Austin's jurisprudence. In that paper he summarized Austin's definition of law. "A law, we understand him to say, is a command (of a definite political superior, enforced by a sanction), which obliges (intelligent human beings) to acts or forbearances of a class." [20] The definition seemed to Holmes to possess little philosophical value. "If names are to mark substantial distinctions, one hesitates to admit that only a definite body of political superiors can make what is properly called a law." For the philosopher, as distinguished from the lawyer, "by whom a duty is imposed must be of less importance than the definiteness of its expression and the certainty of its being enforced." Such social requirements as "the rule that if I am invited to a dinner party in London I must appear in evening dress under the penalty of not being asked to similar entertainments if I disobey," is, in a philosophical sense, at least as truly a law as the New York statute against usury "which juries do not decline to carry out, simply because they are never asked to do so." The critical difference between the social requirements which Austin put outside the law and rules which he brought within its compass seemed to Holmes to lie in the fact that the "sovereign or the political superior secures obedience to his commands by his courts." That difference, insignificant as it may be to philosophers, is of critical importance to lawyers. Because courts give rise to lawyers, a profession has come into being which makes the study of judicial decisions its business. "Rules not enforced by [courts], although equally imperative, are the study of no profession. It is on this account that the province of jurisprudence has to be so carefully determined." [21] For Holmes, that province included nothing more than the rules enforced by the judiciary. Though he believed that there are rules beyond those boundaries which at least philosophically deserve the name of law, they were not for him, any more than they were for Austin, within the province of jurisprudence. He was, accordingly, thoroughly "content to stand by the lines" which Austin had drawn "and to omit ethics [from the province of jurisprudence] until the coming of a second Grotius." [22]

20 *Id.*, 5:4.

21 *Id.*, 4–5.

22 *Id.* at 5. It may fairly be asked whether Holmes did not abandon his own restricted conception of law—rules enforced by courts—when he made a place for

In the spring of 1872, two years after the publication of the essay on Codes and Arrangement, Holmes as University Lecturer gave his lectures on jurisprudence in Harvard College. The character of his audience made it natural that he should consider some of the philosophical deficiencies in Austin's philosophy of law more explicitly than he did in the earlier essay for practitioners. The only surviving record of what he said in his lectures appears in his own summary of their content in a "book notice" which he wrote for the October issue of the *American Law Review* in 1872.[23] In form a review of a recent issue of the *Law Magazine and Review,* the notice was in fact a summary of the criticisms of Austin which Holmes had put forward in his Harvard lectures. He was evidently stimulated to put his criticisms in print by the fact that he had found Frederick Pollock, in one of the essays in the volume being noticed,[24] reaching results which "more or less" coincided with opinions which Holmes had expressed as lecturer.[25] One cannot help feeling that Holmes had some anxiety that he might be considered an imitative and not an originating critic of Austin if Pollock's views were put in print while his went the

---

international law within the province of jurisprudence. The given reason for its inclusion was not that its rules are binding on courts but that it is "a subject which lawyers do practically study," and is made up of "rules of conduct so definite as to be written in textbooks, and sanctioned in many cases by the certainty that a breach will be followed by war." *Id.,* 5. It is quite possible, of course, that Holmes by mere oversight failed to mention the undoubted fact that many rules of international law are recognized and enforced by courts and, to the extent that that is so, fall within the boundaries of jurisprudence as he drew them.

23 *Id.,* 6:723 (July 1872) ; *Harv. L. Rev.,* 44:788. Holmes's reading list indicates that he delivered the last of his twelve lectures on jurisprudence on May 6, 1872, and that he had prepared many of them between October and December 1871. See Little, "Reading," 163, 183, 184. An unsigned review of Holmes's paper on Privity spoke of the reviewer's understanding that the paper dealt with problems which Holmes had dealt with in his Harvard lectures. See *Law Magazine and Review,* 1 (N.S.):1098 (December 1872) .

24 "Law and Command," *Law Magazine and Review,* 1 (N.S.):189 (April 1, 1872) .

25 *Am. L. Rev.,* 6:723. It seems clear that Holmes, in his comment on Pollock's essay, was summarizing the contents of his first series of Harvard lectures—those which he gave as University Lecturer in the Spring of 1872. This first sympathetic intellectual encounter between Holmes and Pollock was to be followed by a personal meeting two years later and thereafter by intimate friendship.

ephemeral way familiar to college lecturers. He had already shown his sensitivity in such matters by his rueful discovery that others had gone before him in suggesting that the law should be classified around duties instead of rights.

In his essay of 1870 Holmes had not directly challenged Austin's central thesis that law is the expression of the sovereign's will. As we have seen, he was then willing to concede that "as a definition of what lawyers call law" Austin's definition was sufficiently accurate. From the summary account which Holmes gave of the content of his University Lectures, it would seem that as teacher he was more critical of Austin's definition of law than he had been as essayist. He pointed out to his students that Austin, like other theorists of sovereignty, seemed to acknowledge that

who is the sovereign is a question of fact equivalent to the question who has the sum of political powers of a state in his hands. That is to say, sovereignty is a form of power, and the will of the sovereign is law, because he has the power to compel obedience or to punish disobedience, and for no other reason. The limits within which his will is law, then, are those within which he has, or is believed to have, power to compel or punish.[26]

Holmes then pointed out something which he had not emphasized in 1870, the fact that there are many forces which set limits to the sovereign's capacity to enforce his will. The danger of war imposes an effective external limitation upon his power to compel obedience to his wishes. The disloyalties and dissatisfactions of the community over which he rules also restrict his power to command. The domestic limits include "conflicting principles of sovereignty (the territorial and the tribal) . . . organizations of persons not sharing in the sovereign power, and . . . unorganized public opinion." A sovereign thus limited is scarcely recognizable as the sovereign of Austin's imagining. When the sovereign is thus, by harsh reality, denied the power which Austin assumed him to possess, what happens to the Austinian notion of law? Holmes suggested to his students that if the sovereign is less mighty than Austin thought

[26] *Id.*

him, "there might be law without sovereignty, and that where there is a sovereign, properly so called, other bodies, not sovereign, and even opinion, might generate law in a philosophical sense against the will of the sovereign." [27]

It may be felt that this reference to the "philosophical" inadequacy of Austin's definition of law implies that Holmes as lecturer was willing to make the same concession which he had made as essayist two years earlier—the concession, that is, that lawyers may take the Austinian definition as sufficiently accurate. If the implication be there, it is undermined by quite explicit statements that the lawyer, like the philosopher, should have a broader concept of law than Austin's. The practitioner's chief concern is with the action of courts, not with the commands of the sovereign. In the essay of 1870 Holmes had stated that the "only concern" of lawyers "is with such rules as the courts enforce." [28] In his lectures he made it clear that he believed that such rules are derived from many other sources than the commands of the sovereign. He reiterated the earlier doubt whether "law, in the more limited meaning which lawyers give to the word, possessed any other common attribute than that of being enforced by the procedure of the courts, and therefore of practical importance to lawyers." [29] He then asked, in effect, what justification there is for Austin's contention that the rules enforced by the procedure of the courts "either philosophically or legally . . . necessarily emanated from the will of the sovereign *as law*." Rules judicially enforced "do not always depend on the courts for their efficacy in governing conduct." [30] Did Holmes, perhaps, make this suggestion more vivid for the students of jurisprudence by repeating the question which he had earlier put to his students of constitutional law: What force leads the President and the Congress, in normal circumstances, to respect a decision of the Supreme Court of the United States? Respect is shown not because the Court has power to enforce its will by issuing its writs to Presidents and Congressmen, but because such other forms of power as tradition and public opinion, govern the conduct of men and of rulers.

[27] *Id.*   [28] *Id.*, 5:5.   [29] *Id.*, 6:723.   [30] *Id.*

In his University Lectures Holmes examined the implications in Austin's thesis that custom, no matter how prevalent it may be in a society, becomes law only when it is adopted by the courts. Austin had insisted that before the act of adoption occurs custom is nothing but "a motive for decision." Holmes did not question, but willingly accepted this proposition. However, he put a discerning if not a devastating question to the Austinians. If it may be said of untamed custom that it is merely a motive for decision—a factor which the court may respect and enforce, or repudiate and reject—may not the same thing be said of statutes and decisions? In what other sense, Holmes asked, is a statute law

than that we believe that the motive which we think that it offers to the judges will prevail, and will induce them to decide a case in a certain way, and so shape our conduct on that anticipation? A precedent may not be followed; a statute may be emptied of its contents by construction, or may be repealed without a saving clause after we have acted on it; but we expect the reverse, and if our expectations come true, we say we have been subject to law in the matter in hand. It must be remembered . . . that in a civilized state it is not the will of the sovereign that makes lawyers' law, even when that is its source, but what a body of subjects, namely, the judges, by whom it is enforced, *say* is his will. The judges have other motives for decision, outside their own arbitrary will, beside the commands of their sovereign. And whether those other motives are, or are not, equally compulsory, is immaterial, if they are sufficiently likely to prevail to afford a ground for prediction. The only question for the lawyer is, how will the judges act? Any motive for their action, be it constitution, statute, custom, or precedent, which can be relied upon as likely in the generality of cases to prevail, is worthy of consideration as one of the sources of law, in a treatise on jurisprudence. Singular motives, like the blandishments of the emperor's wife, are not a ground for prediction, and are therefore not considered.[31]

This passage, of course, foreshadows the substance of Holmes's well-known aphorism that "the prophecies of what the courts will do in fact, and nothing more pretentious, are what I mean by the

[31] *Id.*, 724.

law." [32] It is not my concern to defend or to attack—not even to unravel—the aphorism. What is important at this stage is that we should understand the nature of Holmes's effort when he first emphasized the predictive element in law. His endeavor was principally critical, not creative. When he lectured at Harvard he was not seeking to construct a jurisprudence. His primary effort was to expose a weakness in Austin's thesis that law is always identifiable as the command of the sovereign. Implicit in his thesis, of course, was the suggestion that a competent lawyer—whose primary responsibility is to advise clients—must judge not merely how likely it is that an earlier decision or an applicable statute will be the controlling motive for decision of his client's case, but what other competing motives of more than accidental significance are likely to affect the court's decision.

It has been urged that Holmes's emphasis on the predictive element in law reflected his affiliation with the philosophical pragmatism of William James, Charles Peirce, and Nicholas St. John Green.[33] Perhaps that thesis can be sustained, yet it would seem that Holmes in the beginning, at least, was led toward the prediction theory of law by an impulse more critical than philosophical. In 1872 he was not, I think, searching for a jurisprudence consistent with the philosophical premises of his generation. He was neither considering the nature of truth nor twisting the tail of the cosmos. He was engaged in the more limited and quite hardheaded task of examining the validity of Austin's thesis that law is always identifiable as the command of the sovereign. His method,

32 "The Path of the Law," *Collected Legal Papers* (hereafter *CLP*) , 173. Cf. "Law is a statement of the circumstances in which the public force will be brought to bear upon men through the courts." *American Banana Co.* v. *United Fruit Co.*, 213 U.S. 347, 356 (1909) .

33 For such suggestions see Max Fisch, "Justice Holmes, The Prediction Theory of Law and Pragmatism," *Journal of Philosophy*, 39:85 (1942) ; Jerome Frank, "A Conflict with Oblivion: Some Observations of the Founders of Legal Pragmatism," *Rutgers Law Review*, 9:425, 444 *et seq.* (1954) . It is, perhaps, worth remembering that Holmes asserted to Morris Cohen that as late as 1891 he had not "heard of pragmatism" ("Holmes-Cohen Correspondence," *Journal of the History of Ideas*, 9:19, 1948) .

doubtless, was that of his time, for he sought to discard abstractions on which the prevailing philosophies of law were founded. Surely he was gratified that his bringing of human law into relationship with the predictive process brought him into alliance with those contemporaries in science who were insisting that the laws of nature which are the concern of scientists are merely expert prognostications of the probable sequence which the events of nature will follow.[34] Yet it is hard to believe, I think, that he consciously endeavored to formulate a philosophy of law which would be consistent with the prevailing philosophy of science. When he saw where his effort in criticism had led him I have no doubt that he was satisfied to find himself allied with the contemporary science and philosophy. This satisfaction surely played its part in strengthening his conviction that what had started as a critical inquiry had become a creative achievement.

It was in the Harvard lectures of 1872 that Holmes first questioned the Austinian concept of duty on which he had founded and continued to build his suggested classification of law. Austin had asserted that the command which is law—the command, that is, which brings into being a legal duty—may always be identified as such by the sovereign's threat that a penalty or sanction will be imposed if a certain course of conduct is followed. By posing an example, Holmes suggested that Austin's formula for the identification of legal duties was unsatisfactory. Let us assume, he said, that the sovereign has imposed a tax on those persons who bring iron into the realm. Tested by Austin's formula, this pronouncement would mean that the importation of iron is a breach of duty. "A protective tariff on iron," Holmes replied, "does not create a duty not to bring it into the country." [35] If the subject has a choice between a burdened course of conduct and an unburdened alternative, we cannot properly say that he has a duty to avoid the burden. Yet the Austinian formula would justify the false proposition

[34] See Pollock, "The Science of Case Law," *Essays in Jurisprudence and Ethics* (1882), 238.

[35] *Am. L. Rev.,* 6:724.

76

that the importer of taxable goods violates his duty when he imports them. The application of the same formula led Austin to assert that a party to a contract owes a duty of performance. In his scheme of things the promisor's liability to pay damages signifies the sovereign's command that the promisor should fulfill his undertaking. Holmes, condemning the Austinian test for the identification of duties, intimated that it is as inappropriate to assert that the threat of damages for nonperformance of contracts proves the duty to perform them as it would be to assert that the taxation of imports establishes that there is a duty not to import.

It is important to notice that Holmes's analysis of a promisor's obligation does not suggest that the contractor owes no Austinian duty of performance. Since nonperformance brings the penalty of damages, a promisor, on Austin's premises, may properly be said to owe a legal duty of performance. If, however, one questions the adequacy of Austin's definition of legal duty and accepts the alternative offered by Holmes, there is much force in the contention that liability to pay damages for breach does not establish the existence of a legal duty to perform one's contracts. In 1872 Holmes made the dependence of his analysis of the promisor's obligation upon his restrictive definition of duty quite clear. On later occasions, however, when he played a somewhat teasing game of paradox and again insisted that a promisor owes no duty of performance, he did not trouble to restate—possibly because he had forgotten—the restrictive definition of duty from which the paradox secured its best and earliest justification.[36] Friends and critics alike were misled, perhaps, not only by Holmes's failure to redefine his terms but by the unquestionable fact that while as lecturer he was denying the philosophical validity of Austin's conception of

36 See, for instance, *Holmes-Pollock Letters* (hereafter *HPL*), I, 20–21, 119, 177. As we shall later see, many considerations different from those which led him to his first formulation of the no-duty theory of contract obligation contributed to such later formulations as that in *The Common Law* at 300–302. It is hard to believe, however, that the initial critical impulse which moved Holmes in 1872 had spent its whole force in the later years. Always proud of his original insights, Holmes was unlikely in 1881 to have forgotten his *aperçu* of 1872.

77

duty, as essayist he was contemporaneously building his classification on that conception and showing no hesitation to include the promisor's obligation in his schedule of legal duties.[37]

Holmes did more than call the attention of his students to the errors of John Austin. He offered for their consideration another definition of duty than that which Austin had formulated. The notion of duty, accurately defined, involves "something more than a tax on a certain course of conduct . . . The word imports the existence of an absolute wish on the part of the power imposing it to bring about a certain course of conduct, and to prevent the contrary. A legal duty cannot be said to exist if the law intends to allow the person supposed to be subject to it an option at a certain price." In order to determine whether the sovereign's wish (i.e., the law's requirement) is absolute, we must carry our inquiry beyond the point at which Austin brought his to a stop. "The imposition of a penalty is . . . only evidence tending to show that an absolute command was intended (a rule of construction). But an absolute command does not exist—penalty or no penalty—unless a breach of it is deprived of the protection of the law, which is shown by a number of consequences . . . such as the invalidity of contracts to do the forbidden act;—the rule *in pari delicto potior est conditio defendentis,*—the denial of relief when the illegal act is part of the plaintiff's case, etc." If the imposition of a penalty does not conclusively establish the absolute character of the sovereign's wish, *"a fortiori* in those cases where there is no penalty directly attached to a given act, the existence of a legal duty to abstain from or to perform it, must be determined by these collateral consequences." When no such consequences supplement the ordi-

---

[37] "The Arrangement of the Law—Privity," *Am. L. Rev.,* 7:46; in his footnote in this article, Holmes indicated that he was aware of the difficulty. "We use this word [duty] as near enough for our present purposes, but subject to an investigation, the outline of which has been sketched in our last number . . . as to how far what is commonly called law imposes what are properly called duties." See also "The Theory of Torts," *id.,* 7:660, note 1 (July 1873); *Harv. L. Rev.,* 44:781, note 14. Though in *The Common Law* Holmes reiterated his insistence that classification should be built upon duties rather than rights, he indicated that it might be desirable to "avoid the word duty, which is open to objection . . ." *CL,* 220.

nary liability to a civil action at common law, "it is hard to say that there is a duty in strictness, and the rule is inserted in law books for the empirical reason . . . that it is applied by the courts and must therefore be known by professional men." [38]

The concepts and definitions of duty which Holmes thus put before his students in 1872 were significantly different from those on which he had proposed to build his arrangement of the law in 1870. In "Codes and Arrangement" he had said that a duty, "strictly so called, is only created by commands which may be broken at the expense of incurring a penalty." By illustration he had indicated that the obligation enforced by an action of trover (and presumably debt, covenant, and assumpsit) was a "true" or strict duty. All that he had then excluded from the concept were acts "which the law directly compels," as when the sheriff abates a nuisance or gives possession to the successful plaintiff in a real action.[39] That exclusion was of such trivial importance that the mass of traditional legal relations fell within the scheme of order which Holmes proposed. When, however, in 1872 he repudiated Austin's concept of duty and that which he himself had accepted in the first essay on arrangement he offered an alternative of such extreme narrowness that it could not possibly become the basic element in a serviceable classification of law. Yet after offering his new and restrictive definition, Holmes, in his essay on "The Theory of Torts," [40] continued his attempt to arrange the law around a schedule of duties as they had been defined by Austin. It would seem that his somewhat halfhearted effort to complete the analytical structure in the repudiated Austinian terms was based on the assumption that since judges, practitioners, and text writers found Austin's terminology useful, he could properly use that language to conclude his analytical endeavor.

In the closing paragraph of his summary of the Harvard lectures Holmes very briefly outlined another criticism of Austin which he had offered for the consideration of his students—a criti-

---

[38] *Am. L. Rev.*, 6:724–725.
[39] *Id.*, 5:12.

[40] *Id.*, 7:652 (July 1873).

cism which he was to develop with some fullness a year later in his essay on "The Theory of Torts." Once more the criticism was based on Holmes's belief that Austin's concept of duty was unacceptable. Believing that duties exist whenever penalties are found, Austin supposed that liability to a civil action was not essentially different from the sanction of criminal punishment, and that the civil sanction—like the criminal—implied that the offender who defied the sovereign's command was guilty of culpable fault. He had assumed, accordingly, that a defendant charged with injuring another man's person or property could be held civilly responsible in damages only if he had done the injury wilfully or with actual negligence. Holmes, by contrast, who had come to believe that "liability to a civil action is not a penalty or sanction of itself creating a duty," was led by that denial to question whether such liability necessarily implies culpability. Austin, "who looked at the law too much as a criminal lawyer" did not sufficiently realize that "the object of the law is to accomplish an external result." Since the law's concern is not with the sins of men, but with their actions, it may impose obligations though fault and culpability are lacking. In many circumstances, of course, it is secure "of what it desires in the absence of wilfulness or negligence . . ." Then "it may very properly make wilfulness or negligence the gist of the action, —one of the necessary elements of liability. But in other circumstances it may be thought that this is too narrow a limit; it may be thought that titles should be protected against even innocent conversion; that persons should be indemnified, at all events, for injuries from extra-hazardous sources, in which case negligence is not an element. Public policy must determine where the line is to be drawn." [41]

---

[41] *Id.*, 6:725. The doctrine which Holmes thus expounded to his Harvard students in the spring of 1872 had evidently been formulated in his mind quite recently. We know that in April 1871 he had assumed that culpability is, in almost all circumstances, an essential element in tort liability. Reviewing Campbell's *Law of Negligence* he had then stated that "a culpable state of mind is an element in most wrongs; and negligence and wilfulness, into which negligence shades away, express the more common of these states" (*id.*, 5:536) .

Holmes's disagreement with the Austinian thesis that culpability is an essential element in liability had other sources than the doubt whether law is the command of the sovereign. The data of history had already led him to question facile pronouncements of Austin in justification of the master's liability for the act of his servant. In the essay on Privity, Holmes had urged that such liability is not grounded, as Austin supposed, in the remote inadvertance of the master in employing a careless servant, but is traceable to Roman institutions of slavery.[42] In "The Theory of Torts" a footnote was used to suggest that Austin had again misapplied his principle of remote inadvertance to explain the liability of the owner of an escaped animal for injuries which it may inflict. Austin had justified the owner's liability by ascribing fault to him, not in allowing the animal to go at large, but in keeping a ferocious beast at all. In his critical footnote, Holmes offered the suggestion that the true explanation of the liability in question might be found in "the primitive notion that liability somehow attached upon the thing doing the harm." [43] In the text to which this criticism was a mere annotation, Holmes made it clear that he had begun to come to believe that it would be wiser for the jurist to seek for a historical explanation of vicarious liability than to formulate a fiction which would give it philosophical justification. He suggested, accordingly, that we must recognize that some traditional liabilities without fault come to us as an inheritance from primitive societies. Others, he said, have been imposed by the legislation of judges who have been moved by "more or less thought-out views of public policy" to the conviction that it is sometimes politic to "make those who go into extra-hazardous employments take the risk on their own shoulders." In any case, an accurate arrangement of the law of torts must keep a place for those instances, "some of ancient and some of modern date, in which the cause of action is determined by certain overt acts or events alone, irrespective of culpability." [44]

The essay on "The Theory of Torts," in form at least, was ana-

[42] *Id.*, 7:61–62.   [43] *Id.*, 652, note 2.   [44] *Id.*, 652–653.

lytic in purpose. Holmes was still seeking, in other words, to fill in the details of the scheme of legal order which he had first outlined in 1870. We have seen that at the beginning of his quest he had been inspired by a radical desire to abandon the unphilosophical yet accepted methods of classification which had found their only justification in the forms of action. It was this spirit which had led him to suggest that "torts is not a proper subject for a law book." [45] That spirit had surely spent itself when, two years later, he not only wrote an essay on "The Theory of Torts" but asserted, quite explicitly, that "there is no fault to be found with the contents of text-books" on the law of torts.[46]

What considerations had brought about such a reversal of belief? It would seem that Holmes's disagreement with Austinian details and definitions had rather quickly been transformed into skepticism with respect to the fruitfulness of the entire analytic effort. He had come to believe that the order of time tells more of the structure of law than does the order of logic. It was quite natural, of course, that when he came to believe that law may best be seen as the rules enforced by courts he should abandon the rationalist's protest against the analytic sufficiency of the common law's accepted categories. Having become convinced that "an enumeration of the actions which have been successful, and of those which have failed, defines the extent of the primary duties imposed by the law," [47] Holmes renounced the analytic faith which had first inspired him and set his course by the historian's compass. The concern of the jurist should be with the development of law—the growth, that is, of the rules enforced by courts—rather than with the logical structure of legal concepts. Though Holmes avoided a frank confession of error with respect to his initial endeavors in analysis, a sweeping generalization found in "The Theory of Torts" implied that it had been error to hunt for theory in the categories of reason.

The growth of the law is very apt to take place in this way: Two widely different cases suggest a general distinction, which is a clear one

45 *Am. L. Rev.*, 5:341. See *supra*, pp. 64–65.
46 *Id.*, 7:659–660.   47 *Id.*

when stated broadly. But as new cases cluster around the opposite poles, and begin to approach each other, the distinction becomes more difficult to trace; the determinations are made one way or the other on a very slight preponderance of feeling, rather than articulate reason; and at last a mathematical line is arrived at by the contact of contrary decisions, which is so far arbitrary that it might equally well have been drawn a little further to the one side or to the other.[48]

These, I suggest, are the attitudes which produced *The Common Law,* not those which shaped "Codes and the Arrangement of the Law."

That Holmes was eager to have his theories of law reach and affect the minds of those who stood on "the firing line," is indicated by an incident which evidently blemished in Holmes's mind the reputation of a man who has commonly been supposed to be one of the great judges of the nineteenth century, Justice Doe of the Supreme Court of New Hampshire. In the late spring or early summer of 1872, Holmes sent Doe the proofs of his article on "The Theory of Torts." At the June term of the Supreme Court of New Hampshire, Justice Doe delivered the court's opinion in *Stewart* v. *Emerson.*[49] When Holmes saw the opinion he found that Doe discussed the law's willingness to recognize that most differences are differences in degree.

It may not be easy [said Doe], to fully describe the dividing line, on one side or the other of which all possible cases must fall . . . The general course of the line is well known; its precise location at all points is presumed to be ascertainable by the application of settled principles, although, at certain points, it may be marked in the authorities only approximately by the cases on either side, whose positions are determined from time to time as they arise.[50]

Not surprisingly, Holmes heard in these words an echo of his own voice, and for many years he resented what seemed an unfairness in Doe's failure to credit him with having suggested the notion. In

48 *Id.,* at 654.
49 52 N.H. 301 (1872) .
50 *Id.,* 314.

1910, writing to Dean Wigmore, Holmes expressed some surprise with Wigmore's

predilection for Doe. He seemed to me to write longwinded rather second rate discourses and I thought he did rather an unfair thing when I was a young essayist. I sent him proofs of an article in which I spoke of the gradual working out of a line in the law by the contact of decisions grouped about the two poles of an undeniable antithesis—e.g., night and day. Almost before my article appeared a decision of his used the notion with no credit given, which in those days I felt. Perhaps my memory is wrong as it was long ago, and I would not do injustice to the dead, but I guess I could find it. But at all events I thought there was not a great deal of brandy in his water.[51]

The sense of injury reflected in his letter once more reveals the anxiety which Holmes possessed that his originating contributions of thought or image should be recognized. He had been much grieved to discover that others had preceded him in the suggestion that classification in the law should be built upon duties and not upon rights.[52] He had used the awkward instrument of a book review to make it clear to the profession that he had formulated a careful criticism of Austin before Frederick Pollock's somewhat similar effort had been put in print.[53] In 1882, when he found in the first chapter of Waples on *Proceedings in Rem* many ideas and references which had striking but unacknowledged similarity to suggestions and authorities included both in his essay on "Primitive Notions in Modern Law" and in *The Common Law*, Holmes wrote in some indignation to Thomas M. Cooley, who had provided an introduction to Mr. Waples's book: "It is not merely that he takes for his starting point ideas which I have no reason to doubt were original with me and which I spent much time and labor in stating and proving but that the citations which I gathered

[51] Holmes to Wigmore, Jan. 14, 1910 (HLS). Holmes again indicated that the incident may have prejudiced him against Doe in a letter which he wrote to Roscoe Pound on February 16, 1923 (HLS). If Doe received Holmes's article in proof and wrote his opinion before the issue containing the article was published it is not surprising, perhaps, that he did not give Holmes the conventional credit.

[52] See *supra*, p. 67, note 16.

[53] See *supra*, pp. 71–72.

from various sources occur in such wise as to earmark the indebtedness to my mind." [54] No one of the incidents, taken alone, would indicate that Holmes was driven by an unusual longing for recognition. It does seem, however, that the protestations signify at least a strenuous eagerness for achievement, and perhaps an excess of anxiety for credit. A man of a gentler temperament, while he might not have forgotten Doe's silent adoption of his idea and his image, would probably have forgiven the offense in the recollection of the fact that, within a year of the uncrediting adoption, Doe was to quote a long passage from "The Theory of Torts," giving Holmes full credit for the quotation. [55]

In "The Theory of Torts" Holmes outlined another doctrine which was to become of central importance in his matured philosophy of law. The doctrine was derived in substantial part from his dissatisfaction with Austin's command theory of law and was intimately related to that thesis, already referred to, that the standards of the law, despite John Austin, are external. It asserts that every judge, before he takes decisive action, is compelled to make a preliminary investigation of a question of fact. "For example, the court has to satisfy itself that an ancient statute not found upon the rolls was actually enacted, before it will enforce it." [56] Similarly, if it is alleged that a mercantile controversy should be disposed of in accordance with the custom of merchants, the court is compelled to ascertain by one means or another whether the custom in fact prevails. "If the custom is so publicly known and understood that the conscience of the court permits it to act upon its own knowledge, it will do so." [57] In other circumstances it may be fitting for the judges to receive the testimony of mercantile ex-

[54] Sept. 22, 1882 (copy, HLS). Cooley's reply enclosed the comment of Waples on Holmes's letter. The defense was that the first chapter, as published, was written before Waples had seen Holmes's essay or the same materials, reworked, in *The Common Law* (Waples to Cooley, Oct. 6, 1882; HLS).

[55] *Brown* v. *Collins*, 53 N.H. 442 (1873). It should be noted, perhaps, that Holmes was later able to cite the Brown case in support of an important principle which he developed in *The Common Law* and which had first been outlined in "The Theory of Torts." See *CL*, 107, note 1.

[56] *Am. L. Rev.*, 7:655.

[57] *Id.*, 657.

perts. In either case, however, the court is compelled to conduct—formally or informally—a preliminary investigation of fact.

In some cases the fact, the belief of which controls the action of judges, is an act of the legislature; in others it is public policy, as understood by them; in others it is the custom or course of dealing of those classes most interested; and in others where there is no statute, no clear ground of policy, no practice of a specially interested class, it is the practice of the average member of the community,—what a prudent man would do under the circumstances,—and the judge accepts the juryman as representing the prudent man. But still the function of the juryman is only to inform the conscience of the court by suggesting a standard, just as when the finding is on a custom.[58]

In Holmes's eyes the greatest importance of this interpretation of the judicial process was in relationship to the jury's role in negligence cases. "It has come to pass that negligence is regarded by many whose opinion is entitled to respect as always and in the nature of things a question for the jury." [59] Holmes's thesis required the rejection of that dogma. Just as the court need not summon a jury of merchants to tell it that a custom prevails when the court's conscience is already satisfied that that is the fact, so it need not leave a question of negligence to the jury when it is satisfied that

[58] *Id.*, 658. See also Kent's *Commentaries,* II, *561, note 1.

[59] *Id.* It deserves special notice, I think, that in 1871 Holmes had apparently shared the common opinion with respect to the jury's role in negligence cases. In his review of Campbell on *Negligence* (*supra,* note 41) he had said that "if negligence must be alleged in the pleadings, we suppose it is wholly for the jury to say whether the party has used such care as a reasonable and prudent man would have used under the circumstances of the particular case whatever they may be." Though he then acknowledged that, in logic, it is not inappropriate for the judges to take cognizance of the manifest imprudence in a defendant's conduct, he took it as well settled in practice that negligence is treated as an ultimate fact to be found by the jury and should, therefore, be left to them at large in virtually all cases (*Am. L. Rev.,* 5:536–537). It seems not improbable that Holmes was led to change his view of the jury's role in negligence cases by his associate editor, Arthur G. Sedgwick. Opinions expressed by Sedgwick, reviewing Volume 16 of Gray's Massachusetts Reports (*id.,* 5:537, 538–539), are much more like those developed by Holmes in "The Theory of Torts" than those which he summarized in his review of Campbell. Sedgwick is identified as the reviewer of 16 Gray in Holmes's bound copy of Volume V at the Library of Congress.

an objective standard of prudence has been satisfied or violated. "If negligence means a culpable state of mind, and it is part of the plaintiff's case to prove that, the opinion [that negligence is always for the jury] would be true . . ." [60] When one believes, with Holmes, that liability for negligence is based upon an external standard—what would be the conduct of a reasonable man in the circumstances known to the defendant—then the court, in many cases, is entitled to decide for itself the preliminary question of fact whether that standard has or has not been satisfied before applying the rule of law to the fact so ascertained.

An acceptance of Holmes's analysis might involve, as he recognized, a continual vanishing of the jury's role in negligence cases. In his mind this was manifestly a desirable tendency. For it seemed to him no less absurd to allow one jury after another to decide whether or not a familiar brand of conduct met the objective standard of prudence than it would be to allow successive juries of merchants to say whether or not a mercantile custom prevailed. "It is little better than lawlessness if the same rule is not applied in similar cases thereafter." [61] Whether in fact similarities of careless conduct are so recurrent as to permit the judges at some point in time to substitute a rule of law for the whimsical judgments of that "fugitive tribunal"—the jury—which initially came to the court's assistance, Holmes did not purport to say. "All that is attempted is to point out the theory on which the jury takes any part in these decisions, and that it depends on the discretion of the court whether they shall be appealed to at all, and whether, having clearly decided to the satisfaction of the court, their vote shall still be taken if the same question is raised again." [62]

Having suggested this analysis of the judicial process Holmes then returned to his analytic task. "The legal liabilities defined by a book of torts are divisible into those in which culpability is an element and those in which it is not." With respect to the latter class, it may be subdivided "into the cases where the facts which fix the liability are definitely ascertained, and those where the

[60] *Id.*, 7:658.   [61] *Id.*, 659.

87

boundary line is in course of ascertainment, or from motives of policy is kept purposely indefinite." [63] A chart similar to those which supplemented his earlier articles on Arrangement and Privity was appended to "The Theory of Torts," but it was, I think, the last analytic table which Holmes was ever to prepare.

In what I have said of the shifting of the center of Holmes's interest from the scientific analysis of concepts to their history, I have, perhaps, exaggerated the radicalism of the change. In those essays which he published in the later years of the 1870's, which were rewritten as chapters in *The Common Law,* there persisted a very deep concern with the analytic problems. It might, perhaps, be fairly said that the historical effort in Holmes's later essays was directed to the end of producing from the materials of history support for the conclusions which analysis had led him to defend in his first essays. In the second of his two papers on "Primitive Notions in Modern Law," for instance, he opened the essay with the very explicit statement that "the object of the following investigation is to prove the historical truth of a general result, arrived at analytically" in his essay on Privity.[64] The turning towards history, in other words, did not mean the repudiation of earlier convictions; it merely signified the recognition of the utility of a method of proof which he had not made use of in his first writings.

It should be noticed, also, that concern with the history rather than the structure of doctrine had by no means been absent from the earlier essays on Arrangement. Though "Codes and Arrangement" was almost wholly analytic in purpose and method, even there Holmes had glanced perceptively at a problem of history to which he was frequently to return in later years. He was troubled by the tendency of Anglo-American jurists, whether on or off the bench, to force the common law into a form suggested by the concepts and classifications of the civil law. "Very generally," he said, "where we find [the civil] law retaining its original form in the body of our own, it seems . . . to be a source of anomalies and

[63] *Id.*
[64] "Primitive Notions in Modern Law. No. II," *Am. L. Rev.,* 11:641 (July 1877).

confusion." [65] His short paper, "Misunderstandings of the Civil Law," was an attempt to show characteristic instances in which doctrines having their origin in the Roman law had been carried over, unthinkingly, into the common law. "Doctrines get swerved from their true meaning and extent, because we do not remember their history and origin. A rule of law that has been gradually developed can only be understood by knowing the course of its development . . ." [66] The paper on Misunderstandings examined two instances in which Holmes felt that a careless reception of Roman doctrine had brought distortions and confusion into the common law. The first instance was not of large significance, but it effectively illustrated the point which Holmes was seeking to make. He examined the dogma of cases and texts which assert that persons born deaf and dumb are conclusively presumed to be *non compos mentis*. What Holmes discovered was that judges and authors of the common law had found in the Roman law a principle that the deaf and dumb could not bind themselves to contractual obligations. They had failed to recognize, however, that the Roman doctrine had gone no farther than to say that persons wholly incapacitated in speech and hearing could not by means of speech and hearing—by *stipulatio* as the Roman law called that form of contractual undertaking—enter into binding obligations. Had the common-law judges and lawyers followed the methods of responsible and thorough scholarship they would have seen that a doctrine justified by the forms of Roman law should not uncritically be accepted into the substance of the common law.[67]

This relatively trivial instance of the distorting effect of a shallow Romanism suggested a larger lesson. Anglo-American jurists

---

[65] *Id.*, 5:11.

[66] *Id.*, 6:37, 41–42; *Harv. L. Rev.*, 44:759.

[67] Holmes repeated the same analysis in his annotations of Kent: *Commentaries*, II, *451, note 1. When William James was writing his great work on psychology he evidently asked Holmes a question concerning the legal status of the deaf and dumb. In an unpublished letter dated March 8, 1879, Holmes summarized the points he had made in the *American Law Review* article (James Papers, Houghton Library).

who were seeking to find a scientific arrangement of the common law were too often tempted to make "an ignorant misunderstanding of the Roman classification" central to their ordering of the common law.[68] They had found a refined and elegant structure in the Roman law, and without bothering to discover the civilian justifications—procedural or substantive—for that order, they had imposed it on the institutions and concepts of the common law. Already, in his first essay on Arrangement, Holmes had suggested that there was grave doubt whether the title Bailment deserved a place in a scientific classification of the common law.[69] The same analytical radicalism which led him to question whether Torts was a fitting subject for a textbook led him to challenge the assumptions of such luminaries of learning as Story and Sir William Jones who had written impressive works on Bailments in the common law. When Holmes questioned the scientific justification of textbooks on Torts he based his questioning on the improbable significance, for scientific jurisprudence, of a classification derived from the common-law forms of action. When he challenged the title Bailment he did so in the name of science, but the justification for the challenge, given in some detail in his essay on Misunderstandings, was the shallowness of the learning of those who played with Roman concepts. They had evidently seen no reason to ask whether justifications sufficient in Rome were adequate in London. Holmes's effort was to show what social and legal institutions in ancient Rome explained their concept of bailment and to indicate what very different institutions produced English doctrine defining the rights and responsibilities of the possessor.

In later years Holmes was to give frequent consideration to problems of bailment.[70] Shortly after the publication of the essay on Misunderstandings, however, he seems to have repudiated his early view that Bailment was not a title which should be given a place in the common law. In his edition of Kent's *Commentaries*

[68] *Am. L. Rev.*, 6:42.
[69] *Id.*, 5:11.
[70] See, e.g., "Grain Elevators," *Am. L. Rev.*, 6:455 (April 1872); "Possession," *id.*, 12:688 (July 1878); "Common Carriers and the Common Law," *id.*, 13:609 (July 1879); *CL*, Lecture V.

he referred the reader to his own paper on Misunderstandings of the Civil Law for discussion of "the origin of this title." He went on to say that "the objections there urged against [the title Bailment] require some qualification." It is evident, I think, that just as Holmes came to believe that Torts is a fitting subject for a common-law treatise, so he came to believe that Bailment may be kept as a title in our law. He urged, however, that one subject, commonly brought within its scope, should be excluded. He urged that "there is an important distinction between bailment, properly so called, and giving a thing into the custody of a servant or agent to possess." [71]

In 1879 Holmes concluded an important essay on "Common Carriers and the Common Law" with some general reflections on "the paradox of form and substance in the development of law. In form its growth is logical. The official theory is that each new decision follows syllogistically from existing precedents. But as precedents survive like the clavicle in the cat, long after the use they once served is at an end, and the reason for them has been forgotten, the result of following them must often be failure and confusion from the merely logical point of view." [72] He went to a broader generalization—a generalization which I do not suppose that he considered applicable to his own juristic efforts but which seems to me to throw some light on the process of his own transition from analytic jurist to legal historian. In 1879 he recognized "the failure of all theories which consider the law only from its formal side, whether they attempt to deduce the *corpus* from *a priori* postulates, or fall into the humbler error of supposing the science of law to reside in the *elegantia juris,* or logical cohesion of part with part." [73] Though Holmes never committed himself in the least to the arrogant "apriorist" error, or in full to the humbler error of the logician, it is the fact, I think, that his earliest efforts had led him down a roadway of analytic inquiry which brought him to a dead end. Even while he was traveling that road

[71] Kent's *Commentaries*, II, *558, note 1.
[72] *Am. L. Rev.*, 13:630. Cf. *CL*, 35.
[73] *Am. L. Rev.*, 631. Cf. *CL*, 36.

he came to believe that the bypaths of history which cut across his road, and which from time to time he briefly followed, were those on which he might best proceed towards understanding.

Perhaps the most striking aspect of Holmes's first historical inquiries is their dominant concern with the law of Rome. Both early and late in his speculations concerning the nature of law and its history Holmes went out of his way to question the importance of training in Roman law for the American practitioner. This particular heterodoxy was not surprising after the time when Holmes came to believe that the roots of the common law were Teutonic rather than Roman. It is harder to understand how he doubted the importance of training in the Roman law while maintaining that "the early English law was not the spontaneous growth of the social needs, but was forced by knowledge of the maturer system of Rome." [74] He explained his educational thesis in an unsigned review of his friend James Bryce's pamphlet on *The Academical Study of the Civil Law*. Holmes feared that if the Roman law should become a subject of academic study, the unfortunate tendency of American students and lawyers to become too easily "content with general principles," would find new encouragement. Since the common law "begins and ends with the solution of a particular case," the American student is well advised to avoid the alluring comfort of generalization which is found in the philosophic sweep of the Roman law and its interpreters. Holmes, remembering his own legal education at Harvard, asserted that "the best training is found in our moot courts and the offices of older lawyers"—presumably such lawyers as George Otis Shattuck. These reflections on "academical" study of law did not mean, however, that Holmes thought it foolish for a mature American lawyer, trained to the practicalities and particularities of the common-law system, to pay some regard to the law of Rome. "Every lawyer who aims at being more than a practitioner should know, at least, so much of the Roman law as to intelligently estimate its influence on our own . . ." He further agreed "that it would be

[74] "The Arrangement of the Law—Privity," *id.*, 7:46, at 51.

well if every student could be made to study law philosophically from the beginning. But we should send him for that purpose to Maine and Austin, to the history of our own law in Spence's first volume, and the invaluable little book just published by Mr. Stubbs . . . We should hesitate to send him to Ulpian." [75]

As we have already seen, Holmes, despite his skepticism about the study of Roman law, showed himself in a number of his earliest writings to have become a considerable master of its complexities. He did not, to be sure, examine its doctrine for any other purpose than that of making the structure and the history of English law more comprehensible. Yet he made it abundantly clear in the essay on Misunderstandings that he could find his way with ease and intelligence through Ulpian, Gaius, and the Digest. His essay on Privity, perhaps, was his most learned and perceptive analysis of basic concepts in the Roman law. While he followed in the footsteps of Maine and based his analysis of succession in Roman law on the relevant chapter in *Ancient Law,* he was putting Maine's learning and insights to fresh uses when he traced the concept of succession in the English law to Roman origins and discovered in the institutions of Roman slavery the source of modern doctrine with respect to the liability of a master for the wrongs of his servant. That he was able, while pursuing civilian learning, to cast doubt upon the Austinian thesis that culpability is an element in the English principles of vicarious liability doubtless gave him special satisfaction.

I have suggested that between the time when Holmes began his juristic inquiries in 1870 and the time when he published his essay on "The Theory of Torts" in July of 1873 there had been a significant progression in his thought. He had come to believe that problems of analytic order were less significant than he had initially supposed them to be. As that conviction grew on him his earlier professional commitments came to their end and new ones were assumed. At the end of 1873 his edition of Kent was published. In July he and Arthur Sedgwick had transferred the edi-

[75] *Id.,* 5:715–716 (July 1871). Cf. "The Bar as a Profession," *CLP,* 153.

torship of the *American Law Review* to other hands.[76] In June he had relinquished the last of his three lectureships at Harvard. And, most important, in March he had formed his partnership for the practice of law with George Otis Shattuck and William A. Munroe.

On the external face of things the termination of a group of essentially academic and speculative responsibilities and the assumption in their place of the obligations of an active practitioner would indicate that Holmes's career was about to take a wholly different course from that which it had followed. There is good reason to believe that an important consideration leading him to turn from the pursuit of learning to the life of a practitioner was the blunt necessity that he should earn a living.[77] He and his wife may well have come to wonder whether they could indefinitely live their married life as members of Dr. Holmes's household. If they should at long last cut the apron strings some regular source of income would be a necessity. Such considerations as these surely played an important part in Holmes's decision that the time had come for him to test his capacities at the bar. One may assume, I take it, that Mr. Shattuck, the effective man of affairs, recognized that Holmes's contributions to the life of the firm would be significantly different from his own—that Holmes would not be a getter of business or a planner of industrial and financial enterprise. It might be expected, however, that his remarkable learning and his exceptional intellectual power would add promise of a very special sort to the new firm's prospects.

No contemporary record survives, I think, to tell us with precisely what expectations Holmes made his move into active practice. Perhaps he faced the possibility that the firm's successes and his own would so tax his energies that he would be compelled to abandon further systematic juristic inquiries. If he did, he could not have done so with enthusiasm for he was not a man to look happily upon the abandonment of an effort once begun. Though

[76] The new editors were Moorfield Storey (1845–1929) and Samuel Hoar (1845–1904).

[77] See his letter of August 17, 1879, to James Bryce, quoted *supra*, pp. 24–25.

he may have come to believe that some of his first ventures in jurisprudence had led him down dusty pathways to dead ends he had also seen new roads of promise and had set his course in new directions. One may feel wholly sure, I think, that he took the turning into active practice still resolved that his final distinction should be as a thinker, not as practitioner.

4

Traveler and Practitioner

*W*hen *Holmes concluded* the first phase of his major endeavors in scholarship and turned his course towards the practice
of law he freed his spirit, at least briefly, from the clutch of conscience. Between 1870 and 1873 he had held a tight rein on those
qualities of temperament which might have jeopardized achievement—gayety, romanticism, and zest for living. When he had
made his trip to England in 1866 he had shown that these were
strong elements in his nature—elements so dangerously strong,
perhaps, that he dared not give them any play while he sought the
eminence which ambition had chosen. With Kent, the *American
Law Review,* and the Harvard lectures behind him, it was not surprising that the young man of thirty-three decided that the summer of 1874 might be used for the postponed indulgence of his
own neglected tastes and the exposure of his wife to a different
world from that to which she had been consigned for two years in
the household of Dr. Holmes. In May of 1874 Holmes and his wife
sailed for England and the continent.

Mrs. Holmes was the diarist of the journey, and in her record
of the summer's travels there is sketched a revealing portrait of the
diarist herself, the one self-portrait of its author which survives.[1]
Its pages show us a timid and somewhat reluctant traveler: Saturday, May 30, at sea; "Will never, never, never put myself in such

[1] The diary is among the Holmes papers at Harvard Law School.

a fix again. 14 days more of it perhaps. Women on deck beginning to get sick." Mrs. Holmes's spirit evidently did not suffer bores easily; at least on shipboard: "Mrs. Mathews becoming a nuisance"; and when ashore in England, a corrosive eye: "Mr. and Mrs. Tuckerman simply disgusting. I have seldom seen a man who combined in such small quarters such gigantic defect of manners, mind and heart linked to so fitting a partner as his wife." After attending a *soirée* at Lord and Lady Belper's Mrs. Holmes described her host as "a twinkling hippopotamus," and remarked that Lady Belper looked like "Miss Jane Norton without the Norton." She reported a scene at Lady Augusta Stanley's:

The Dean very disagreeable in black stockings, long coat, black sash and ribbon round his neck. Overheard some joke between him and two or three fat old ladies covered with feathers, lace and chains about "St. Peter's daughter—and he, you know, was not a married man"—at which point up went the fans and the Dean's hand to conceal his face from his own joke—altogether the whole impression not of a gospel of humility and simplicity. Fat old ladies with immense bosoms and larger stomachs both adorned with gold and precious stones. One thin old lady with a cap and veil of heavy black lace with a red feather held in place by a diamond cluster, a black satin overdress and red satin petticoat and a roll of white cardboard tied up with red ribbon and attached to her belt by a red ribbon which roll she used for an ear trumpet.

On the evening of June 23, remembering that her first Dixwell ancestor in America was a fugitive regicide, Mrs. Holmes accompanied her husband to a ball—"a regular London jam"—at Devonshire House. "It was delightful. I was called 'My Lady' by the servants and as I went up the great marble circular staircase step by step the blood of the Dixwells rose from a long sleep and was at home again." The Duke of Devonshire was "a fine looking old man but very shy. Lots of men with ribbons and orders. Lots of diamonds, lots of middle-aged women fat and comfortable. Many younger faces full of discontent." While assessing the English traits around her Mrs. Holmes was suddenly confronted by her *bêtes noires:*

That portable trunk of nuisances Mr. Tuckerman and his green-eyed monster of a wooden-mouthed wife were there, so delighted to see us in such good society,—did not see us when they were there the last time . . . Thought they had passed in music and out of sight when Tuckerman came back and said: "A friend of yours, Mr. Holmes, wants to see you. I shall bring her here." "Yes," said Wendell. "Where is she? Who is it?" "Oh, I'll not tell. Is your wife jealous? Is she jealous by nature a little bit?" "Not at all." "Oh, you have need to be. There has been cause for it in this case I assure you." Scandal in high life! Four pair of strange English eyes and one eye-glass directed upon the group full of interest, and gossip in our case mingled with a little sentiment and an instantaneous glance which seemed to say "I too have suffered," and Miss Minton appeared—the last person under the last circumstances in the world!

Two days later, while attending a garden party at Lambeth Palace, Miss Minton was again on the horizon.

She likes me little; I saw the look. Also her friend Mrs. Tuckerman who tried to speak and managed to say that she had meant to call upon me today but as she had met a very —————— mump. For which I bowed and we passed on. Two steps brought us to her husband who would be seen and who would shake hands and from whose hand mine slipped like a minnow. He also said, "Meant to have called today but —————— grump." "Ah yes," said Wendell, "just met your wife. Very good." To which Tuckerman replied "Curious old house." Wendell said, "Very," and the sweet creature went after his party and Wendell for champagne and got claret cup.[2]

Though Holmes may have been indifferent to the charms of Miss Minton he was not wholly impervious to those of other ladies. On June 28 the Holmeses dined at Mr. John Campbell's—one of the clan, doubtless, with whom Holmes had so much enjoyed himself during his visit to Scotland in 1866.[3] Mrs. Holmes reported

---

[2] It seems likely that Mrs. Holmes was writing of Charles K. Tuckerman (1821–1896) who had been American Minister in Greece from 1868 to 1872 and had settled down to an expatriate's life. *His Personal Recollections of Notable People at Home and Abroad* (2 vols., London, 1895) reveals qualities not wholly unlike those which Mrs. Holmes described.　　　[3] *Shaping Years*, 241–244.

that the evening "was delightful. All Scotch from the butler to the terrier. Everybody very cordial and pretty, and I don't know when I have had such a pleasant time." At the foot of his wife's account of the evening an entry was added in Holmes's hand: "I sat next to Mrs. Willoughby whom I love. O.W.H., Jr." Before a week was out, Mrs. Holmes, recording the fact that a book for her husband had been left off at 9 Bolton Street from Mrs. Willoughby, added the entry: "Wendell off on the rampage." On the evening of July 9, Mrs. Holmes further reported: "Wendell to see his charmer and return the book. Brought the book back with him."

When the Holmeses left the world of fashion they moved either in that of letters or in that of intellectual affairs. On July 7, with Henry Adams' friend Charles Milnes Gaskell as host, they dined with Robert Browning. "Pretty good time; rather stupid," reported Mrs. Holmes. "Browning said that he had a great dread of comets. All the sad events of his life from his birth until now had been connected with commet [sic] years—his wife in '61.[4] He said very pleasantly when we rose to leave, with what seemed a genuine pressure of the hand 'Well goodbye, and don't *forget* me.' " On another evening they dined with Anthony Trollope, where Mrs. Holmes sat between her host and Tom Hughes—he, we may presume, no longer worrying about the seriousness of Holmes's intentions with respect to his daughter.[5] Lunching with Leslie Stephen shortly after their arrival in London, the Holmeses found James Russell Lowell a fellow guest, and Mrs. Holmes enjoyed her glimpse of Thackeray's two daughters—the younger, married to their host. Dining with Lady James, Mrs. Holmes was seated between Russell Gurney, Recorder of London, and Sir Fitzroy Kelly, Chief Baron of the Exchequer—"delightful old man of eighty, who . . . asked me just as the ladies rose if he might ask how long Mr. Holmes had had the pleasure of possessing me as his charming wife. I told him two years. 'And have you a family?' 'No,'

[4] In the summer of 1874 much public attention was being given to Coggia's comet.
[5] *Shaping Years,* 230–231.

'Ah le bon temps viendra.' " [6] Sir James Hannen, judge of the Court of Probate and Divorce, suggested that Holmes might like to visit his court. "It seemed to please the old man (not so very old) to have me know something about him, evidently thinking that his name was a terror in the States to disobedient wives."

Much as Holmes enjoyed the dinners, garden parties, and balls of London, he spent a very large portion of his time in the company of men who shared his professional and intellectual interests. On the evening of June 17 he dined at the Alpine Club with Leslie Stephen where it is probable that he fell in with another member, Frederick Pollock, whose paper, "Law and Command," Holmes had noticed in the *American Law Review*.[7] A few days before, Holmes had met Pollock's father at the Metropolitan Club, a meeting which brought in its wake a visit to the law courts on June 19 in the company of the senior Pollock. Sir Frederick, in his journal, told of how the young Bostonian "came to sit by my side in Judges' Chambers to see our practice. Afterwards I took him to see the Middle Temple Hall, and the Public Record Office. He was moved by the sight of Domesday Book." [8] There was a tea with Carlyle; there were breakfasts with Sir Henry Maine and with John Lothrop Motley, and numerous calls with Bryce, Dicey, and Morley on various illustrious persons. These excursions into the masculine world of London and its community of thought surely made Holmes feel that this was the world to which his mind and spirit were most closely akin.

Many years later he wrote to an English friend and described the hold which London had on him.

I always feel twice the man I was, after I visit London. Personality there is in higher relief than in my world here [in Boston] with its limited experience and half culture. (This does not mean that I am not a good American—I think small beer of any man who does not commit himself to his crowd, except under very exceptional circum-

[6] Holmes quoted this interchange on a number of occasions. See, e.g., *HLL*, II, 849. See also *supra*, p. 8, note 17.

[7] See *supra*, p. 71.

[8] *Personal Remembrances of Sir Frederick Pollock, Second Baronet, Sometime Queen's Remembrancer* (London, 1887), II, 264–265.

stances.) . . . I have been so bored . . . by the assumption that various of my acquaintances must be thinking something tremendous because they said nothing, and that I could not be serious because I said a lot, that I have come to loathe the very expression "reserved power." You have to pay your way in London. No one takes you on faith—and I love it. You must be gay, tender, hard-hearted when something misses fire, give your best, and all with lightness. London Society is hard to get into, not from any requirement of 16 quarterings, but because, to borrow a phrase from Admiral Maxse, there are too many interesting people in London. You must interest, and must interest people who, being in the center of the world, have seen all kinds of superlatives.[9]

Holmes's affectionate and admiring turnings to London were often, I think, tired rejections of Boston—perhaps, even, the exhausted repudiations of his own seriousness. There, at home, he was committed to the task of proving his intellectual eminence, not in his father's way, by brilliant talk, but by dedicated labor. The shadow of Beacon Hill and the shadow of Dr. Holmes did not darken Holmes's spirits while he gave them the freedom of London. There he found refreshment in a display of conversational excellence—in stylishly surviving a battle of spriteliness and wit. Much evidence supports the thesis of Sir John Pollock, son of Holmes's friend, that Holmes was enormously gifted as a conversationalist. Sir John, who had been an attentive listener to the talk of some of the most notable conversationalists of his times—Meredith, Arthur Balfour, John Morley—has testified that

of all that I have heard it seems to me that the talk of Oliver Wendell Holmes was on the whole the best . . . [H]e would catch a subject, toss it into the air, make it dance, and play a hundred tricks, and bring it to solid earth again. There was no trace of flippancy, but a spice of enjoyment even in the serious treatment of a serious subject . . . As he talked he drew inspiration from his company; he challenged and desired response, contradiction and development . . . Talk was a means of clarifying ideas, of moving towards the truth; but it was a great game too.[10]

9 To Lady Burghclere, Sept. 17, 1898 (copy, HLS).
10 *HPL* (2nd ed., 1961), I, xxix, xxx.

The sport, in Holmes's judgment, was played with more style and brilliance in London than in Boston or Washington, and it was no wonder that he who loved the game should find refreshment in playing it with the best and the most skilled competitors.

Though Mrs. Holmes's diary indicates that she too found excitement in the social air of London, there are some indications that she was more responsive to the occasional simplicities than to the frequent refinements which she encountered. She saw much of the scholars and men of affairs—Sir Henry Maine, Leslie and James Fitzjames Stephen, Sir George Otto Trevelyan, John Morley, James Bryce, and Albert Venn Dicey. But the man whom she found most appealing among her husband's friends was Sir John Kennaway who, eight years before, had been Holmes's evangelical host in Devonshire and who, in later years, by correspondence, continued to give him "a well-meant poke about [his] immortal soul." [11] On an evening when Holmes was dining with friends a caller on Mrs. Holmes was announced. "Result—a tall brown bearded man" who pleased his hostess by the simple announcement: "I am called Kennaway."

He staid $\frac{3}{4}$ of an hour with me, and when he went off he said "Why, this is awfully lonely for you. If I were not going to dine from home myself I should take you with me now whether you liked it or not" . . . I like him very much indeed—better I think than any of the others. Wendell's embroidered shirt is very fine and all is merry as a marriage bell.

While Mrs. Holmes could prick bubbles of pretension with a quick and scathing word ("Washington is full of famous men and the women they married when they were young" [12]), she evidently found none of the satisfaction and refreshment which her husband did in the virtuosity of talk. The shyness and reserve of New England made her an appreciative but slightly mistrustful observer of the world of social and intellectual fashion. Her tastes

[11] Holmes to Lady Castletown, Aug. 17, 1897 (copy, HLS). See also *Shaping Years*, 240.

[12] Quoted by Catherine Drinker Bowen, *Yankee from Olympus* (New York, 1944), 362.

were more responsive to the tranquilities of the country than to the confusions of the city. Doubtless the inclinations of an anchorite grew with the years, but it is not unlikely that her husband would have said of her in 1874 what he stated in 1912: "She is a very solitary bird, and if her notion of duty did not compel her to do otherwise, she would be an absolute recluse, I think . . . She and I are a queer contrast in that way, as in many others."[13] It is probable, I think, that one of the other ways in which Holmes saw himself and his wife as queerly contrasted was in their attitude towards intellectuality. No surviving records or memories of Mrs. Holmes indicate that she shared, or pretended to share, his exuberant interest in the world of ideas. In his later years he found a number of ladies who did the one or the other. It may well be that Mrs. Holmes looked upon them as pretentious bluestockings who encouraged his somewhat dangerous virtuosity.[14] Beyond that, however, I suspect that, not sharing his insatiable appetite for ideas, she saw herself as excluded from that segment of his life which was spent, whether in the company of men or women or quite alone, in the pursuit of knowledge and the quest for ideas. Reasons such as this, it seems to me, make her preference for the straightforwardness of Sir John Kennaway to the subtleties of Leslie Stephen comprehensible.

On July 11 the Holmeses left London for Paris. As soon as the travelers arrived on the continent their life, as reflected in Mrs. Holmes's diary, became that of conventional tourists. In each other's company they saw the traditional sights in every city they visited (including "horrible Americans with a little boy" and "disgusting Americans who flirted with waiters"), and had casual words in railroad cars or hotel lobbies with other travelers. Neither in Paris, Geneva, Milan, Venice, nor Turin did Holmes

13 To Lady Scott, Jan. 6, 1912 (HLS).
14 The story is told of his first meeting with a bright young lady. While Mrs. Holmes sat in the background, her husband fixed the visitor's attention. "[A] steady stream of the deepest philosophy poured from his lips. The beautiful sonorous voice flowed on . . . Just at the critical zenith of words" Mrs. Holmes spoke up: "George—you do talk pretty!" (Richard Walden Hale, *Some Table Talk of Mr. Justice Holmes and "The Mrs.,"* privately printed, 1935, 11).

meet or converse with an illustrious person. In Switzerland he looked, doubtless with some nostalgia, on the Alps which he and Leslie Stephen, then both unmarried, had climbed in the summer of 1866. In Venice the Holmeses joined forces with Bostonians who had been their companions on the Atlantic crossing. After two concluding days in Paris, on Sunday, August 2, they were back in the familiar surroundings of London. Though the season of highest gayety had passed, Holmes was able to breakfast with Bryce, dine with W. K. Clifford, make a series of calls, and go to *A School for Scandal* before he and his wife went to stay with Henry Cowper, Holmes's "dearest friend" at Ampthill in Bedfordshire.[15] That country interlude was followed by a few more days in London—given over, largely, to the galleries—and then hurried trips to Oxford and Cambridge. The surviving diary of Mrs. Holmes came to an abrupt end on the evening of August 14 after a full day in which Henry Sidgwick, the philosopher-friend of the Englishmen with whom Holmes had become most intimate, had shown them the sights of Cambridge. Whether after the Cambridge visit the Holmeses wandered farther afield—Devonshire, perhaps, to stay with Sir John Kennaway—we do not know.[16] The next record of their whereabouts is the entry in Holmes's reading list indicating that the vacation concluded on September 6—presumably the date of their arrival in Boston. Another eight years were to pass before they should again return to England, but in the visit of 1874 Holmes, if not his wife, had made or intensified friendships and associations which were to mean much to him in the intervening years.

While Holmes was in London he had received a note from

[15] Though many letters written to Holmes by Henry Cowper (1836–1887), barrister and M.P. for Hertfordshire from 1865 to 1885, survive among the Holmes papers, the other side of the correspondence has not, apparently, been preserved. Cowper's niece, Lady Desborough (1867–1952), became one of Holmes's most intimate English friends.

[16] An entry in Mrs. Holmes's diary, for August 4, reported an invitation from Sir John to come to Devonshire on August 15. A letter to Holmes from Lord Coleridge, dated October 7, 1874 (HLS), indicates that the Holmeses had been staying with the Kennaways in early August.

Sir Henry Maine thanking him for having sent him a copy of his essay on "The Theory of Torts." Maine had found the paper "both ingenious and original"—praise from a master which Holmes must have found especially gratifying.[17] He had also received the first letter in that series which was to stretch across the decades from Frederick Pollock. At their first or second meeting Holmes had apparently given Pollock a copy of his notice of Pollock's own paper on "Law and Command" and an offprint of "The Theory of Torts." On July 3, Pollock wrote to Holmes of the pleasure which he had found in both of the essays. He wholeheartedly endorsed Holmes's contention in the first that "the only definition of law for a lawyer's purposes is something which the Court will enforce," and he expressed pleasure that in the second paper Holmes had so clearly exposed "the fallacy of treating legal negligence as a state of the negligent's consciousness." [18]

The letters from Maine and Pollock have significance less for their contents than for what they show of the abiding interests of their recipient. When in the spring of 1873 Holmes had concluded his Harvard teaching, given up the editorship of the *Review*, substantially finished his work on Kent, and joined the partnership of Shattuck and Munroe, it looked to the world as if he had turned his back on scholarship and theory and turned his face towards the market place. Yet Sir Henry Maine, who had included in his letter an expression of regret that Holmes was "likely to be absorbed wholly in practical work in the future," had opened his note with the salutation: "My dear Professor Holmes." May not the salutation be taken to indicate, perhaps, that Maine had found in the talk and the manifested interests of the visiting American a continuing commitment of available time and enthusiasm to those inquiries which had absorbed his best energies for three years? Surely the fact that Holmes in the summer of 1874 put his writings in the hands of new English

17 Maine to Holmes, July 26, 1874 (HLS). Maine concluded his letter by saying that he had "had the very great pleasure in making the acquaintance this summer of a colleague of yours and of his wife, Mr. and Mrs. H. Adams."

18 HPL, I, 3.

acquaintances who might be expected to find them interesting indicates that though the hours of each working day might henceforth be given to the practice of law he did not plan, on his return to Boston, to abandon wholly that search for understanding on which he had previously been engaged. The September homecoming might be to new obligations, but it would also be to old interests.

When the Holmeses found themselves back in Boston it seems that they returned, for a time, to Dr. Holmes's household at 296 Beacon Street. Before many months had passed, however, they made the break which, however much it may have been desired, had probably been financially inadvisable—perhaps impossible—while Holmes was giving his energies to scholarship rather than practice. By the spring of 1875 they were living in their own apartment at 10 Beacon Street, within a few minutes walk from the office of Shattuck, Holmes & Munroe, within easy reach of the Court House (which provided quarters for the Social Law Library), and next door to the Boston Athenaeum. This long-delayed declaration of independence marked an emancipation which was surely no less grateful to the younger Mrs. Holmes than it was to the Doctor's eldest child. Until the late winter of 1883, after Holmes was on the Supreme Judicial Court, he and his wife made the apartment at 10 Beacon Street their home.

George Otis Shattuck and William Adams Munroe, the lawyers with whom Holmes had entered into partnership in March of 1873, had been associated in practice for three years as Shattuck and Munroe. Shattuck was then a man of forty-four and Munroe was fourteen years his junior—two years younger than Holmes. Before either of the junior members of the firm had begun the study of law, Shattuck had been known as one of the most gifted lawyers at the Boston bar, and by 1873 was clearly one of its leaders. He was counselor to many important financial, mercantile, and manufacturing interests, yet also was an active and prominent member of the trial bar in Boston. It was upon the basis of his achievements and his reputation, one may be sure, that the promise of the new firm was primarily built. Munroe was but thirty years old and had scarcely had the time to make a large impression at the bar. He evidently lacked the aggressive force of Shattuck and never showed the speculative bent of Holmes. He lived in another social world than theirs: active in the Baptist Church, he did not receive, and, so far as we know, was not interested in receiving the traditional honors of the Back Bay—membership in the Massachusetts Historical Society, the Harvard Board of Overseers, or the Saturday Club. He was a quiet and industrious lawyer who was somewhat overshadowed, one suspects, by his more powerful partners. A few surviving notes from Munroe to Holmes indicate that they enjoyed friendly, if not intimate relation. On his death in 1905, writing to John C. Gray, Holmes said of Munroe: "He really was a noble spirit for whom I had deep respect and admiration." [19]

The records of the office of Shattuck, Holmes, and Munroe do not survive, and it is difficult, accordingly, to reconstruct the nature of its practice and the division of responsibilities between the partners. Court records indicate that the firm, while active in litigation, was not among the Boston offices with the heaviest load of courtroom business. In those cases which Shattuck, Holmes, and Munroe tried in the state courts, the firm seemed generally to be representing a commercial or business client. They might act for a merchant in seeking damages for breach of contract or they might defend him against a claim for personal injury or property damage. They might act for a fire insurance company, threatened with insolvency as a result of the Great Boston Fire of November 1872, when it sought to collect on deposit notes given by policy holders in part payment of premiums. With some frequency they represented litigants in controversies with state or municipal authority. They do not seem, however, to have been involved in the litigation of large social or political issues, being satisfied to handle the more humdrum civil controversies of private interests. They do not seem to have made the administration of trusts and estates as crucial to the economic success of the firm as did other Boston offices with partners coming from the same social back-

[19] Sept. 6, 1905 (HLS).

ground as that of Shattuck and Holmes. They were, in other words, less specialists in the law of property than general practitioners dealing with the commercial, industrial, and banking affairs of downtown Boston. In 1901 Holmes stated that his "keenest interest" was excited, "not by what are called great questions and great cases, but by little decisions which the common run of selectors would pass by because they did not deal with the Constitution or a telephone company, yet which have in them the germ of some wider theory, and therefore of some profound interstitial change in the very tissue of the law." [20] It is not unlikely, I think, that this proclivity of the judge had been fostered by the experience of the practitioner.

In one area it seems that both Shattuck and Holmes, and therefore the firm, could fairly claim a specialist's peculiar competence. As the representatives of Boston's commercial and mercantile interests they found themselves often appearing in the federal Court of Admiralty or litigating questions of maritime law in the state courts of Massachusetts. They might find themselves concerned with defending suits for personal injury suffered in Boston Harbor, defending a British vessel from a seaman's wage claim, seeking to protect a vessel against a stevedore's *in rem* proceeding, or defending the owner of a vessel lost in the Pacific from the salvage claim of a mate who had brought a lifeboat to the Marquesas after twenty-three days of hunger and horror. In each of these cases—and others not unlike them—Shattuck, Holmes and Munroe were dealing with the law of the sea, a law which obviously had a strong hold on the historical tastes of Holmes and which developed a specialist's competence in its refinements. Yet it should not be supposed that this branch of practice came to the Shattuck firm by reason of its love of romance. It came to the office because the firm handled the commercial affairs of men and companies whose business took them down to the sea in ships.

On many occasions Holmes spoke with some sadness of the fleeting anonymity of a practicing lawyer's achievement. "You argue a case in Essex. And what has the world outside to do with

<hr>

[20] "John Marshall," *OS*, 134.

that . . . ?" [21] Of the most distinguished lawyers the only record
"which remains . . . is but the names of counsel attached to a
few cases." [22] Yet Holmes's oratory—perhaps also his philosophy—
was able to take comfort in the conviction that "the glory of
lawyers, like that of men of science, is more corporate than individual. Our labor is an endless organic process." [23] The practitioner, whose achievement seems so transitory, must not forget
that in his argument he has "confirmed, or modified or perhaps
[has] suggested for the first time a principle which will find its
way into the reports and from the reports into the text-books and
so into the thought of the common law, and so into its share in
governing the conduct of civilized men." [24] "When I hear that
one of the builders has ceased his toil, I do not ask what statue
he has placed upon some conspicuous pedestal, but I think of the
mighty whole, and say to myself, He has done his part to help the
mysterious growth of the world along its inevitable lines towards
its unknown end." [25]

Somewhere in the unpublished records of the state and federal
courts in Massachusetts there may stand a forgotten statue on an
inconspicuous pedestal—a statue made by Holmes's hand and giving, in the form of argument, new and exciting shape to the
common law. The published records and a large number of file
papers which have been searched do not reveal such a statue. They
show instead what Holmes's own words might have led one to
expect, a chronicle of effective advocacy in miscellaneous cases
and causes. In such a record one does not expect to find the revelation of a philodsophy of law, the unfolding of the advocate's
own conviction, or even the outline of his economic or political
commitments. The briefs or arguments of a lawyer who has made
himself a specialist may, taken as a whole, tell us something of
his own view of public affairs and of his own jurisprudence.
Lawyers, however, who take their cases as they come and argue

21 Undated speech to the Essex Bar Association, *OS*, 48, 49.
22 "Daniel S. Richardson," *id.*, 56, 57.
23 *Id.*
24 "Speech to Essex Bar," *OS*, 49.
25 "Daniel S. Richardson," *id.*, 58.

today a case in commercial law, tomorrow a case in tort, and, while they prepare to advocate particular resolutions of those controversies, draft a client's will, represent an insurance company in receivership, and arrange the release of a vessel seized on *in rem* process by the federal marshal, are not likely to leave in the archives of the courts many traces of their own ultimate convictions. One may search the records expecting to discover traces of proficiency and style, but not anticipating the revelation of the inner springs of the lawyer's own convictions.

It is the case, of course, that just as the client can be judged by the lawyer he retains, so the advocate can be judged by the company he keeps. The Shattuck firm spoke for the dominant interests in its community, not for the oppressed of Boston and New England. There is no surviving indication, I think, that the firm ever represented a laboring man in a suit against his employer or counseled a labor union in its internal or external affairs. In so far as the administration of criminal law was concerned it does not appear that Shattuck, Holmes, or Munroe was involved with any regularity in the defense of persons accused of crime. If any of the partners had a social conscience his practice did not reveal it. In the practice of some lawyers at the Boston bar one can see the reflection of a personal concept of justice in the professional career in law. Moorfield Storey built a practice which gave expression to his humanitarian instincts, and Louis D. Brandeis made his work at the bar a means of advancing social and economic reform. They chose to fulfill their political philosophy through a selective practice—a practice so general, to be sure, that they would speak for all types of interest, but selective, none the less, in its persistent inclusion of causes which bespoke their own personal concern.

With some justification it may be urged that by their representation of the business and commercial interests of Boston, Shattuck, Holmes, and Munroe expressed their respect for the achievements and aspirations of the men who governed those interests. Had any one of the partners been deeply anxious to contribute something towards a radical change in the social order his practice would have reflected that anxiety. There is, in fact, every reason to suppose that Holmes possessed a somewhat awed respect for the qualities of mind and temperament which the more prominent clients of his office possessed. Though he often testified that business problems and business affairs were as disagreeable to him as they were mysterious, he commonly added to that testimony a word of admiration for the gifts of those men who had successfully mastered them. The admiration came in part from his instinctive esteem for action—"I prefer the kitten when it chases its tail to when it laps milk" [26]—and in part from his high regard for men of commanding power. One of his firm's clients he described, almost affectionately, as "fierce" and as a "powerful Philistine with insight." [27] Another "splendid old Philistine who had fought his way to wealth" might be disappointing for his inability to articulate his premises, but he gained Holmes's respect for his fierceness and his energy.[28] Holmes once suggested to President Taft that instead of seeking to put John D. Rockefeller in jail, the government should "put up a bronze statue to him." [29] That Holmes felt this admiration for those men who had found success in economic power did not mean that he sought out or enjoyed their company. He did not.[30] The community of ideas in which he lived and the world of affairs in which they moved might briefly come together in the courtrooms of the Commonwealth, but the path which Holmes followed when he was not at work seldom crossed that on which his clients traveled. He had high regard for the force of the tycoon's character but small sympathy for the quality of his mind. Grateful as he believed that we should be for the achievements of

[26] To Lewis Einstein, October 21, 1906 (LC; copy HLS).

[27] *HLL*, I, 417; II, 1300. The person referred to was Albert Winslow Nickerson (1840–1893), industrial entrepreneur and investor.

[28] *Id.*, II, 930. At the time of George H. Norman's death Holmes is quoted as saying that few people he had known "have had so high a pressure of life to the square inch." See *id.*, note 2.

[29] To Lewis Einstein, October 28, 1912 (LC; copy HLS).

[30] "I don't quite sympathize with your scorn of Rockefeller. I don't enjoy that kind of society, but I believe him (typically, I don't know much about him personally) to be a great man, and I think we should do justice to those who do big things however little we want to dine with them." To Lewis Einstein, June 13, 1918 (LC; copy HLS).

the industrial giants, he acknowledged that "there would be compensations . . . if we had to drop from James Hill to Aeschylus and Aristotle." [31]

Through a letter written in 1918, Holmes gave us a fleeting glimpse of the participation of his firm in large affairs. "I often think," he said, "of the tremendous ability shown in commercial transactions that leave no mark in history—except in some occasional case like that of Jim Hill and his railroad. I once as a young man was the penman for an agreement on half a sheet of foolscap by which the Atchison and the Denver and Rio Grande ended a private war and divided an empire, and as my partner who was the lawyer on the Atchison side and I walked away I spoke of the big thing that had been done and how it would be forgotten in the years, as it was . . ." [32] Though not himself the counselor to the railroad, Holmes was sufficiently close to the transaction by which Boston's financiers determined the fate of the Southwest to feel a romantic and an awed regard for their power and energy.

Since the advocate is spokesman for his client's cause and not the preacher of his own philosophy, his briefs can seldom be taken as proof of his own conviction. In the arguments of a lawyer who is more than a tradesman at the bar, one may, of course, discover a style of thought which has substantive significance, or perhaps find a recurrent attitude towards the total process of adjudication which tells something of the lawyer's own mind. But surely it would have been the purest accident if Holmes as advocate had been able, with any regularity, to achieve the immediate end which he was seeking in the courtroom—his clients' victory in litigation—by making no other argument than that which was consistent with his own philosophy. In fact he must have thought himself fortunate on these few occasions when he found himself

[31] Remarks at the Alpha Delta Phi, 1912, *OS*, 166. Cf. *HPL*, I, 167.

[32] To Lewis Einstein, April 26, 1918 (LC; copy HLS). It seems likely that the transaction in question was that which occurred in October 1878, by which the war between the Atchison, Topeka, and Santa Fe Railroad and the Denver and Rio Grande was brought to a close by the leasing of the latter's lines to the Atchison. See Glenn Danford Bradley, *The Story of the Santa Fe* (Boston, 1920), 170.

able, in presenting his client's cause, to speak his own philosophic mind.

The eye of even a casual reader would notice, I think, in a number of Holmes's briefs filed with the Supreme Judicial Court, the mind of a lawyer possessing unusual gifts. It would also see in Holmes's methods of advocacy a striking tendency to build an argument not simply on the given precedents but on explicit and articulate principles of theory and philosophy. The argument for the defendant executor in *Sherwin* v. *Wigglesworth* [33] provides a revealing instance of these special qualities in Holmes's briefs.

In the Sherwin case the issue before the Court was whether a landowner is liable for real estate taxes which accrue against the property between the time when a petition for its condemnation by the federal government is filed and the time when condemnation is finally decreed. In arguing that no such liability should be recognized, Holmes was somewhat embarrassed, perhaps, by the fact that in a case which he had argued before the same Court six years earlier he had based an argument that the value of lands condemned by the United States should be measured as of the date of the final award, and not as of the date when the petition seeking condemnation had been filed, on the fact that federal and state statutes clearly stated that the government's title did not vest until the date of the final decree.[34] Though the Court on that earlier occasion had been forced to concede that the title did not pass from the owner to the United States until final condemnation had occurred, Chief Justice Gray was able to reject the logic of Holmes's argument and to hold that valuation should be ascertained as of the date when the petition for condemnation had been filed.

How could Holmes, who had led the Court to commit itself to the doctrine that title to land was not divested from its owner until the date of condemnation, hopefully formulate in the second

[33] 129 Mass. 64 (1880). Holmes's briefs in cases argued before the Supreme Judicial Court are to be found in the Social Law Library at Boston.
[34] *Burt* v. *Merchants' Insurance Co.,* 115 Mass. 1 (1874).

case an argument which would immunize the owner from taxes accruing before that date? I suspect that it was not natural for him to deal with the problem as the Court did—to assert, quite simply, that "it would be most unjust to charge the owner of lands with . . . taxes imposed after [the land] has been designated and set apart for the public use." [35] Holmes, preferring a lawyer's to a moralist's argument, presented the Court with an elaborate analysis of the common law's traditional and contrasting ways of looking at an owner's relationship to personal property and of treating his relationship to real property. The contract which Holmes had in mind was most usefully and clearly shown in doctrine with respect to inheritance.

The law of the domicile governs the distribution of personalty irrespective of the *situs* of the particular chattels making up the inheritance. The inheritance is treated as a *universitas* or ideal unit consisting of the total rights and obligations of the deceased (excepting the real estate) now vested in the person of the principal administrator.

The inheritance of real estate, by contrast, is governed by the law of the state in which it lies. The law of taxation gives the same significance as does the law of inheritance to the differences between personal and real property.

The several chattels which a man may own are not regarded as so many several objects, but simply as so many attributes of the subject of taxation; they are only members of that university of rights which the State protects the subject in enjoying. For this protection it taxes the individual, considering the items of his property merely as means of measuring the amount. On the other hand, the State does not regard real estate in this way. It deals with it only as a specific object and does not tax it unless within the territorial limits. Why? Because the tax paid on land is not compensation for the general protection of the owner, but for the protection of that land specifically.

It was because these principles had been accepted that the Massachusetts legislature had never seen fit to impose an *in personam* liability for real estate taxes. The claim of government for such

[35] 129 Mass. at 65–66.

taxes must be against the lands themselves, and not against their owner.[36]

A unanimous Court decided the case in favor of Holmes's client. As I have already indicated, however, the opinion of the Chief Justice, Horace Gray, made no reference to or apparent use of the elaborate analytical effort of Holmes. The Chief Justice disposed of the problem before the Court by the application of a simple rule of justice. Though one may feel that the lawyer—Holmes—and the Judge—Gray—were both right in believing that this particular owner of this specific parcel of land should not be obliged to pay the tax in question, the issue, Why? remains for resolution. It is not the logic, but the style of thought which the two men brought to the resolution of that problem which has significance. The contrast between the fashions of thinking of Holmes and of Gray marks, I believe, something more important than the different modes of thought of two individuals. It marks a change of attitude between two generations.

The contrast is accentuated by the extraordinary similarities between the public careers of the two men. Each began his life with the favoring assurance of "background"; each passed through Harvard College and the Harvard Law School to the Boston bar. Gray, born in 1828, had begun his practice in 1851 and had been named an Associate Justice of the Supreme Judicial Court, as its youngest member, in 1864—three years before Holmes was admitted to the bar. Gray moved to the chair of the Chief Justice in 1873, and presided over the Commonwealth's highest Court until he became an Associate Justice of the Supreme Court of the United States in 1882. When he resigned that post in 1902, Holmes, having in his turn become the youngest Associate Justice on the Supreme Judicial Court and later its Chief Justice, was selected to fill Gray's seat in Washington.

The man in whose wake Holmes moved forward had imposing qualities of person and of mind—qualities, in their way, not less

---

[36] The issue of a taxpayer's personal liability for real estate taxes was not settled in Massachusetts until 1909. The position argued by Holmes in the *Sherwin* case was then rejected; *Dunham* v. *Lowell*, 200 Mass. 468 (1909).

impressive than those of the younger man. It would not have been inappropriate to describe him in the phrase which Emerson somewhere applied to another: "A large composite man, such as nature rarely organizes." Gigantic in frame and commanding in manner, Gray was possessed of a vast fund of accurate legal knowledge and blessed with a phenomenal memory. Distrustful of literary graces in judicial opinions, he wrote with solid clarity and on many occasions with condensed brevity. Yet he was plagued by the didactic impulse, and with considerable frequency found entirely irresistible the temptation to display his accumulated store of learning in encyclopedic opinions. A judicial opinion could properly be more than a reasoned resolution of a controversy; it could be a monograph in legal history. When Gray discovered that no complete collection of the instances in which coastal fishing vessels had been recognized as exempt from capture could be found in a single published work, he decided that it would be "worth the while to trace the history of the rule, from the earliest accessible sources, through the increasing recognition of it, with occasional setbacks, to what we may now justly consider as its final establishment in our own country and generally throughout the civilized world." The result was a twenty-eight page essay in legal history.[37] Called upon in a dissent to consider the jury's role in criminal cases, Justice Gray produced an opinion of seventy-three pages in length—an erudite review of the history of jury trial in England and the United States.[38] By those who see legal history as the sequence of cases in time and logic, he was quite properly conceived to be a legal historian of exceptional competence. There can be no question but that he made important contributions to knowledge of the legal past in a number of his judicial opinions and in extra-judicial writings.[39] In cast of

[37] *The Paquette Habana*, 175 U.S. 677, 686 (1900).

[38] *Sparf and Hansen v. United States*, 156 U.S. 51, 110 (1895).

[39] See, e.g., *Pomeroy v. Trimper*, 8 Allen 398 (1864); *Jackson v. Phillips*, 14 Allen 539 (1867); *Commonwealth v. Macloon*, 101 Mass. 1 (1869); dissenting opinion in *Sparf and Hansen v. United States*, 156 U.S. 51, 110 (1895); *United States v. Wong Kim Ark*, 169 U.S. 649 (1898); *The Paquette Habana*, 175 U.S. 677 (1900). See also his appendices in *Quincy's Reports* (1865); note to *Commonwealth v. Rox-*

mind he was not unlike Chancellor Kent and Mr. Justice Story; learned, in the traditional fashion of lawyers, clearheaded, after the manner of able judges, he was a man of considerable force and capacity. Yet his most ardent admirers admitted that his intelligence was not philosophical and that his inclination to write opinions of inordinate length deprived them of any semblance of artistry.[40]

For the whole of the ten-year period in which Holmes was appearing with regularity before the Supreme Judicial Court, Gray was its Chief Justice. Unhappily no surviving record tells us what each thought of the gifts of the other. All that we know of their personal relationship is that the Chief Justice, in 1880, attended the first of Holmes's Lowell Lectures on *The Common Law*,[41] that Gray once reprimanded Holmes for appearing before the Court in a light, instead of a black, cutaway coat; [42] that when Holmes, as Chief Justice of Massachusetts, decided that the members of his court should wear judicial robes—as their predecessors had not done for more than a century—Gray hailed the decision and offered his friendly offices as advisor in tailoring; [43] that Gray,

---

bury, 9 Gray at 503; comment on *The Dred Scott Case*, in *Monthly Law Reporter*, 10 (N.S.):66 (1857).

40 From 1879 to 1881 Louis D. Brandeis served as law clerk, on a part-time basis, for Gray. His admiring comments on the Chief Justice may be found in Alpheus Mason, *Brandeis: A Free Man's Life* (New York, 1946), 58–59. Appreciative estimates of Gray's capacities and achievements are found in the Proceedings of the Bar and of the Supreme Judicial Court, 182 Mass. 613, and in the proceedings of the Supreme Court of the United States, 187 U.S. See also memoirs of Horace Gray by Charles Francis Adams and George Frisbie Hoar in *Proceedings of the Massachusetts Historical Society*, XVI (2nd series), 251 (1902); *id.*, XVIII (2nd series), 155 (1905). See also Francis C. Lowell, "Horace Gray," *Proceedings of the American Academy of Arts and Sciences*, XXXIX, 1 (1906). At the time of Holmes's appointment as Chief Justice of the Supreme Judicial Court the significant difference between the intellectual and literary style of Gray and Holmes was noted in legal periodicals. See *Albany Law Journal*, LX, 76 (August 5, 1899).

41 Boston *Daily Advertiser*, Nov. 24, 1880.

42 Richard W. Hale, *Some Table Talk of Mr. Justice Holmes and "The Mrs."* (privately printed, 1935), p. 11.

43 Gray to Holmes, January 29, 1901 (HLS). The story of the decision to resume the wearing of judicial robes is told in *Massachusetts Law Quarterly*, 2:425

at an auction of Chancellor Kent's library, purchased a book on which Holmes had cast a covetous eye, and though Gray promised to leave the volume to Holmes in his will, he neglected to do so.[44] When Theodore Roosevelt announced that he was nominating Holmes to fill Gray's place on the Supreme Court of the United States, the retiring Justice wrote a friendly note to Holmes congratulating him and the public on the nomination.[45]

Surely Gray was pleased that another son of Massachusetts who, in the Commonwealth, had followed in his footsteps from one judicial office to another should be chosen to fill his place on the nation's highest court. Yet one may fairly wonder whether Gray was not among those solid men of Boston who looked with some uneasiness upon the philosophical and literary inclination of Holmes's mind. Both Gray and Holmes in 1901 delivered addresses honoring the memory of John Marshall. The tribute of Gray had all the pietistic devotion appropriate to the occasion.[46] The peculiar gifts of its author were revealed, however, in the snippets of anecdote which Gray's industry had discovered in the pages of obscure pamphlets and journals. To show that the effort was not merely that of an orator but was that of a scholar as well, Justice Gray appended to the tribute an extensive bibliography. By contrast, Holmes's brief, reflective tribute asked some rather disturbing questions.[47] He wondered whether Marshall's work "proved more than a strong intellect, a good style, personal ascendancy in his court, courage, justice and the convictions of his party." He did not publicly put in words the thought which he expressed privately, that he was "inclined to rebel a little at Marshall's long-winded establishment of the almost obvious," [48]

(1917). A petition from the Suffolk Bar requesting the change in habits is among the Holmes papers at Harvard Law School.

[44] *HLL*, I, 343.

[45] Gray to Holmes, August 13, 1902 (HLS).

[46] *An address on the Life Character and Influence of Chief Justice Marshall* (Washington, 1901).

[47] "John Marshall," *OS*, 131, 134.

[48] To Lewis Einstein, August 22, 1926 (HLS).

but it is not unlikely that, if Gray saw Holmes's tribute to Marshall, he felt some of Theodore Roosevelt's concern that Holmes showed insufficient reverence for the nation's idols and too little respect for the devotional forms of American patriotism.[49] May it have been, perhaps, that Gray wondered from time to time whether Holmes, who saw Marshall, Kent, and Story as "an innocent lot [who] didn't need caviar for luncheon," did not see Gray as belonging in mind and heart to the tradition, if not the time, of those giants—"a God-fearing simple time that knew nothing of [our] stinking twisters but had plain views of life"?[50]

In *Sherwin* v. *Wigglesworth,* Holmes was unable to persuade the Chief Justice to follow the somewhat circuitous route of theory towards the desired end. Though the Court arrived at the destination which Holmes wanted them to reach, Gray had taken a short-cut—the path of justice—to get there. Three years before, Holmes had made a similar effort, but on that occasion he not only failed to lead the Court down the road of theory which he had mapped; he lost his case as well. The argument in question, that in *Temple* v. *Turner,*[51] is interesting in two aspects. It shows the skillful capacity of Holmes to blend history and principle into a forceful argument. It also illustrates his professional and intellectual familiarity with the peculiarities of the maritime law. The task before him was to sustain the decision which he had secured in the Superior Court—the holding, that is, that the master of a vessel, not being its owner, who had hired a seaman to serve on shipboard is not personally liable if the seaman's wages remain unpaid at the conclusion of the voyage. Holmes was compelled to acknowledge that in the Court of Admiralty it had for a long time been settled that though the master is acting for the owner when he hires the vessel's hands, and thus can bind both owner and vessel to the performance of the contract, he also may be sued for breach of the contract of employment. Holmes urged that such

49 Roosevelt to Henry Cabot Lodge, July 10, 1902; *Selections from the Correspondence of Theodore Roosevelt and Henry Cabot Lodge: 1844–1918,* I, 517–519.
50 *HLL,* II, 1015.   51 123 Mass. 125 (1877).

an anomalous personal liability of an agent contracting for another should not be imposed in these common-law proceedings.

The obscurity which has surrounded this class of questions arises from the fact that admiralty law has been a compound of doctrines springing from various stages of society, and cannot be understood except by the aid of history, which will also help to rid it of its incongruities. Modern authorities properly reduce the relation of shipmaster and owners to an ordinary case of agency; but the law of agency, as now understood, is for the most part modern.

In its beginnings the law of Rome did not know vicarious liability, save as it was involved in the imposition of liability on the master for the acts of his slave. For the act of a freeman no other person than the actor himself could be held liable. It was natural that during that early period both the maritime and the non-maritime law should have held that the shipmaster, not the owner, is liable on contracts which he had made on behalf of the enterprise. "On special grounds of policy" the Roman praetor came to recognize that the shipmaster might, in certain cases, impose a liability on the vessel's owner. "The medieval maritime law showed a further development. The master could bind the ship, although he was in no sense the agent of the owners to whom the ship belonged." As these added liabilities came to be recognized, the reason for continuing the personal liability of the master disappeared. The law of agency had been born and had grown to maturity and today it is "a part of the law of agency that a man may make himself a mere conduit pipe, through which a contract moves from his principal. And, as the responsibility of the superior is wholly determined by that law, it is supposed that the same is true of the inferior . . ." [52]

In this argument Holmes was asking the Court to make an imaginative, not merely a mechanical, use of history and of precedent. If one accepts his history as accurate—and there seems to be no reason to question its accuracy—the problem of policy seems inescapable. If, in addition to the original liability of the ship-

[52] *Id.*, at 127.

master, born when no law of agency existed, other liabilities have been established upon the foundations of an evolving law of agency, is there any good reason for keeping alive the old liability? In effect Holmes was making the point which he was again to make in later years: "It is revolting to have no better reason for a rule of law than that it was so laid down in the time of Henry IV. It is still more revolting if the grounds upon which it was laid down have vanished long since, and the rule simply persists from blind imitation of the past." [53]

A few brief sentences by Horace Gray disposed of Holmes's argument.

> The general rule is everywhere recognized that a seaman has a threefold remedy for his wages, against the master, the owner, or the ship, and may proceed, at his election, against either of the three in the admiralty, or against the master or the owner at common law . . . "It is an established rule," said Dr. Lushington, "so ancient that I know not its origin, that the seamen may recover their wages against the master" . . . [T]he reason commonly assigned, and a sufficient one for these cases, is that, according to the usual practice in the merchant service, the master makes an express contract with the seaman . . . It is not to be presumed, without the most positive and satisfactory proof, that the crew gave exclusive credit to the owner.[54]

It is not my purpose to condemn the Court's decision or to acclaim the vision of Holmes. What seems to me to be significant to the presentation and the decision in the *Temple* case are the styles of thought which they reveal. Perhaps had Gray been advocate and Holmes judge in this cause each would have had the other's style. I think that unlikely, however, for it was surely not a characteristic effort of Gray or his generation to make emancipating rather than dogmatic use of history. That did become the habit of Holmes—and perhaps because of Holmes, of his generation. When Gray discovered that the cases were clear, he justified their continued force as law by discovering a contract—quite fictitious, to be sure—which would make reason seem to sanctify authority.

[53] "The Path of the Law," *CLP*, 187.
[54] 123 Mass. at 128.

Holmes, by contrast, asked that a better justification than either authority or fiction could provide should be given for treating old doctrine as current law.[55]

The advocate's obligation to his client may lead him vigorously to support positions which as scholar or jurist he would not defend. It is not surprising, accordingly, that instances may be found in which Holmes pressed on the Court propositions which he had already repudiated in essays and book notices in the *American Law Review* and annotations of Kent's *Commentaries*. There was an occasion, for instance, on which Holmes urged that a promisor's liability is dependent, not upon his manifested intention, but upon the actual intention by which his mind was governed when he gave his promise.[56] In a negligence case he went so far in the repudiation of his own published view that the standard of negligence is external, as to cite John Austin as authority for the proposition that culpability is a necessary element in liability for negligence.[57] In a case involving constitutional issues, Holmes urged that the owner of a factory could not validly be required to reimburse the city for its expenses in raising the grade of the owner's lands surrounding the factory in order to improve drainage and thus promote the health of the residents of the city. Holmes did not press his constitutional protest so far as to deny that the

[55] In a portion of his brief not published or summarized in the reports, Holmes made a further argument of some technical interest. He suggested that though in a court of admiralty the maritime law with respect to the shipmaster's liability might be binding, the court of common law to which the seaman had chosen to come should enforce its own familiar principles of agency. "The plaintiff has selected his tribunal, and his case must be determined by common-law rules." The Court did not explicitly deal with the problem but seems to have assumed that the substantive law of the sea was as binding on the court of common law as it would be on a court of admiralty. Cf. Holmes's opinion for the Court in *Kalleck* v. *Deering*, 161 Mass. 469 (1894).

[56] *Connecticut Trust Co.* v. *Melendy,* 119 Mass. 449, 452 (1876).

[57] *Hill* v. *Winsor,* 118 Mass. 251 (1875). It was in a supplementary letter to Gray, C.J., filed with the record and briefs, that Holmes called the Court's attention to the passage in Austin's *Jurisprudence* (3rd ed.), 440—the passage which Holmes had criticized in his "Theory of Torts," *supra*, pp. 79–80. *Hill* v. *Winsor*, decided against Holmes by a majority of the Court, became a leading case in Massachusetts.

state and city could require the landowner to bear an appropriate share of the expenses of a public measure designed to secure the public health. He evidently conceded that the power being exercised could fairly be classified as that of police. He did urge, however, that there was an unconstitutional inequality resulting from the variable costs of elevating wholly dissimilar tracts of land.[58] Quite probably Holmes was aware that his effort to upset the law for its inequality was "the usual last resort of constitutional arguments." [59]

A more discerning eye than mine might find in Holmes's briefs some materials of large substantive importance—the formulation, perhaps, of a theory of liability or a principle of immunity which foreshadowed things to come or things in process of coming. Such matters I have not discovered. What seems to me to be revealing and significant in the Holmes briefs is not the substance of conviction which they reveal, but the form of argument which they illustrate. With considerable frequency one finds him turning to authorities remote both in time and space from contemporary Massachusetts. When he wanted to authenticate the proposition that an employee is chargeable with the negligent failure of his employer to warn third parties that his employees are in a precarious position endangered by that third person's conduct, he did not cite the Massachusetts cases in support of the proposition. Instead he quoted from the Digest: *"Eadem est persona domini et procuratoris."* [60] When he urged that the defendant's violation of a statute leading to plaintiff's injury does not give the plaintiff a cause of action unless the statute was intended to benefit persons in the plaintiff's position, he supported the proposition with a long string of English authorities running from Rolle's Abridgment, title *Action sur case,* to the most recent decision of Baron Bramwell.[61] The lawyer who had edited Kent's *Commentaries* had lost, quite naturally, that parochialism which is distrustful of

---

58 *Nickerson* v. *Boston*, 131 Mass. 306 (1881).
59 Holmes, J., in *Buck* v. *Bell*, 274 U.S. 200, 208 (1927).
60 Brief in *Hill* v. *Winsor, supra,* note 57.
61 Brief in *Jenks* v. *Williams*, 115 Mass. 217 (1874).

the decisions from another land and of another day. It is fair to say, I think, that Holmes's briefs showed not only an extraordinary breadth of legal knowledge, but an unusual desire to utilize English authority as the continuing foundation of the Massachusetts law.

So far as I have discovered there was but one case before the Supreme Judicial Court in which Holmes used economic theory to support a legal argument. In *Whitcomb* v. *Converse*,[62] he was seeking to protect the member of a partnership who had agreed to give his time to the common enterprise from a claim to contribute equally with the other partners towards the satisfaction of unpaid partnership debts. "On principle," Holmes argued,

it is submitted that the defendant cannot be liable. If A. and B. agree to labor together a year for their joint advantage, and to share profits, and they make no profits, each loses his labor. If A. and B. are partners in shoemaking for a year, A. to furnish leather or money to purchase leather, and B. to make it into shoes, A. and B. to divide the profits, and they make no profits, B. loses his labor as before. But B. cannot be held to insure A.'s contribution on any principle which would not equally make A. insure B. Even the seeming difference in the nature of the respective contributions is not a true one. Before the goods are sold and the question of profit or loss settled, B.'s labor has been converted into capital, in the strictest sense of the word, by the change in form and increased value which it has given to the leather. The same is true when the labor of B. is selling instead of changing the form of goods. He increases their value for A.'s purposes by helping them to market, and his labor is an element in the price which they fetch.

Gray, C. J., quickly disposed of the labor theory of value. Conceding that a single *nisi prius* decision and an early edition of Lindley on *Partnership* sustained Holmes's contention, the Chief Justice referred to the last edition of Lindley, rejecting Holmes's thesis, and cited a cluster of English and American decisions holding that where "a partnership is created not merely in profits and losses, but in the property itself . . . if the assets of the partner-

[62] 119 Mass. 38 (1875).

124

ship, upon a final settlement, are insufficient to satisfy this obligation, all the partners must bear it in the same proportion as
other debts of the partnership." Did the Chief Justice take a little
malicious pleasure, perhaps, in adding to the authorities by which
Holmes's position was undermined a reference to the 12th edition
of Kent's *Commentaries?* [63]

In 1876 and 1877 Shattuck and Holmes were involved in the
litigation of a hotly contested suit in admiralty—proceedings in
which their clients were Captain Joseph Nickerson and his son,
Albert—the "fierce old Philistine" so admired by Holmes. The
libellants, insurance companies incorporated in Louisiana, were
represented by Richard Henry Dana, Jr., author of *Two Years
Before the Mast,* and his son. The steam vessel *Concordia,* owned
by the Nickersons, while carrying a cargo of cotton from New
Orleans to Liverpool had departed from her normal course and
in making for a port in Nova Scotia where she expected to take
on coal, had stranded. Vessel and cargo were a total loss. Thereupon the insurers of cargo, having paid the shippers for their loss,
brought suit in admiralty against the Nickersons, charging that
the deviation and consequent disaster were caused by the un-
seaworthiness of the vessel at the time of her departure, a condition known to the owners. Shattuck and Holmes, in the District
Court, had persuaded Judge Lowell that the charges had not
been proved and that the deviation had been necessitated by a
leak in the *Concordia's* boilers resulting from an undiscoverable
and latent defect in their construction.[64] The Danas appealed the
case to the Circuit Court and it came on for hearing before
Mr. Justice Clifford, of the Supreme Court of the United States,
sitting on Circuit in Portland, Maine, in August of 1877.

In the journals of Richard Henry Dana the younger, who sat
at his father's side in Justice Clifford's courtroom and who also
was allowed to present a portion of the argument for the libellants,
there survives an account of the proceedings:

[63] *Id.,* 43.
[64] No opinion in the final disposition of the case was published. An earlier, in-
terlocutory issue was reported in 2 Lowell 310 (1874).

The judge . . . came in at 10 a.m. dressed in his black gown and in his portly and pompous manner . . . After I was through Mr. Holmes began. He made a decided attempt at oratory. He never spoke in a conversational tone. His sentences were well ballanced [*sic*] and telling. He endorsed and made himself responsible for his clients, at which I was surprised, as he should have known better as a point of legal practice, and then the well known slippery character of the Nickersons, especially old Joe, made it rather absurd, but probably had its favorable affect for him on the judge. The best example of rhetoric was calling our witnesses "wreckers," while the only testimony in which the word was used was that some wreckers had stolen some cotton lying on the beach. The witnesses he referred to were, in fact, a retired Cunard captain, and the present Port Warden of Halifax, the telegraph operator, the justice of the peace of the place, etc.[65]

Printed briefs and arguments survive and indicate that the case was fought by the Danas and by Shattuck and Holmes with considerable energy and some bitterness. In the Danas' brief they suggested that the Nickersons and their shipping associates were not the most highminded of merchants.

They form a body of fourteen men doing business in Boston, mostly connected by blood or marriage, owning and managing very largely in steam vessels, possessing large influence over others so engaged, and able to advance or greatly injure masters, mates, engineers and other subordinate officers engaged in the steam business. These powers they used freely, with little regard to propriety or even decency, and sometimes to the great disadvantage of the libellants, who were corporations of distant States of the far South.[66]

Mr. Dana, senior, had further indicated to Justice Clifford that Shattuck and Holmes in their conduct of the case had been somewhat overreaching, forcing the libellants to prove all sorts of technical matters, such as their incorporation, and after proof was

[65] Manuscript journal of R. H. Dana, I, 296 (Massachusetts Historical Society). The journal entry is published in Bliss Perry's *Richard Henry Dana, 1851–1931* (Boston, 1933), 104–105.

[66] Brief for the libellants in *New Orleans Mutual Insurance Co.* v. *Joseph Nickerson, et al.* (Case #778, 779, 780, Circuit Court for the District of Massachusetts, 1877) at 26; Library of Congress.

made conceding that the facts were as the libellants had alleged them to be. He further charged that they had endeavored by somewhat abusive implications to discredit the thoroughly creditable witnesses offered by the libellants.

Holmes's response to these accusations against his clients and his firm was no less vigorous than the charges. In the course of Holmes's argument to the Court, Mr. Dana interrupted, seeking clarification of Holmes's thesis. To that interruption Holmes abruptly responded: "I am stating my case." "Mr. Dana.—I want to get light." "Mr. Holmes.—You must allow for some feebleness of intelligence on my part." "Mr. Dana.—I shall not do that." [67] Turning to the charge that his clients and his firm had shown excessive zeal, Holmes spoke to Justice Clifford as follows:

I sincerely trust that I may never forget, until my brother on the other side bids me forget it, that I owe to him some of the first kind advice that I ever had when I came to this bar; and so I shall trust that the comments of the counsel on the other side will end as they began. But I want it distinctly understood with regard to any suggestions of intimidation of witnesses that will be found scattered through this book of evidence, that the counsel for the respondents take the full responsibility for their acts, and we believe that there has been nothing done throughout the case, from beginning to end, so far as we know anything about it, and so far as every step that is disclosed in the record goes, that has not been perfectly legitimate and proper; and we believe further, that nothing will be found in the record, or is true outside of it, which in the least warrants the imputations upon our clients which the counsel on the other side has allowed himself to make.[68]

Holmes's argument before Justice Clifford, preserved in a pamphlet of some fifty-four pages, reveals an unfamiliar aspect of his professional talent. His address was that of an advocate, not that of a scholar. The occasion did not, of course, call for the acute analysis of precedent and the imaginative interpretation of history. The issues before the Court required the weighing of conflicting

67 *Opening Argument for Defendants by O. W. Holmes, Jr. in New Orleans v. Joseph Nickerson, et al.* (Boston, 1878) at 4; Library of Congress.
68 *Id.*, 8.

evidence, the persuasive construction of testimony, and a faithful commitment of enthusiasm to the client's cause. Holmes's oral argument in the case of the *Concordia* shows that his gifts included those capacities—that he was not, in other words, a mere book lawyer, but a man capable of effective and powerful advocacy of his client's cause. Though he liked to insist that he had no love for facts,[69] he was capable of working with and through them when that was required by his professional responsibility.[70] We cannot know, of course, whether it was the ability of Holmes or the capacity of Shattuck which led Justice Clifford to affirm Judge Lowell's decision in their favor, but the Justice, in an unreported decision, found in favor of the Nickersons. Though he allowed an appeal by the Danas to the Supreme Court of the United States, the case was later settled and the appeal was dropped.[71]

There was but one occasion on which Holmes argued a case before the Supreme Court of the United States. In 1902, recalling the event, he remembered "thinking that it needed only a black boy with gold bangles, holding a leash of greyhounds at one end of the bench, to be a living picture by Paul Veronese."[72] The case which brought him before the Court in the October Term of 1878 was *United States* v. *Oakes A. Ames and Oliver M. Ames, 2d, ex-*

[69] See, for example, *HLL*, I, 128: "My difficulty in writing about business is that all my interest is in theory and I care a damn sight more for ideas than for facts."

[70] Another occasion on which Holmes found himself entangled in complicated issues of fact involved patent litigation. See *Wonson* v. *Peterson*, Fed. Cas. #17,934 (1878). Holmes was associated with Chauncey Smith in representation of the defendant who was charged with infringement of a patent for improvement in paints for ships' bottoms. The defendant's brief, extensively annotated in Holmes's hand and preserved in Holmes's library at the Library of Congress, contains elaborate discussions of the chemical components of oxide of copper and sulphuret of antimony. It is likely, I take it, that Holmes became involved in this patent litigation because the interests involved were maritime. Smith and Holmes were not successful in their contention that no infringement of the complainant's patent by the defendant had been shown.

[71] The appeal and its withdrawal are recorded in the file papers of the United States Circuit Court in the custody of Records Service Center at Dorchester, Massachusetts.

[72] "Twenty Years in Retrospect," *OS*, 154, 155.

ecutors of Oakes Ames. William A. Munroe, Holmes's partner, was intimately associated with the Ames Plow Company—the concern in which Oakes Ames, the congressman notorious for the Crédit Mobilier scandal, had made his initial fortune. It was perhaps this association which led the Shattuck firm to represent the estate of the deceased congressman in complicated litigation in the federal courts.[73] During the Civil War, a vessel, the *Rob Roy,* and her cargo had been taken as a prize by Union forces in New Orleans. In the District Court in Louisiana, condemnation proceedings were initiated. One Mansfield appeared in the proceedings as claimant—that is, as owner—of the cargo of cotton, and gave bond with sureties to satisfy such prize decree in favor of the United States as might be entered. Thereupon the cotton was released to Mansfield. The prize proceedings went forward and concluded with a decree of condemnation in a sum exceeding $200,000. When the United States sought satisfaction of the cargo decree from Mansfield and his sureties it appeared that they were insolvent. The government then discovered that Oakes Ames, Oliver Ames, and Peter Butler had in fact been dormant partners of Mansfield in the venture in question, and that after the release of the cargo it had been sold advantageously and the proceeds distributed among the partners. The United States accordingly brought proceedings in equity in the United States Circuit Court in Boston seeking to collect its unsatisfied claim from the estate of the deceased partner, Oakes Ames, and from the other surviving partners.

Shattuck and Holmes successfully defended Mansfield's partners before Judge Shepley.[74] On an appeal to the Supreme Court of the United States that decision was affirmed in an opinion by Mr. Justice Clifford, with Bradley, J., dissenting.[75] Holmes's argument as presented in his brief in the Supreme Court made the full-

[73] The records of the Probate Court in Taunton, Massachusetts, indicate that Shattuck, Holmes, and Munroe represented the executors of Oakes Ames when the estate, with assets of nearly three million dollars, was found to be insolvent.

[74] Fed. Cas. #14,440 (1878).

[75] 99 U.S. 35 (1878).

est possible use—as, indeed, it had to—of every technical barrier which stood in the government's way.[76] It was hard, if not impossible, to deny the equity of the claim asserted, yet there was established common-law doctrine which says that a judgment recovered against one of several partners is a bar to a later suit against the others, and there were principles with respect to the significance of *in rem* proceedings in admiralty which also worked to immunize the executors of Oakes Ames from liability. On behalf of the executors Holmes persuaded the Supreme Court that the powers of a court of equity could not be exercised to override the applicable principle of the common law and a controlling rule of the court of admiralty. Though Mr. Justice Bradley dissented, he wrote no opinion, and one can only surmise that he believed that a court of equity could, legitimately, find ways of circumventing the obstructions which Holmes had discovered in the path of justice and had skillfully used for the protection of his clients' interests.

In the same season which brought Holmes before the Supreme Court there was an exciting and substantial possibility that he would leave the bar and assume judicial office.[77] In July 1878 the United States circuit judge for the First Circuit, George F. Shepley of Portland, Maine, had died. It was the consensus of professional opinion in Boston that the resulting vacancy might best be filled by promoting the district judge, John Lowell, to the circuit judgeship. A number of the leaders of the Boston bar urged on the Department of Justice that if Lowell should be advanced to the Circuit Court, Holmes would admirably fill the vacancy on the District Court. Holmes's intimate friend, John C. Gray, half brother of Horace Gray, wrote more fully of the possibility than anyone else. He addressed his communication to Charles C. Beaman, a college classmate of Holmes's, then in the Department of State under William M. Evarts:

Mr. Holmes, has been solicited by several members of the bar, not his personal friends, to be a candidate for the office, and he has con-

[76] A copy of Holmes's brief, with annotations in his hand, is preserved in the Holmes library at the Library of Congress.

[77] Holmes wrote to Pollock of the possibility on December 9, 1878 (*HPL*, I, 10).

sented to accept it, should it be tendered to him, though he does not want to take any personal step himself.

The business of the court, since the repeal of the bankrupt law, will be mainly in admiralty, and of admiralty law Holmes's knowledge is singularly exact and profound. His appointment would be a very popular one with the bar . . .

It would be a pecuniary sacrifice for Holmes to take the place,[78] but as you know, he is an ardent follower of the law for the law itself, and he would be a worthy successor of Judges Sprague and Lowell. It is a rare chance to get a man of first rate calibre for the position. His equal is certainly not to be found here among those who would be willing to take it.

Excuse the liberty I take in thus addressing you, but I trust the interest we both feel in our common friend will induce you to pardon me and to do all that you can with propriety do on his behalf. There is no time to be lost as Congress meets next week. Holmes's wounds and sufferings in the war ought to help his chances.[79]

Another communication, addressed to Charles Devens, Attorney General (later to be Holmes's associate on the Supreme Judicial Court), and signed by eight Boston practitioners (including Gray), also emphasized the special qualifications of Holmes for dealing with admiralty matters.[80] A younger member of the bar, Godfrey Morse, wrote to President Hayes directly and spoke of Holmes as "an able, learned, upright and good man and lawyer, who would honor the bench, and, in my judgment, would be satisfactory to the bar who have a most favorable impression of his uprightness and abilities." [81]

As always, there were competing claims and conflicting considerations. Some persons evidently thought that it would be inadvisable to promote Lowell to the Circuit Court. The President for a

---

78 At this time the salary of a district judge was $4000.

79 Gray to Beaman, Nov. 29, 1878 (General Records of the Department of Justice, National Archives).

80 The covering letter, dated Nov. 30, 1878, was signed by J. B. Richardson. Those signing the petition were Gustavus A. Somerby, A. A. Ranney, Nathan Morse, Seth J. Thomas, Edward Avery, Augustus Russ, and Richardson. The original is in records of the Department of Justice in the National Archives.

81 This letter, dated Dec. 5, 1878, is also in the National Archives.

time considered naming his Attorney General, Devens, to the vacancy. When he learned that Devens did not seek or want the post, the administration seriously considered asking Holmes's partner, Shattuck, to take the circuit judgeship. That possibility was discarded, however, and it was determined to advance Lowell and seek an appropriate man to fill his place on the District Court. The post was offered to Charles Allen (later Holmes's associate on the Supreme Judicial Court) but he refused it. During this whole period of uncertainty, the junior senator from Massachusetts, George Frisbie Hoar, was pressing the name of his friend and associate, Thomas L. Nelson of the Worcester bar, on Devens and the President. Senator Hoar in his *Autobiography* tells of the conclusion of the struggle. When Charles Allen rejected the district judgeship, the Attorney General and Hoar went to the White House.

In the meantime a very strong recommendation of Mr. Oliver Wendell Holmes, Jr. . . . had been received by the President. He felt a good deal of interest in Holmes. I think they had both been wounded in the same battle. But, at any rate, they were comrades. The President then said: "I rather think Holmes is the man." I then gave him my opinion of Mr. Nelson, and the President said to Devens: "Do you agree, Mr. Attorney-General?" Devens said: "I do." And the President said: "Then Nelson be it." [82]

The nominee consented to accept the post, and Nelson it was. The junior senator had managed to make his word decisive. When he was senior senator and twenty-four years later stood in Holmes's way to the federal judiciary, his word did not prevail.[83]

When Holmes wrote to Pollock of the possibility that he might receive the apointment, he said that if it should come to him he would "hardly know whether to be glad or sorry." He made it clear, however, that though it would cost him a severe pang to

[82] *Autobiography of Seventy Years* (New York 1903), II, 416–419. Senator Hoar was mistaken in believing that Holmes and President Hayes had been wounded in the same battle.

[83] See John A. Garraty, "Holmes's Appointment to the U.S. Supreme Court," *New England Quarterly*, 22:291 (1949).

leave his partners, he would suffer that pain in order to enjoy the opportunity of working in the way he wanted to.[84] This did not mean, I take it, that he longed to possess the power of a judge over the person and the property of his neighbor. It meant, I think, that he was eager to occupy a position which would enable him to make a philosophy of law an operating reality. As practitioner he had found that he could do little—and it was indeed very little—to give the shape of theory to American law. As writer and scholar, working through long evenings, he had continued the effort to which his first years in the profession had been dedicated. As judge he would not be compelled to give over entirely that phase of his effort towards achievement. He would also be able by the decisiveness of authority to make his voice heard and his convictions felt in the actual process of adjudication. It is not surprising, accordingly, that he had shown a thorough willingness to accept the office of judge if it should be offered him.

One is tempted, of course, to ask what Holmes's destiny might have been had he been named to the federal District Court in 1878. It seems unlikely that he would have written and published the two important essays "Common Carriers and the Common Law" and "Trespass and Negligence" at the time when they were written and published. Had they not appeared when they did, the chance of his being invited to deliver the Lowell Lectures—the Lectures which became *The Common Law*—would have been significantly reduced. The publication of that volume was probably the most important factor in securing his appointment to the Supreme Judicial Court. Would the appointment have been offered him—with or without *The Common Law* to his credit—if he had been a judge of the United States District Court? Had he stayed on the District Court would he, perhaps, have been later promoted either to the Circuit Court or to the Supreme Court of the United States? [85] If it was ordained in the stars that, by the one route or

84 *HPL,* I, 10.
85 When Circuit Judge Lowell resigned in 1884, Judge Colt of the United States District Court in Rhode Island, not Judge Nelson of the District Court in Boston, was named to fill the vacancy on the Circuit Court.

the other, he should find himself an Associate Justice of the Supreme Court in December 1902, would his contribution to that Court's functioning have been significantly different if he had brought to it the experience of a federal trial judge rather than that of an appellate judge of a state court? These questions, of course, are unanswerable. One may, however, safely conjecture that had Holmes gone on to the District Court in 1878, he would have found himself, while there, less free as scholar and judge to fulfill his talent for giving philosophic shape to common-law principles than he did as essayist, lecturer, and appellate judge of a state court possessing general jurisdiction in law and equity. It seems most unlikely, accordingly, that, whatever disappointment Holmes may have felt when Nelson and not he was chosen for the District Court, the regret was with him in his later years.

5

German Philosophy
and Teutonic History

*O*n October *12, 1930,* Holmes wrote reminiscently to a friend: "I have by my side a champagne cork drawn . . . when my work *The Common Law* came out and marked 'First copy of book, March 3, 1881.' (I remember that I hurried to get it out before March 8, because then I should be 40 and it was said that if a man was to do anything he must do it before 40.) " [1] Manifestly the special "anything" which Holmes had resolved to do was not the achievement of an active and successful practitioner. The "anything," furthermore, was not accomplished in the first productive years of scholarship—the years between 1869 and 1874. Though that period saw the publication of the early unsigned essays and reviews and the 12th edition of Kent, and included the lectureships in Harvard College, these marked the beginnings, not the fulfillment, of achievement. Attitudes and convictions took form in those first years and they were to survive in *The Common Law,* but the book was, almost in whole, made of research and writing carried on by Holmes while he was making his living at the bar. The achievement by which he wanted to be judged at the age of forty was *The Common Law.*

Perhaps the dimensions of the achievement will be better appreciated if a preliminary word is said of the provenance of the

1 To Mrs. Charles S. Hamlin (copy, HLS) .

volume as a whole and of its several parts. The published book was the fruit of twelve lectures which Holmes delivered in Boston under the auspices of the Lowell Institute in November and December of 1880.[2] When he was invited to deliver those lectures he had published five signed articles in the *American Law Review*.[3] These appeared in successive volumes of the *Review* between 1876 and 1880. The first two were concerned with Primitive Notions in Modern Law.[4] The next two, related closely to each other, dealt with Possession and with Common Carriers and Common Law.[5] The fifth was entitled "Trespass and Negligence." [6] In whole or in part each of these essays, variously reworked and revised, was incorporated in *The Common Law*.[7] The volume also included portions of Holmes's earlier unsigned papers on "Privity" and "The Theory of Torts." [8] The lecture on The Criminal Law and the three on Contracts had not been elsewhere published.

[2] The twelve lectures were given on successive Tuesday and Friday evenings at Huntington Hall, 187 Tremont Street. The first lecture was on November 23, 1880. The titles of the lectures, as distinguished from the chapters in the published version, were as follows: (1) The Beginnings of Legal Liability. (2) The Criminal Law. (3) Torts. Unintentional Wrongs. (4) Torts. Malice and Intent. (5) The Bailee at Common Law. (6) Possession. (7) Contract. History. (8) Contract. Elements. (9) Contract. Conditions. (10) Successions. By Descent or Will. (11) Successions. By Conveyance. (12) Summary of the Course.

[3] It is not known exactly when Holmes received the invitation to deliver the Lectures. In June of 1880 he wrote to Pollock that his nights had "been largely devoted to preparing a course of lectures for next winter" (HP, I, 14). In his reading list for 1880 Holmes noted that he was "at work writing Lectures for Lowell Inst. wh. occupied evenings, begun about Jan. 1" (Little, "Readings," 202). A. Lawrence Lowell, in a letter to the author, dated May 19, 1942, stated that it was on his suggestion that his father suggested to Holmes that he might give the Lowell lectures.

[4] *Am. L. Rev.*, 10:422 (April 1876); *id.*, 11:641 (July 1877).

[5] *Id.*, 12:688 (July 1878); *id.*, 13:609 (July 1879).

[6] *Id.*, 14:1 (January 1880).

[7] In its published form, Lecture One, "Early Forms of Liability," was based largely on "Primitive Notions in Modern Law, Part I." The fifth and sixth lectures, on "The Bailee at Common Law" and on "Possession and Ownership," incorporated most of the two articles on those subjects. Lectures Three and Four, on Torts, were built upon the recent article on "Trespass and Negligence" and the earlier essay "The Theory of Torts." The two concluding lectures on Successions included excerpts from the early article on Privity (*Am. L. Rev.*, 7:46) and "Primitive Notions in Modern Law: Part II" (*id.* 11:641).

[8] *Id.*, 7:46 (October 1872); *id.* 652 (July 1873); *Harv. L. Rev.*, 44:738, 773.

In 1919 Holmes was mildly distressed when his pontifical critic, John M. Zane, published in the *Illinois Law Review* some adverse reflections on his achievement.[9] Holmes indicated that he did not know whether later scholarship had shown that his book contained many or serious errors. "I think the material thing to be that I gathered the flax, made the thread, spun the cloth, and cut the garment—and started all the inquiries that since have gone over many matters therein. Every original book has the seeds of its own death in it, by provoking further investigation and clearer restatement, but it remains the original and I think it already is forgotten how far that is true of the *C.L.*" [10]

Though Holmes may have been somewhat over-sensitive to criticism and a little stubborn in his reluctance to abandon a position once taken, he was wholly justified in the conviction that if he was not the founder of a school of thought and scholarship, he was the first lawyer, English or American, to subject the common law to the analysis of a philosopher and the explanation of a historian. Shortly after the book's publication he wrote to John Norton Pomeroy of his purpose. The book, he said,

is intended to give the rationale of the cardinal doctrines of the common law—using analysis only where that is sufficient, but resorting to history where the particular outline of a conception or a rule could not be explained without it. I do not understand any other science of the law than this and yet so far as I know my attempt stands almost alone.[11]

It is not easy for those generations whose learning is built upon the foundations of scholarship laid in the last two decades of the nineteenth century to recognize the unquestionable truth of Holmes's assertion that the effort he made in *The Common Law* was an originating venture. Impressive institutional histories had, of course, been written on the Continent, but their legal framework was that of the Roman law. Brunner, to be sure, had pub-

9 John M. Zane, "A Legal Heresy," 13 *Illinois Law Review* 431 (1919). See also his "German Legal Philosophy," 16 *Michigan Law Review* 287, 349 (1918).

10 *HLL*, I, 184.

11 August 8, 1881 (copy HLS).

lished his work on the origins of the English jury. Yet scarcely any English or American historians of law and legal institutions had attempted to examine the growth of the common law with the scientific accuracy and philosophical perspective which the jurists on the continent and Henry Maine in England brought to their consideration of the Roman law and of the primitive legal institutions in other lands. The darkness and the legends of English constitutional history had, it is true, given way before the Germanic industry of Palgrave, Kemble, and Bishop Stubbs, but no such diligence as theirs had yet inspired the lawyers or historians of the nineteenth century to turn their attention to the growth of English institutions in the realm of private law. In 1884 Edward A. Freeman, the Regius Professor of Modern History at Oxford, spoke in a lecture of the progress which had occurred in the study of legal history between the time of Blackstone and his own day. For many generations "a vast body of professional lawyers [had piled up] a gigantic mass of error instead of the truth." Now, however, in 1884, "we can span the gap which parts Blackstone from Maine and Pollock." Further, "Law has now become a mainstay of history, or rather a part of history, because the knowledge of history is coming to be received as part of the knowledge of law." [12] Twenty years after Freeman spoke these words, Pollock in his turn discussed the condition of English legal history at the time when Henry Maine wrote his *Ancient Law*. It was, he said,

very imperfectly known, and what was known was concealed under huge masses of comparatively modern formalism . . . Constitutional law (and that from a political more than from a legal point of view) was the only department which could be said to have found an adequate historian. On the whole, historical knowledge of English law before the twelfth century was not to be found, and after the twelfth century was pretty much what Blackstone had left it . . . Clearly the English materials were not in a fit state, when Maine was writing "Ancient Law," to be used with effect for any purpose of historical general-

[12] Edward A. Freeman, "History and its Kindred Subjects," *The Methods of Historical Study* (London, 1886), 43, 71, 72.

isation or comparison; and he had no choice but to leave them alone for the most part, and build on other and at that time safer ground.[13]

Though it is the fact, I believe, that Holmes was the first of the English and American lawyers to attempt something like a full-scale study of the common law in which its basic concepts would be considered both historically and analytically, he was not the only lawyer who was concerned with the opportunity of inquiry along new avenues. In 1875, Digby's *Introduction to the History of the Law of Real Property* had revealed much of the spirit of the true historian. A young legal scholar in Boston, Melville Bigelow, in 1875 had published his *Cases on Torts,* a volume which not only acknowledged the influence of Holmes's suggested analysis of that portion of the law but showed that Bigelow, like Holmes, with the industry of the historian, was searching into the antiquities of the English law to aid in understanding its present substance. In 1879 he had made an important contribution to the resources of historical scholarship when he published his *Placita Anglo-Normannica: Law Cases from William I to Richard I,* a volume which Holmes read in manuscript. On its appearance in England, Pollock sang its praises, adding an Englishman's lament that

it is not exactly an honour to English learning and jurisprudence that we leave our brethren on the other side of the Atlantic to compete almost unaided with the insatiable industry of German scholars for the elucidation of our legal antiquities . . . The history of law is yet to be written as it deserves. Probably the man to do it, when it is done, will be either a German or an American." [14]

Time proved that Pollock was more discerning as critic and historian than he was as prophet, for the genius which he awaited came from England, not from across the Atlantic. But it was not until after the publication of *The Common Law* that the brilliance of Maitland's mind and pen made itself felt throughout the world of legal and historical scholarship.

[13] Maine, *Ancient Law* (Pollock, ed., 1906) , Introduction, xx, xxi, xxii.

[14] 48 *Saturday Review* 327 (Sept. 13, 1879) . In the same year in which Holmes delivered his Lowell Lectures, Bigelow published his *History of Procedure in England from the Norman Conquest* (London, 1880) .

It was not until 1885 that the *Law Quarterly Review* was established, nor until two years later that the Selden Society was founded. James Fitzjames Stephen had reluctantly come to see that even a dedicated Benthamite may improve his analysis of criminal law if he looks upon the history of its growth. His *History of the Criminal Law,* in three volumes, was not published, however, until after Holmes's lectures on the common law had been delivered.[15] At the Harvard Law School, James Bradley Thayer and James Barr Ames had begun their research in legal history, but until the *Harvard Law Review* was born in 1887 they did not begin to publish their most important essays in legal history.

To emphasize Holmes's increasing concern with the history of law is not to assert that he had resolved, in the middle of the 1870's, to transform himself from legal philosopher into legal historian. He had merely come increasingly to believe that a valid jurisprudence, whether for the scholar or for the practitioner, must take far more serious account of the materials of history than had the common-law lawyers of the eighteenth and nineteenth centuries. He followed the historian's path, however, not for the purpose of increasing understanding of the past but to the end of comprehending the character of legal institutions. Neither his impulse nor his achievement was that of Maitland. Yet his growing concern for the tough actualities, rather than for the fruitful legends, of the past led him more and more to see the legal scholar's endeavor as descriptive rather than normative. In the long stretch of time during which the common-law lawyer had turned an indifferent back to the realities of history, the profession's concern had been less with the "is" than with the "ought" in law. Though Bentham and Austin had looked with despising contempt on the complacent mind of Blackstone, they shared his conviction that the legal order was a means towards the achievement of a moral end. To the utilitarian, the means must be redirected towards the

---

[15] The *History of the Criminal Law* (London, 1883) was the three-volume consequence of Stephen's effort to prepare a new edition of his first analytic work on the criminal law, *A General View of the Criminal Law* (London, 1863).

true goal, the greatest happiness of the greatest number. To Black-stone the common law was the most fitting and ingenious means for fulfilling the law of nature. When, in the later years of the nineteenth century, English and American lawyers began to accept the standards of "scientific" accuracy on which the historians were insisting, the tendency to shift the role of legal scholarship from that of prescribing to that of describing was under way.[16]

As we have already seen, the earliest of Holmes's writings on law had been concerned more with problems of scientific analysis than with those of historical explanation. He had sought to refine and improve the Austinian scheme of order and had questioned the sufficiency of such fundamental elements in Austin's jurisprudence as the concept of sovereignty, the notion of law as command, and the hypothesis that culpability is an essential element in civil liability. He had also shown an intermittent and developing interest in uncovering the rational origins of apparently irrational rules of law. In the first years of his juristic endeavors—the period, that is, in which he was preparing the new edition of Kent and writing his articles on arrangement of the law—there are relatively few indications that he was probing new areas of learning. His education in the classics made it easy for him to work in the materials of Roman law. The settled traditions of Anglo-American legal scholarship made it quite natural that the field of his attention should be centered on the post-conquest law of England and the civil law of Rome. Holmes had suggested a number of radical views with respect to the arrangement of the law and he had made a somewhat different effort from that of his contemporaries when he sought to apply the fresh perspective of Maine's *Ancient Law* to the institutions of the common law. There is little to suggest, however, that in his earliest years he was affected by the new school of learning which traced the roots of English legal institutions to Germanic sources and sought to extend comprehension of their reality. Perhaps if Holmes had been able from the first to read German he would earlier have affiliated himself with the newer move-

[16] See, Freeman, "History and its Kindred Studies," in *The Methods of Historical Study* (London, 1886), 43, 70–79.

ment in legal history. His reading list, his reviews, and his citations in portions of Kent indicate that he was aware that the winds of new doctrine were beginning to blow.[17] Yet it is evident that before 1874 he made no systematic effort to follow the course which continental learning had, since mid-century, been taking.

There is no direct evidence to support the proposition that it was through the talk and the writing of Henry Adams that Holmes was encouraged to abandon the essentially conventional inquiries of English lawyers and search for guidance among the German scholars. Yet it surely is likely that President Eliot's young appointees to the Harvard College Faculty—friends as they already were and both deeply interested in the history of legal institutions—each followed the other's inquiries and enthusiasms with attentive interest. We know that they were both members of "The Club," that group of "clever, ambitious young fellows" in the Harvard community who dined with regularity in each other's company.[18] We also know that books which Adams was enthusiastically reviewing and discussing in the pages of the *North American Review* appeared contemporaneously on Holmes's reading list and

[17] See, e.g., his note on Village Communities, in Kent's *Commentaries* (12th ed.), IV, *441, note 1, referred to *supra*, p. 19.

[18] See Ernest Samuels, *The Young Henry Adams* (Cambridge, 1948), 217. Another link between Henry Adams and Holmes is suggested by entries appearing in Holmes's reading list for 1870–1871. Notations there appear that "with Adams" Holmes either read or "went over" Smith on *Contracts,* Williams on *Real Property,* Stephen on *Pleading,* and Langdell's *Cases on Contracts* in the last months of 1870 and the first weeks of 1871 (Little, "Reading," 182). The notations indicate that Holmes "finished with Adams" on February 1871. Though one may be tempted to surmise that Holmes was giving Henry Adams a glimpse of important aspects of the common law as Adams embarked on his academic journey through the legal institutions of England and the continent, the surmise seems unwarranted. Henry's younger brother, Brooks, entered the first year at the Harvard Law School in February 1871, the middle of the academic year. Holmes's notations in his reading list indicated that he "finished with Adams" on February 11. A note from Brooks Adams to Holmes (HLS), not signifying the year, but merely dated "Cambridge, 13 Feb.," stated that though Holmes had "set such an absurdly small value on what you have done for me" he was taking "the liberty of sending the enclosed check— saying with Rosalind: Wear this for me,—one out of sorts with fortune, /That would give more but that her hand lacks means." While Holmes was giving tutorial help to Brooks Adams, Brooks was living at Wadsworth House in Cambridge with his brother Henry.

soon began to play a most important part in fixing the direction and affecting the substance of his thought. It therefore seems clear that Adams's expressions of conviction may be taken to reflect—perhaps even to have shaped—the developing beliefs of Holmes.

When Adams reviewed Maine's *Village Communities,* Nasse's *Agricultural Communities,* and Sohm's *Die altdeutsche Reichs- und Gerichtsverfassung* in the *North American Review* he dealt not only with those specific volumes but with the currents of scholarship which had inspired him and his colleagues to follow new lines of historical inquiry—new, that is, for the Latin-speaking world of Harvard and the Inns of Court.[19] In the course of that review Adams asserted a proposition to which Holmes within a very few years was wholeheartedly to subscribe. No English lawyer or historian, said Adams, had ever used the materials to which the "plodding, obscure, and far from lively German"—Nasse—had given his discriminating attention.

The Englishman has accepted feudal law; he has, very unwillingly but at least frankly, accepted Roman law as modifying feudal law; but he still does battle with desperate energy against the idea that Germans as such, before they were either feudalized or Romanized, had an actual system of personal and proprietary law of their own, a system as elaborate, as fixed, and as firmly administered by competent and regular courts, as ever was needed to guarantee security of person and property in a simply constructed, agricultural community. From these laws and this society, not from Roman laws or William the Conqueror's brain, England, with her common-law and constitutional system, developed.[20]

Adams then urged that it was high time that English and American scholars should become aware of what the Germans had done in accurate explanation of the backgrounds of English legal history. Surely it is no coincidence that Holmes's reading list, shortly after Adams's review was published, for the first time, includes the titles Adams had commended.

In the same review Adams uttered some general and perceptive

19 *North American Review,* 114:196 (January 1872).
20 *Id.,* 197–198.

reflections on the contrast between juristic traditions and achievements in England and in Germany. These also seem to tell much of the character of Holmes's aspiration and suggest that his fundamental effort was to fulfill the hope of Adams that a new spirit would inspire the efforts of Anglo-American legal scholarship. The works of Nasse, Sohm, and their German contemporaries

are the works of jurists rather than of historians, and there never has been a time when the training of an English lawyer admitted of the possibility of such speculations. No doubt this was an advantage in some respects. It implied that English law had maintained itself in a course of development little disturbed from without; that it was jealous of foreign ideas and external influence; that it frowned upon unpractical theorizing. An Austin was a solitary and not a welcome apparition to the English bar. Perhaps it was well for the common law that it should have grown in this practical and healthy way; that it should have drawn assistance from the civil law only by stealth, and without acknowledgment of its thefts . . . But for history the disaster was enormous. In proportion as Englishmen made themselves good lawyers they have become bad historians. The whole fabric of the common law rests on a quantity of assumptions which as history are destitute of any sound basis in fact, and these assumptions have decisively influenced the ideas even of those English historians who, technically speaking, knew no law . . . In Germany the case was different . . . The German lawyer was also a jurist, and his study of codes . . . has forced him to develop a faculty for comparison and criticism, for minute analysis and sweeping generalization, such as no Englishman, except perhaps Austin and Maine, has ever dared to conceive. It is evident that this state of things is now rapidly passing away in England, and it may be that in the process of overthrow the English law will suffer; but even if this prove to be the case, some compensation may be drawn from the chance that English critical literature will spring into new life, and that English history will perhaps at last be written.[21]

I have already said something of Holmes's early attention to the Roman law. On that matter Adams, reviewing a recent translation of *The Ancient City* by Fustel de Coulanges—a book which Holmes read and re-read in the early 1870's—had protested that

[21] *Id.*, 198–199.

Roman institutions have alone been studied with care, but they have necessarily been studied by themselves rather than as a part of a general subject. Hence Roman law has come to be regarded as the type and source of all law; and the history of the Roman law appears to bound the ambition of the most curious student . . . Even Sir Henry Maine is true, after a fashion, to the classical tradition. Roman law is to him, too, the pure, typical, legal history, to be illustrated rather than to be used for illustration, to be studied as the end rather than to be used as a subject for classification.[22]

Adams then proceeded to outline the thesis which was dominating his mind—the thesis, that is, that the time had come for "creating something that can claim the name of scientific legal history." More specifically, he suggested that it should now be clear to the student of English law that "no really thorough historical acquaintance with his subject is possible without tracing the stream of legal institutions back through the German hundred, as well as through the Roman city, to its Aryan source.[23]

The fruit of Adams's convictions and teachings appeared in 1876 in the *Essays in Anglo-Saxon Law*. All of the contributors to the volume—Adams himself, Henry Cabot Lodge, Ernest Young, and J. Laurence Laughlin—were champions of the essentially political thesis that the strength of Anglo-American institutions came from Teutonic origins. They looked with scorn upon those historians of English institutions who paid no regard to contemporary continental learning and persisted in the traditional faith that the roots of all civilizing decency are traceable to Roman soil. Differ-

22 *Id.*, 118:390, 391 (April 1874).

23 In the same issue of the *North American Review* Adams, reviewing the recently published French translation of Rudolf Sohm's book on the procedure of the Salic law, spoke again of these matters. After emphasizing the fact that the law of the Salian Franks was the law which "was administered in England for seven centuries until the Plantagenets succeeded in substituting a better in its place," Adams went on to observe that "English historians have done little to clear away the darkness which rests on this portion of their history. Perhaps in time they will wake to the necessity of at least translating the commonest German books which bear on the subject; not the flighty and diffuse essays of Von Maurer, but the . . . books of Sohm and Brunner, Thudichum, Heusler, and so many other German scholars" (*id.* 397).

ing in some details with the views of Bishop Stubbs, Kemble, Freeman, and Green, Adams and his disciples attempted, through a more detailed examination of Anglo-Saxon law than any English or American historian had yet undertaken, to show that these historians were at long last traveling on the right road towards understanding. Adams and his students, like Bishop Stubbs and the other English Germanists, were not legal but institutional historians. Yet they had not feared to treat of law, and had turned to its history to prove their thesis. Just as one may say that the work of Maitland in legal history might never have been done had not German scholars—supported by Green, Freeman, and the others—opened the way, so it may be said that Holmes's inquiries would not have led him to *The Common Law* had not Adams persuaded him that new approaches to English legal history might have significant consequences. So far as one can see, Holmes never let himself become involved in the essentially romantic issue whether the democracy of the town meeting was traceable to the forests of Germany.[24] He was persuaded, if not by the words of Adams and his associates, at least by the guidance which they had given him, that "the main roots of our law are Frankish." That conviction formed perhaps the most important foundation stone of Holmes's writing in the second half of the 1870's and, therefore, of *The Common Law*.

In November 1881, after Adams had turned his back on English institutional history, he wrote a note to Holmes announcing that Holmes would shortly receive a box of books which might prove useful to him in his "investigations." The books, very clearly, were those which had constituted Adams's working library while he was engaged in his studies of Anglo-Saxon law. Adams had abandoned *sac* and *soc* and had turned to American his-

---

[24] This statement should, perhaps, be qualified by a reference to Holmes's little essay on Village Communities in his annotations of Kent. See, *supra*, p. 19. Holmes had there spoken of the village communities "once common throughout the Aryan world," which "served as a model for the New England townships" (*Commentaries*, IV, *441, note 1). It is significant perhaps that in Holmes's own copy of Kent he corrected "the New England townships" to read "some" New England townships.

tory—"Mr. Jefferson is feeling the knife"—and he hoped that Holmes might put the volumes which had once meant so much to Adams to good use. If Holmes would do that Adams would "feel as though I were still teaching—by proxy." [25] Although Holmes's letter of appreciation does not, apparently, survive, in letters to Pollock and Laski he indicated that he had not forgotten Adams's kindness.[26] On another occasion he chided Adams for talking "very absurdly" in the *Education* as if his work had been futile. "I, for one," said Holmes, "have owed you more than you in the least suspect . . . Of course you may reply that it is all futile—but that is the dogmatism that often is disguised under skepticism . . . If a man has counted in the actual striving of his fellows he cannot pronounce it vain . . . I thought that you might not dislike this IOU along with my wishes for a happy New Year.[27]

In 1877, in a long unsigned review of *Essays in Anglo-Saxon Law,* Holmes publicly expressed the warmest appreciation of the methods and achievements of Adams and his associates.[28] Noting with some amusement the "almost polemical renunciation of English models"—"due, we presume, to the influence of Mr. Adams"—Holmes commended the four essayists for their "German exactness in details" and concluded his notice with the reflection that such studies as those under review "prepare the ground for a truly philosophic history of the law" without which "the foundations of jurisprudence will never be perfectly secure." Yet he was not wholly satisfied that Henry Adams had

25 Adams to Holmes, Nov. 3, 1881 (HLS). Many of the volumes, with Adams's bookplate, are preserved in Holmes's library in the Library of Congress.

26 *HPL,* II, 18; *HLL,* II, 1031.

27 Dec. 31, 1907 (Massachusetts Historical Society; copy, HLS).

28 *Am. L. Rev.,* 11:327 (January 1877). The identification of Holmes as author of the review is based on the close parallel between comments on the essays noted in Holmes's "Black Book," under the date of November 9, 1876, and the points made in the published review. A letter from Henry Adams to Holmes, dated December 5, 1876 (HLS), quite clearly indicates that Holmes had told Adams something, at least, of what he meant to say as reviewer. Adams's reply contained characteristic expressions of satisfaction that his thesis would anger English scholars. "The Best Germans," he said, "will be with me, and there is no man in England whose opinion, unbacked by proof, is worth having."

been true to the standards which he purported to respect. "All scientific study nowadays is microscopic, even the study of history; and broad generalizations may depend at least on the reading of a text as well as on the structure of a fibre." Henry Adams had been so eager to sustain the thesis that in the purity of Germanic democracy as preserved in Anglo-Saxon institutions there could be no place for private courts that he had either dismissed unfavorable documentary evidence as forgery or maintained a discreet silence about the existence of such tribunals. Holmes showed his own familiarity with detail by reproving Adams for his failure explicitly to take into account relevant provisions in the laws of Edward the Confessor or to consider the significance of the practices of manor courts in manors of ancient demesne—provisions and practices which did not fit the scheme of things which Adams preferred. He charged his friend with the acceptance of the improbable hypothesis that private jurisdiction was a sudden creation rather than the consequence of gradual growth. In his comments on the essays of Lodge, Young, and Laughlin, Holmes showed that he was no stranger in the world of German scholarship. He intimated a general doubt, however, whether the essayists had not shown an excess of faith in the omnipotence of historians. "It must not be forgotten that there is a limit to historical explanation, as it is called. Some things (the origin of the notion of property, for instance) receive more light from an analysis of human nature." [29] In that suggestion Holmes indicated that he had not become so committed to the methods of the legal historian that he had abandoned the goals of the legal philosopher.

In 1922, Holmes's young friend, Harold Laski, asked him when *The Common Law* was conceived, and "where did the idea of comparative historical work spring from: was it from reading (and meeting?) Sir H. Maine?" [30] Holmes's reply was in terms of generality.

You ask me what started my book. Of course I can't answer for unconscious elements. I don't think Maine had anything to do with it ex-

[29] *Am. L. Rev.*, 11:330.   [30] *HLL*, I, 427.

George Otis Shattuck

Ersayhin Anglo Saxon law (Continued)

legal procedure - taxibin : Continued

The sixth of seven pages of Holmes's notes on Essays in Anglo-Saxon Law as recorded in his "Black Book" and dated November 9, 1876.

60. Possession - Roman

Lehrbuch des Pandektenrechts. Von Dr. Bernhard Windscheid, Professor an der Universität Leipzig. Vierte Auflage. Düsseldorf, Julius Buddeus. 1875.

Zweites Kapitel. Der Besitz. §§ 148—164.

The top half of the first of three pages of Holmes's notes on Windscheid's analysis of possession in the Roman law. The notes are dated December 9, 1877.

cept to feed the philosophic passion. I think the movement came from within—from the passionate demand that what sounded so arbitrary in Blackstone, for instance, should give some reasonable meaning—that the law should be proved, if it could be, to be worthy of the interest of an intelligent man—(that was the form the question took then). I went through much anguish of mind before I realized the answer to that question that I have often given since. I don't think of any special book that put me on the track—though the works that I cited such as Lehuërou helped. I rooted round and made notes until the theory gradually emerged.[31]

The shifting course of interest, and, perhaps, of influence, is indicated with unmistakable clarity in Holmes's reading lists. It is not, I think, a distorting effort to produce order, to classify his reading in three categories—the anthropological, the historical, and the philosophical. Of course the boundaries dividing the areas of learning were not precise and clear. Maine's work was scarcely less important to anthropologists than it was to jurists; Savigny's *History of Roman Law* was as influential in jurisprudence as it was in legal history. Wake's *Evolution of Morality* was a study of history and of philosophy. Yet the compartments of learning and of interest are not without significance and may fairly be used to clarify the progression in Holmes's thought.

Ever since his first reading of *Ancient Law* when he was a law student, Holmes had made it his business to keep abreast of anthropological studies relating to primitive institutions. McLennan's *Primitive Marriage*, Waitz's *Anthropology*, and Tylor's *Primitive Culture* provided the starting point for such specialized

---

[31] *Id.* 429–430. There is good reason to suppose that from the very beginning of the decade Holmes had formulated the hope, if not the plan, of doing a new kind of work on legal philosophy. Reviewing Ram's *Science of Legal Judgment* (New York, 1871) in October 1871, he had said that a treatise "on the sources of the law which shall strike half way between the latitudinary theorizing of Savigny and the too narrow exclusiveness of Austin, will form a chapter of jurisprudence which is not yet written, and which it is worthy of the ambition of an aspiring mind to write" (*Am. L. Rev.*, 6:134). It was surely something more than a coincidence that for Holmes's lectures on Crimes, Torts, Possession, Contract, and Succession in the common law of England, there were equivalent chapters in Maine's *Ancient Law*.

studies as Laveleye's *De la propriété et de ses formes primitives,* Giraud-Teulon's *Origines du mariage et de la famille,* Paul Viollet's *Caractère collectif des premières propriétés immobilières,* von Maurer's *Einleitung zur Geschichte der Mark-, Hof-, Dorf-, und Stadt-Verfassung und der öffentlichen Gewalt,* and Lea's *Superstition and Force.* By Maine and Laveleye, Holmes was persuaded that communal preceded private ownership. This persuasion meant, of course, that he could not take seriously the eighteenth century's dogma that private property is either sanctioned by the social compact or sanctified by the eternal law of nature. It did not, however, mean for Holmes, any more than it did for Maine, that a socialist ordering of property should become the objective of the nineteenth-century government. It was towards a view of law and its history, not towards a philosophy of government and its destiny, that Holmes's readings in anthropology led him.

It is not surprising that Holmes's professional interest in historical writing did not extend to what he termed "literary history." "A history of Economics, Law, or Philosophy, *bon*—but the works of literary gents in the general field are too unquantified in premise and conclusion to suit me. My notion of literary history is 'Gallants staked whole estates upon a single cast of the die.' " [32] As man of letters, Holmes turned from time to time to the pages of Gibbon, Carlyle, Macaulay, and Froude. While he was making himself a productive scholar, however, it was in the works of Fustel de Coulanges, Stubbs, Freeman, Lehuërou, Laferrière, and Kemble that he found what he was seeking. His concern was with the social and legal institutions of history, not with its heroes and its villains, its chronicles and its wars.

As one who felt an impelling obligation to keep abreast of contemporary learning in the law, Holmes could not neglect the tendency in the jurisprudence of his time to seek in Roman law some universal principles of order. This led him necessarily be-

---

[32] *HLL,* I, 46. The quotation which Holmes remembered was from Green's *Short History of the English People.*

yond the newest English studies of the law of Rome to the massive works of German scholarship on which civilian learning throughout the world was built. Even before he had mastered the language of that scholarship he discovered its general direction and some of its substance either in French and English translation or in second-hand descriptive analysis.[33] When he had conquered the dismal tongue of civilian erudition he fought his way through the pages of such works as Schuerl's *Lehrbuch der Institutionen,* Windscheid's *Lehrbuch des Pandektenrechts,* Jehring's *Geist des Römischen Rechts,* and Keller's *Der römische Civilprocess.* As we shall later see in more detail, what most impressed and repelled him in the German interpretation of Roman law was the philosophical foundation on which so much of that interpretation was based. He discerned in the works most frequently acclaimed—particularly in Savigny—Kantian or Hegelian presuppositions. In the company of William James, Chauncey Wright, Nicholas St. John Green, and the other "members" of the Metaphysical Club, Holmes had come very early in his philosophic pilgrimage to share their deep distrust and antagonism to the *a priori* categories of Kant and the conceptual dialectic of Hegel.[34] A philosophy of law, an analysis of legal history, which was built on Kantian or Hegelian foundations must be repudiated and cast aside. His distrust of the German aptitude for forcing the Roman law into a shape prescribed by Kant's categories and Hegel's logic sometimes carried him so far as to see that law itself as somehow infected by a false metaphysics. This led him, one suspects, to look with particular favor upon other legal orders than the Roman—

[33] In 1870 he read Savigny's *History of the Roman Law during the Middle Ages* in the English translation of Cathcart, Lindley's edition of Thibault's *Introduction to the Study of Jurisprudence,* Savigny on *Possession,* in Perry's translation. In the following year he read Tomkins and Jencken, *A Compendium of the Modern Roman Law,* Abdy's edition of *The Commentaries of Gaius and Rules of Ulpian,* Prichard's and Nasmith's translation of Ortolan's *History of Roman Law.* These are but samples of the readings relating to Roman law which continued throughout the decade.

[34] See Philip Wiener, *Evolution and the Founders of Pragmatism* (Cambridge, 1949).

orders which had not yet felt the distorting hands of the disciples of Kant and Hegel and which might, therefore, be interpreted and understood in very different terms from those prescribed by German metaphysics.

The fact that Holmes saw a significant relationship between German civilian scholarship during the nineteenth century and the metaphysics of Kant and Hegel is indicated by his philosophical reading during the period when the essays which were incorporated in *The Common Law* were being written. In 1877 his reading list carries the following works: Kant's *Metaphysics of Ethics* and his *Metaphysics of Law,* the *Logic* of Hegel with prolegomena by Wallace, Edward Caird's *Critical Account of the Philosophy of Kant,* and James Hutchison Stirling's Hegelian lectures, *The Philosophy of Law.* These speculative excursions of Holmes's were carried out in the same period in which he was soaking himself in the work of the German civilians. When he read Bruns, Gans, and Puchta on possession he could not escape the Hegelian flavor. When he turned to Savigny's *System of Modern Roman Law* (in a French translation) he found it easy to see distasteful presuppositions in such Kantian pronouncements as that "all Law exists for the sake of the moral freedom indwelling in every individual Man." [35] Though he evidently saw that Jhering shared his own suspicion of the metaphysical foundations on which his fellow countrymen had built their jurisprudence and their interpretations of legal history, it does not seem that Holmes was willing to recognize that Jhering was, to a very considerable extent, his philosophical ally. Though he read the four volumes of Jhering's *Spirit of the Roman Law* (again in a French translation) in 1879, there is, I think, no indication that he ever recognized that Jhering had uttered protests no less vigorous than his own against the beatitude of logic and sanctity of will in German legal thought.

Holmes, I think, sought to master the German language not because it would lead him through the German tracts on Roman

[35] The quotation is from Ratigan's translation of the second book, entitled by the translator *Jural Relations* (London, 1884) 1.

law. The learning which he sought was that of which Henry Adams had made him aware—the studies of early Teutonic institutions which had provided the underpinnings of the *Essays on Anglo-Saxon Law.* As Holmes developed his capacity to read German with some ease, his reading list begins to record the titles of such works as *Beispruchtsrecht und Universalsuccession im Deutschen Rechte,* Rudolph Sohm's *Der Process der Lex Salica* and his *Frankischen Reichs-und Gerichts Verfassung,* Behrend's *Zum Process der Lex Salica,* and Heusler's *Die Gewere.* Annotations of his essays and of *The Common Law* indicate that these were but a few of the studies of Germanic law and custom with which Holmes was making himself familiar. I believe that it can be said without qualification that none of the studies of Germanic law—whether of German, French, or English authorship— bore the metaphysical watermark which Holmes's astute and possibly suspicious eye had found in the standard works on Roman law. If the roots of the common law could be traced to Teutonic rather than to Roman soil they would, therefore, be uninfected by what seemed to Holmes to be a fatal philosophic infirmity. One might discover in the growth of the common law tendencies wholly different from those which not only had distorted understanding of the civil law, but had even warped that law itself.

To the extent that contemporary scholarship was concerning itself with English legal history, Holmes kept himself abreast of all developments. Forsyth on *Trial by Jury,* Güterbock's *Bracton and His Relation to the Roman Law,* Twiss's edition of Bracton and of *The Black Book of the Admiralty,* and Thorpe's *Ancient Laws and Institutes of England*—all these works and many others poured learning into Holmes's devouring mind. This reading, it should be emphasized, was not the leisurely exposure of an interested intelligence to current professional thought. It was the concentrated instruction of an aspiring mind. One of Holmes's favorite reflections was that "culture"—["odious word"] [36]—"often means having more wood in your woodpile than you have in your

36 Letter to Mrs. C. P. Curtis, Jan. 18, 1926 (HLS).

furnace, and of a size that won't go in." [37] In the 1870's Holmes was feeding his furnace, not stacking his woodpile.

Another word seems desirable with respect to his attitudes towards Roman law and German philosophy. As we have seen, Holmes had from the beginning of his professional career shown a vigorous interest in providing a new analysis and a new ordering of the common law. There is some reason to believe that he was fearful that English lawyers and scholars, impressed as they had come to be by the profundity of German learning with respect to Roman law, would seek to impose the philosophic shape of that learning upon the chaos of the common law. This danger was not, I think, negligible. I have already pointed to the Roman influence upon Austin's analysis of law, to the effort which Bryce was making to bring more Roman law into English legal education, and to the fact that the most original of all the contemporary English legal historians, Sir Henry Maine, in his first book, *Ancient Law,* had done much to arouse the English legal world to the seductive charms of Roman jurisprudence. Savigny, of all the German jurists, seems to have had most fascination for English lawyers. John Austin had said of his work on Possession that "of all books upon law [it is] the most consummate and masterly; and of all books which I pretend to know accurately, [it is] the least alloyed with error and imperfection." [38] Maitland testified that Savigny's *Geschichte des römishen Rechts* "first opened [my] eyes as to the way in which law should be regarded." [39] As we shall later see, Pollock and other analysts of the law of contract built much of their doctrine upon foundations which Savigny had laid. Seeing the Kantian imprint upon the work of Savigny, it is not surprising that Holmes was worried lest Anglo-American jurisprudence, at a most critical juncture in its development, should find itself burdened with disastrously abstract presuppositions.

If the suggestions which I have made regarding the lines of force by which Holmes's mind was governed during the 1870's be

[37] To Mrs. J. R. Green, Nov. 9, 1913 (copy, HLS). Cf. *Shaping Years,* 252.
[38] *Lectures on Jurisprudence* (4th ed., London, 1873), I, 55.
[39] H. A. L. Fisher, *Frederick W. Maitland* (Cambridge, 1910), 18.

sound, one might expect to find that the central philosophic thesis of *The Common Law* was that Kantian and Hegelian metaphysics had corrupted jurisprudence. One might expect also to find that the volume's controlling historical thesis would not be unrelated to that and would emphasize the Germanic rather than the Roman elements in the law of England. These expectations I shall seek in later chapters to justify. The philosophic and the historical theses have not infrequently been overlooked because the most memorable passage in the volume—that with which it opens—seems to show less concern with philosophy and with history than it does with the nature of the judicial process.

The life of the law has not been logic: it has been experience. The felt necessities of the time, the prevalent moral and political theories, intuitions of public policy, avowed or unconscious, even the prejudices which judges share with their fellow-men, have had a good deal more to do than the syllogism in determining the rules by which men should be governed. The law embodies the story of a nation's development through many centuries, and it cannot be dealt with as if it contained only the axioms and corollaries of a book of mathematics.

This is a protest not against a false philosophy or against a misleading history. It is the repudiation of a traditional understanding of the judicial process.

In the pages of *The Common Law* itself, Holmes did not make it wholly clear whom he considered the sinners to be. The generality of his protest was so broad that he seemed to have nothing significantly different in mind than what Jhering had referred to when he objected to the excesses of logic among the German jurists.[40] But when one looks behind the first page of *The Common Law* to an unsigned book review which Holmes had published in the *American Law Review* in March 1880, one can see that Holmes was directing his opening fire, in significant part at least, at the dean of the Harvard Law School, Christopher Columbus Langdell. What Holmes had said in his review of the second edition of Langdell's *Selection of Cases on the Law of Contracts*

---

40 See, e.g., *Geist des römischen Rechts,* Theil 3, Abth. 1.

enormously clarifies the significance of the most familiar passage in *The Common Law*. This is what Holmes said of Langdell's casebook.

It is hard to know where to begin in dealing with this extraordinary production,—equally extraordinary in its merits and its limitations. No man competent to judge can read a page of it without at once recognizing the hand of a great master. Every line is compact of ingenious and original thought. Decisions are reconciled which those who gave them meant to be opposed, and drawn together by subtle lines which never were dreamed of before Mr. Langdell wrote. It may be said without exaggeration that there cannot be found in the legal literature of this country, such a *tour de force* of patient and profound intellect working out original theory through a mass of detail, and evolving consistency out of what seemed a chaos of conflicting atoms. But in this word "consistency" we touch what some of us at least must deem the weak point in Mr. Langdell's habit of mind. Mr. Langdell's ideal in the law, the end of all his striving, is the *elegantia juris,* or *logical* integrity of the system as a system. He is, perhaps, the greatest living legal theologian. But as a theologian he is less concerned with his postulates than to show that the conclusions from them hang together. A single phrase will illustrate what is meant. "It has been claimed that the purposes of substantial justice and the interests of contracting parties as understood by themselves will be best served by holding &c. . . . and cases have been put to show that the contrary view would produce not only unjust but absurd results. *The true answer to this argument is that it is irrelevant; but"* &c. (pp. 995, 996, pl. 15) . The reader will perceive that the language is only incidental, but it reveals a mode of thought which becomes conspicuous to a careful student.

If Mr. Langdell could be suspected of ever having troubled himself about Hegel, we might call him a Hegelian in disguise, so entirely is he interested in the formal connection of things, or logic, as distinguished from the feelings which make the content of logic, and which have actually shaped the substance of the law. The life of the law has not been logic: it has been experience. The seed of every new growth within its sphere has been a felt necessity. The form of continuity has been kept up by reasonings purporting to reduce every thing to a logical sequence; but that form is nothing but the evening dress which the newcomer puts on to make itself presentable according to conventional requirements. The important phenomenon is the man underneath it, not the coat; the justice and reasonableness of a decision, not its consistency with previously held views. No one will ever have a truly philosophic mastery over the law who does not habitually consider the forces outside of it which have made it what it is. More than that, he must remember that as it embodies the story of a nation's development through many centuries, the law finds its philosophy not in self-consistency, which it must always fail in so long as it continues to grow, but in history and the nature of human needs. As a branch of anthropology, law is an object of science; the theory of legislation is a scientific study; but the effort to reduce the concrete details of an existing system to the merely logical consequence of simple postulates is always in danger of becoming unscientific, and of leading to a misapprehension of the nature of the problem and the data.[41]

We may assume, I think, that in his opening lecture in the Lowell Institute series Holmes did not name names when he spoke of the sins of logicians in the law. It is not unlikely that Langdell, Thayer, Ames, and Gray—the entire Faculty of the Harvard Law School—were in the audience, and the lecturer would hardly have pointed a finger of scorn at the attentive Dean. Yet some of the audience, perhaps Langdell himself, had surely read the unsigned review of the Dean's casebook and therefore saw fangs in the opening generalities which the majority of the audience did not see. One may have special confidence that John C. Gray took malicious satisfaction in the unstated, *ad hominem,* reference which Holmes had in mind. Within a very

41 *Am. L. Rev.,* 14:233. The review also contained a notice of Anson's *Principles of the Law of Contract* (Oxford, 1879). Writing to Pollock on April 10, 1881, Holmes once more again commented on Langdell's Casebook on Contracts. "A more misspent piece of marvellous ingenuity I never read, yet it is most suggestive and instructive. I have referred to Langdell several times in dealing with contracts because to my mind he represents the powers of darkness. He is all for logic and hates any reference to anything outside of it, and his explanations and reconciliations of the cases would have astonished the judges who decided them. But he is a noble old swell whose knowledge ability and idealist devotion to his work I revere and love" (*HPL,* I, 17).

few years Gray was to communicate to President Eliot of Harvard his deep distrust of Langdell's approach to law.

In law the opinions of judges and lawyers as to what the law is, *are* the law, and it is in any true sense of the word as unscientific to turn from them, as Mr. Langdell does, with contempt because they are "low and unscientific," as for a scientific man to decline to take cognizance of oxygen or gravitation because it was low or unscientific . . . Langdell's intellectual arrogance and contempt is astounding. One may forgive it in him or Ames, but in an ordinary man it would be detestable. The idols of the cave which a school bred lawyer is sure to substitute for the facts, *may be much better material for intellectual gymnastics than the facts themselves and may call forth more enthusiasm in the pupils,* but a school where the majority of the professors shuns and despises the contact with actual facts, has got the seeds of ruin in it and will and ought to go to the devil.[42]

The importance of Holmes's opening generalities with respect to the roles of logic and experience in the judicial process did not depend, of course, upon their applicability to Langdell, for they asked not simply for a turning away from his peculiar exaggerations but for a radical renovation of legal thought. Doubtless Holmes's call for a realistic analysis of the judicial process was inspired by his philosophical proclivities and antipathies, yet it could stir enthusiasm in minds less hostile than was his to metaphysical abstraction. His words had force and meaning not merely to philosophers but to practitioners and judges—to lawyers who cared little for history and less for philosophy but who sought for generality that was true to their own experience. There is some reason to suppose that Holmes's lectures also stirred the interest of law students—among them, perhaps, some from the Harvard Law School who were not unwilling to hear a new voice teaching another doctrine than that which they had learned in Cambridge. The newspaper accounts of the Lowell Lectures remarked upon the fact that "no other course in the Institute in recent years has been attended by so large a proportion of young men—an evidence

[42] J. C. Gray to President Eliot, Jan. 8, 1883 (Harvard Archives).

both of the interest they have in the law and the power of Mr. Holmes to interest them." [43] The youthful interest may also have bespoken an awareness by a younger generation that the time had come for a new reading of history and a new analysis of the common law.

[43] Boston *Daily Advertiser,* Saturday, Jan. 1, 1881, p. 1, c. 10. The account of the concluding lecture reported that at its close "Mr. Holmes gave a few minutes . . . to a picture of the scope, beauties, pleasures and horrors of the law, and then took leave of his audience."

6

Self-Preference, Externality, and Crimes

$\mathcal{T}$*he greater portion* of Holmes's first lecture, "Early Forms of Liability," had initially been published as the first of two essays on "Primitive Notions in Modern Law." It had appeared in the *American Law Review* for April 1876.[1] In the essay and its revision Holmes's historical endeavor was that of tracing the origins of three contemporary rules of law. The first rule holds the owner of an animal of "known ferocious habits"[2] liable for damage which the animal may do to the owner's neighbor. The second rule is this: "A baker's man, while driving his master's cart to deliver hot rolls of a morning, runs another man down. The master has to pay for it."[3] The third rule, embodied in an Act of Congress of 1851, permits the owner of a vessel which does injury in certain circumstances to limit the amount of his liability to the value of the offending ship.[4] The analytical jurist's facile justifica-

[1] *Am. L. Rev.*, 10:422.
[2] *CL*, 6.
[3] *Id*. Holmes, the lecturer, had seen fit to add color to the situation which the essayist had first described. In "Primitive Notions" the imagined case of master and servant had been thus set down: "A man's servant, while driving his master's cart, carelessly runs another down; and the master asks why he should be liable for the illegal act of another" (*Am. L. Rev.*, 10:423–424).
[4] *CL*, 6–7.

tion for the first rule of law had been that the owner of the animal had been guilty of remote heedlessness in "having such a creature at all." [5] The liability of the master, under the second rule of law, "from the time of Ulpian to that of Austin," had been rationalized by the assertion that the master was "to blame for employing an improper person." [6] With respect to the limitation of the shipowner's liability the justification offered in Congress had been that "if a merchant embark a portion of his property upon a hazardous venture, it is reasonable that his stake should be confined to what he puts at risk,—a principle similar to that on which corporations have been so largely created in America during the last fifty years." [7] Tracing each of the three rules to the conceptions and processes of primitive societies—Jewish, Greek, Teutonic, and Roman—Holmes sought to show how different were the considerations which led to their creation from the reasons given for their surviving force.

The first paper on Primitive Notions made it clearer, I think, than did the published lecture that Holmes's ultimate interest was more in the philosophy than in the history of legal liability. The essay opened with the explicit assertion that Holmes was seeking in the materials of history confirmation of the thesis which he had offered in "The Theory of Torts." [8] That thesis, as he summarized it in "Primitive Notions" was this:

> More generally than has been supposed, civil liability depends not on culpability as a state of the defendant's consciousness,—that is to say, upon the particular defendant's having failed to do the best that he knew how to do,—but upon his having failed to come up to a more or less accurately determined standard in his overt acts or omissions.

Holmes went on to say that in his earlier essay he had glanced incidentally at the historical origin of liability in some cases which Austin, following the jurists of the mature period of Roman law, had interpreted on grounds of culpability; and to point out that it sprung from the much more primitive notion, that liability attached directly

5 *Id.,* 6.　　　　　　　　　　　6 *Id.*
7 *Id.,* 6–7.　　　　　　　　　　8 See *supra,* p. 80 *et seq.*

1 6 1

to the thing doing the damage. This suggestion will be found to have occurred to earlier writers who will be quoted. But we shall endeavor in this article to explain that primitive notion more at length, to show its influence on the body of modern law, and to trace the development from it of a large number of doctrines which in their actual form seem most remote from each other or from any common source; a task which we believe has not been attempted before. If we are successful, it will be found that the various considerations of policy which are not infrequently supposed to have established these doctrines, have, in fact, been invented at a later period to account for what was already there,—a process familiar to all students of legal history.[9]

This passage makes it clearer than did the first lecture as published that Holmes's historical inquiry was carried on in order to refute the Austinian thesis that personal fault is an essential element of civil liability. It is not easy, perhaps, to see that effort in refutation as a part of the first published lecture, for one of the most striking elements in Holmes's thesis with respect to early forms of liability—civil and criminal—is that the primitive mind, permeated with a superstitious animism, ascribed malevolent intention to all moving things—whether in fact animate or inanimate—which do injury to others. It is this animism which explains, in his judgment, the processes common to many early systems of law, by which the moving "thing"—whether it be dog, vessel, slave, or falling limb of tree—is either condemned by destruction or transferred to the victim of "its" injury. In the pages of Tissot's *Droit Pénal* and Tylor's *Primitive Culture* Holmes found that the learning of a comparativist and of an anthropologist confirmed his own early suspicion that the passion for vengeance, planted in minds which ascribe life and malevolence to moving things which do damage, explains many bewildering aspects of early principles of legal liability.[10] He was convinced,

9 *Am. L. Rev.*, 10:422, 423.

10 In "Primitive Notions" Holmes, somewhat characteristically, indicated that he had reached some of his most significant conclusions with respect to the problem under consideration before "his attention had been called to [relevant] provisions of the Roman law . . . and still longer before he had seen the works of MM. Tissot and Tylor" (*Id.* 432). He then cited his annotations to Kent to establish his own

in any case, that these elements deserved an attention which neither metaphysical nor analytical jurists had given them.

I have suggested that in the published lecture Holmes did not make it wholly clear what relationship his analysis of primitive concepts of liability bore to his thesis that personal culpability is not an essential ingredient of liability. The lecture might even seem to suggest that ancient history confirms Austin's contention. The lecturer did, after all, urge that the primitive passion for revenge was released only against those "things" to which a culpable intent was ascribed. It might, therefore, seem that the data which Holmes had assembled, far from refuting the thesis of Austin, gave it the support of comparative history. In the essay on Primitive Notions there is, however, a greater clarity of argument than in the published lecture. Holmes did not deny—in fact, as we shall see, he insisted with considerable force—that in primitive and early times fault (whether real or imagined) was conceived to be a necessary element in liability. He urged that the primitive mind was quite indifferent to the question whether the owner of the offending thing which was surrendered or destroyed shared in the fault of his property. As the animistic superstition dissolved, however, the primitive legal process against the "thing" survived. It came to be recognized that through condemnation or transfer of offending property its owner was being penalized. How was the penalty against him to be justified? Ingenious and inventive minds, feeling a moral or inherited obligation to justify liability by discovering culpable fault on the part of the owner-defendant, asserted that there was blame in the owner of the dog, slave, or tree, in his careless management of his property or affairs. Neither the Roman jurists nor Austin had seemed to recognize that in fact a lack of care by such a defendant was not a prerequisite to his liability. The owner of offending property or the employer of a careless servant is not protected from liability—limited

---

priority of insight in relationship to the personification of vessels in the court of admiralty. In the essay, but not in the lecture, he had also used the psychological testimony of Bain to support his interpretation of the primitive mind. See *Am. L. Rev.*, 10:430, note 1.

or unlimited—by showing that he was wholly without fault in having taken ownership or in having employed the careless servant. As Holmes interpreted that phase of legal history with which his first lecture was concerned, the movement of doctrine was in fact a movement from the primitive liability of things with fault to the matured liability of persons without fault.

Two somewhat controversial aspects of the first lecture deserve attention. In an almost casual aside, Holmes indicated that he assumed that a single theory of liability should control both civil and criminal matters. "The first subject to be discussed," he said, "is the general theory of liability civil and criminal." [11] It is possible, of course, that this was a historical and not a philosophical assumption—that Holmes, in other words, had in mind the fact that the line between civil and criminal law, clear as it may have become in modern jurisprudence, had little if any significance in primitive systems of law. In view, however, of the theses of later portions of *The Common Law,* it seems entirely clear that Holmes was speaking philosophically when he suggested, thus succinctly and indirectly, that the external theory of tort liability which he had outlined in "The Theory of Torts" should also govern in the criminal law.

The second question deserving of special attention is whether Holmes, in questioning the Austinian justification for vicarious liability and the legislative defense of limited liability in admiralty, intended to cast doubt upon the rules thus speciously justified. One may be persuaded by later lectures in *The Common Law,* by later essays—perhaps by later judicial opinions which he delivered—that Holmes thought the law unwise which imposes liability on the careful master of the careless servant and questioned the policy which, to the advantage of shipowners, treats vessels as if they were persons. Upon the basis of the first lecture itself, however, it is not possible to say, I think, that Holmes intended to suggest that reasons other than those which Austin and congressmen had given were not adequate to support

[11] *CL,* 2.

as operative rules of law doctrine born of primitive psychology in barbaric times.

In the first essay on Primitive Notions, though Holmes had developed the contention that the primitive roots of criminal and civil liability are traceable to the thirst for vengeance, he did not explicitly consider certain psychological aspects of that appetite, which soon received his attention. It is not unlikely that when he first wrote of primitive notions he accepted the common belief that the relatively simple mind of the barbarian had not troubled itself with the distinction between an injury inflicted intentionally or negligently and an injury done by sheer accident.[12] Holmes had not then, perhaps, formulated his historical generalization that the progression of legal thought with respect to elements of civil and criminal liability had been a movement from liability with personal fault to liability measured by an external standard. We know that he had already come to believe that the law of civil liability in his own day was built upon an external standard of blame.[13] In the essay on Primitive Notions he did not indicate that he considered that the archaic concept of liability was differently grounded. In his first Lowell Lecture, however, he stated very explicitly that the noxal processes which he had described—the processes, that is, which were directed against animate and inanimate offenders—"started from a moral basis, from the thought that some one was to blame."[14]

There has been much discussion, and considerable misunderstanding, I believe, of this historical thesis of Holmes. It is, therefore, worth the effort to discover the evolution and search out the meaning of the proposition as it was stated in *The Common Law*.

---

12 In the first lecture he spoke of "an opinion which has been held, that it was a characteristic of early law not to penetrate beyond the external visible fact, the *damnum corpore corpori datum*" (*CL*, 4). This reflection was taken from his essay of 1880 on Trespass and Negligence (*Am. L. Rev.*, 14:4). Is it possible, perhaps, that Holmes was indirectly acknowledging that he had been of that mistaken opinion when he published the paper on Primitive Notions?

13 "The Theory of Torts," *Am. L. Rev.*, 7:652 (July, 1873). See *supra*, p. 81.

14 *CL*, 37.

If one turns to the essay "Trespass and Negligence," which Holmes published in 1880, he there finds that the suggestion, not made in Primitive Notions but presented in the Lowell Lectures, that the noxal actions started from a moral base, was briefly set forth. Referring to his own earlier essay Holmes repeated the proposition that the "strange procedure" against inanimate objects "originated in the thirst for vengeance against something towards which a barbarian could entertain that feeling." [15] He then pronounced a rule, or assumption, with respect to psychology which became, I think, the keystone of his historical thesis. "Vengeance," he said, "is founded on the thought that a wrong has been done, and the feeling of blame, however much the opinion may be distorted from the truth by passion. Even a dog can distinguish between being stumbled over and being kicked." [16] This, I believe, is the first occasion on which Holmes indicated his belief that the animistic superstition carried with it the fiction that moral blame infects the offending thing. Though in Tylor's *Primitive Culture* this imputation was taken to be a necessary element in an animistic view of nature,[17] Holmes had not brought that assumed necessity into the open when he wrote of Primitive Notions. When, however, he came to write of Trespass and Negligence, he had evidently come to believe that emphasis upon the moral implications of animism would strengthen his suggested analysis of the progression of theory with respect to the elements of criminal and civil liability. Perhaps what led him to see an orderly progression was his persuasion, first expressed in "Trespass and Negligence," that in the English law in the times of Glanville and Bracton the personal liability of criminal defendants was limited to their intentional wrongs.[18] This reading of English legal history—questionable as it

[15] *Am. L. Rev.*, 14:15.

[16] *Id.* The same suggestion, rephrased, appeared in his first lecture. "Vengeance imports a feeling of blame, and an opinion, however distorted by passion, that a wrong has been done. It can hardly go very far beyond the case of harm intentionally inflicted: even a dog distinguishes between being stumbled over and being kicked" *CL*, 3.

[17] Tylor, *Primitive Culture* (Boston, 1874), I, 285–287.

[18] *Am. L. Rev.*, 14:16–17.

may have been—made it easy for Holmes to search for a similar moral principle in primitive institutions.

Not many years after the publication of *The Common Law,* Maitland in England, Brunner in Germany, and Wigmore in the United States turned their attention to some of the problems of legal history on which Holmes had touched in his first lecture.[19] None of them, I think, purported to reject the particular point which Holmes had made with respect to the moral implications of animism—the source, as Holmes saw it, of the primitive liability of offending "things." Yet each of them found in early records a great deal of evidence to support their thesis that "the law begins with making a man act at his peril and gradually becomes moralized until liability is connected with fault." [20] The historical tendency, established by the research of Maitland, Brunner, and Wigmore, is, according to one commentator, "exactly the opposite to that described by Justice Holmes." The same critic expressed astonishment that Wigmore, who proved the tendency which Holmes denied, should have stated that Holmes was the only writer who publicly agreed with him on the fundamentals of the legal history of liability in tort.[21]

It may well be that the conciseness of Holmes's presentation of his thesis with respect to the psychology of animism contributed to misunderstanding. I suspect, however, that Maitland and Wigmore recognized that the central thesis in Holmes's first lecture related to another matter than that with which they were principally concerned. They did not, I think, anywhere reject his thesis that when noxal actions were born they carried with them a superstitious presupposition that the "thing" condemned was morally culpable.[22] Their questioning of Holmes's contention concerned

19 Pollock and Maitland, *The History of English Law* (2nd ed., London, 1898), II, 470–476; Brunner, *Über absichtslose Missethat im altdeutschen Strafrechte* (1890); Wigmore, "Responsibility for Tortious Acts," *Harv. L. Rev.,* 7:315, 383, 441 (1894).

20 Isaacs, "Fault and Liability," *Harv. L. Rev.,* 31:955 (May 1918).

21 *Id.,* 955 and 955–956, note 2.

22 An essay of P. F. Girard in the *Nouvelle Revue Historique de Droit* 12:31, 38 (1888), without referring to Holmes's analysis, suggested that such an interpretation of primitive psychology as his was inaccurate. The doubting passage was quoted

his suggestion that the relatively mature law of England, at least into the age of Glanville and Bracton, made personal fault of the defendant an essential element of criminality.[23] Holmes had first made that suggestion in the essay on Trespass and Negligence and had repeated it in his first lecture. In neither instance, however, did he endeavor to justify the truth of the proposition by an elaborate citation of authority. He went no farther than to say that "the early English appeals for personal violence seem to have been confined to intentional wrongs" and that when Bracton spoke of "lesser offences, which were not sued by way of appeal, such as blows with the fist, flogging, wounding, insults" he instanced "only intentional wrongs." [24] Holmes recognized that the theory which he propounded was not consistent "with an opinion which has been held, that it was a characteristic of early law not to penetrate beyond the external visible fact, the *damnum corpore corpori datum.*" [25] Yet he did urge that the primitive assumption that fault was an essential ingredient of criminality survived in the law of medieval England.

When one turns to the second lecture, "Criminal Law," it is with the expectation that the historical inquiry begun in the first will be carried forward from primitive into more recent times. One anticipates, accordingly, that the almost casual suggestion of the first lecture that moral culpability was an essential element of guilt in the twelfth century, will be justified. The lecture opened with a reiteration of that thesis, but no further effort to set forth its historical justification was made. One quickly sees that the sec-

---

by J. H. Wigmore in a revision of his *Harvard Law Review* essays and is quoted in the revision as published in *Selected Essays on the Law of Torts* (Cambridge, 1924), 64, note 1. In his article Girard cited *The Common Law* but did not deal with the psychological thesis which Holmes had outlined.

[23] There are some modern scholars who have assembled materials of English legal history which tend to give support to Holmes's thesis. See, e.g., Isaacs, *supra*, note 20, at 962 *et seq*. It would seem that Maine believed that "the ideas of moral responsibility . . . often seem more clearly realised at very ancient than at more advanced periods . . ." *Ancient Law* (10th ed., London, 1906), 135; Winfield, "The Myth of Absolute Liability," 42 *Law Quarterly Review* 37 (1926).

[24] *CL*, 3, 4. *Cf. Am. L. Rev.*, 14:16–17.

[25] *CL*, 4.

ond lecture is analytical, not historical in purpose. Perhaps the change of purpose and of pace was owing, at least in part, to the fact that the second lecture was not a revision of an earlier essay but was prepared specially for the lecture series—perhaps with somewhat greater haste than other segments of the Lowell Lectures. Holmes addressed his second audience on the assumption that his interpretations of history—precise or sweeping as they may have been—had been largely persuasive. He, therefore, started his analysis with two historical presuppositions: first, that the roots of the criminal law were planted in the passion for vengeance, and, second, that this passion, reflected both in the primitive noxal actions and in English criminal law of the later middle ages, was accompanied by an assumption that the offender—whether thing or person—was guilty of moral blame.

It is not surprising that one whose philosophical inclinations had from the first been towards empiricism should look with considerable suspicion upon such metaphysical analysis of the criminal law as that in which Kant and Hegel had engaged. Ingenious as their speculations may have been, they had become cobwebs of abstraction in which the minds of commentators were trapped. Francis Wharton had built his influential *Treatise on Criminal Law* upon Kantian premises. Like other jurists of his day, Wharton repudiated the utilitarian thesis that the purpose of punishment was prevention of crime. Terroristic penalties, he asserted,

undertake to punish the offender, not merely for what he has actually done in the past, but for what others may possibly do in the future. Terrorism, also, treats the offender not as a *person,* but a *thing;* not as a responsible, self-determining being with rights common to all members of the same community, to whom justice is to be distinctively meted as a matter between him and the State, but as a creature without any rights, on whom punishment is imposed so that others should be deterred from acts requiring punishment. The theory . . . violates the fundamental principle of all free communities,—that the members of such communities have equal rights to life, liberty, and personal security.[26]

26 *A Treatise on Criminal Law* (8th ed., Philadelphia, 1880) , I, 8. Wharton paid great respect to the views of Theodore D. Woolsey, who emphasized the moral

Though Wharton, a faithful Kantian, considered that Hegel's analysis of punishment as the negation of negation was somewhat speculative, he nonetheless saw much merit in his emphasis upon the retributive purpose of the criminal law.

Certainly Hegelianism, in adopting and sustaining philosophically the theory of a just retribution as the sole primary basis of punishment, exhibits a healthy contrast to the sentimentalism of humanitarian philosophers who ignore the moral and retributive element in punishment, making its primary object to be the reform of the alleged criminal, and example to the community.[27]

The central purpose of Holmes's chapter on Criminal Law was to defend the preventive theory of punishment against such attacks as these. The defense which he formulated against the Kantian analysis took the following shape. Building upon the thesis of his first lecture, that the passion for revenge was the initiating force behind both civil and criminal liability, he described the tendency of public, as distinguished from private prosecution, to dominate the effort to discourage acts of private vengeance. "If people would gratify the passion for revenge outside of the law, if the law did not help them, the law has no choice but to satisfy the craving itself, and thus avoid the greater evil of private retribution." [28] When the State assumed the responsibility of providing an alternative to private vengeance it did not, of course, wipe out of the human heart the passion which endangered public order. The thirst for vengeance, accompanied still by an imputation of blame to the offender, was allayed, if not satisfied, by the punishment of the defendant under public authority. One of the objects of the criminal law may thus still be stated to be gratification of the desire for vengeance. Sir James Stephen spoke with percep-

and religious justifications for the punishment of criminals and rejected out of hand the preventive justification as stated by Bentham. See his *Political Science or The State* (New York, 1878), I, 334, 352. Holmes accepted Wharton's interpretation of Kant as accurate (*CL*, 43).

[27] Wharton, Sec. 13, note 1, p. 15. This must be one of the very few instances on which views which Holmes supported were characterized as "sentimental."

[28] *CL*, 41-42.

tive accuracy when he said that "the criminal law stands to the passion of revenge in much the same relation as marriage to the sexual appetite." [29] While Holmes showed a strong desire—perhaps an excessive longing—to discover one all-sufficient explanation for punishment, he was compelled by his thesis that its roots were traceable to the longing for revenge to make a small concession to Hegel. Retributive elements, he acknowledged, still color the passion for vengeance and, to the extent that the passion finds its satisfaction in punishment, the demand for retribution is fulfilled.[30]

Kant's denial that the purpose of punishment could be preventive was the necessary corollary of his categorical imperative: Each man is to be treated as an end and not as a means. By rejecting the imperative, Holmes undermined the corollary. The basic rejection had two foundations, the one philosophical or ethical, the other "scientific" or descriptive. Holmes's ethics began with the proposition, explicitly asserted, that "at the bottom of all private relations, however tempered by sympathy and all the social feelings, is a justifiable self-preference." [31] This statement, of course, is something more than a descriptive account of human nature. A man's self-preference is not merely a fact of his constitution; it is a virtue of his character. Holmes's ethical pronouncement was, on this occasion, framed in anti-Kantian terms, but it was in substance no different from his affirmation of 1873 that "in the last resort a man rightly prefers his own interest to that of his neighbors." [32] The rightness of self-preference was established, as it were, by a natural, rather than a categorical imperative—a command of nature that each creature should struggle to achieve as triumphant a life as he could. This ethical principle, which Holmes had asserted in 1873 against the utilitarian thesis of Mill, he now avowed against the metaphysical proposition of Kant. In the interval between the two pronouncements Holmes had read

29 *A General View of the Criminal Law of England* (London, 1863) 99, cited *CL*, 41.

30 *CL*, 45.

31 *Id.*, 44.

32 "The Gas-Stokers' Strike," *Am. L. Rev.*, 7:583 (April 1873); *Harv. L. Rev.*, 44:795. See *supra*, p. 48.

James Fitzjames Stephen's *Liberty, Equality, Fraternity*—that remarkable and powerful assault on the gentle and hopeful liberalism of Mill.[33] I see no reason to suppose that Holmes appropriated for use against Kant weapons which Stephen had forged for use against Mill. Holmes had already shown his distrust of the dogmatic twins bred in the house of liberalism, Equality and Altruism. Yet he must have found a measure of satisfaction when he heard Stephen's sword smashing the china and the furnishings (if not the daughters themselves) in the mansions of Mill. Stephen, asserting his fidelity to the school of Locke, Bentham, and Austin, had announced that in any analysis of laws, political or ethical, "the first idea of all is force, the power to reward and punish." [34] In Stephen's eyes, the primacy of force was still a fact in the nineteenth century. Neither "the law of force" nor "the law of the strongest" had been abandoned—nor did Stephen believe that either should be.[35] Pretensions of equality are little more than pious frauds:

What equality is there between the rich and the poor, between the strong and the weak, between the good and the bad? In particular, what equality is there between the well-born and well-bred man, the son of a good, careful, prudent, prosperous parent, who has transmitted to him a healthy mind and body, and given him a careful education; and the ill-born, ill-bred man whose parents had nothing to teach which was not better unlearned, and nothing to transmit which would not have been better uninherited? [36]

Holmes's protestations against the Kantian emphasis on equality did not, of course, have the truculent vigor of Stephen's remonstrance against the egalitarian theme of contemporary liberalism. It may not, accordingly, seem wholly fair to suggest that the two friends shared a dogged respect for strength and a tough suspicion of weakness. There were, of course, significant differences

---

[33] Holmes read the first edition of the book in August 1873, after the publication of his own comments on the Gas Stokers' Strike.

[34] *Liberty, Equality, Fraternity* (London, 1873) , 196.

[35] *Id.*, 222.

[36] *Id.*, 233–234.

between the philosophies of Holmes and Stephen. The Englishman built his ferocious ethics upon foundations which he called
religious.[37] Surely Holmes considered that Stephen's ultimate re-
liance upon faith was no less corrupting in his philosophy than
it was, in Holmes's eyes, in the philosophy of James. The tough-
ness of Stephen and the softness of James were equally tainted by
a lingering and clutching faith which Holmes had renounced.
Though Holmes's skepticism thus went farther than Stephen's, I
find it hard to believe that the former's rejection of Kant's egalitarian metaphysics sprang from an essentially different soil than
Stephen's repudiation of Mill's utilitarianism. The ethics of each
was molded in the age of Darwin.[38]

Another political or juristic principle which Holmes emphasized gave special significance to his ethics of self-preference. "The
first requirement of a sound body of law," he said, "is, that it
should correspond with the actual feelings and demands of the
community, whether right or wrong." [39] If it be a fact of human
nature that self-preference governs individual conduct, then the
law must build its doctrine on that stubborn actuality. Acknowledging that there is an "ever-growing value set upon peace and the
social relations"—a tendency which might ultimately mean that
"the social instincts shall grow to control [human] actions absolutely, even in anti-social situations"—Holmes insisted that the
growth of altruism had not, as yet, gone so far. "As the rules of
law are or should be based upon a morality which is generally ac-

---

[37] In the Preface to the second edition of *Liberty, Equality, Fraternity* (1874),
xviii–xx, Stephen commented, with his usual vigor, on Frederic Harrison's reflections
on "the Religion of Inhumanity or 'Stephenism'"—a religion which rejected "the
harp and tabor idea of heaven [and] the gridiron theory of hell" and argued that
"so long as we have a hell, any hell will suffice."

[38] Stephen, the Englishman, could speak in public more frankly of the American character than could Holmes, but I wonder whether the Brahmin streak in
Holmes's nature did not relish Stephen's reflections on the "success" of equality in
the United States. Stephen had the British temerity to ask whether "the enormous
development of equality in America, the rapid production of an immense multitude
of commonplace, self-satisfied, and essentially slight people is an exploit which the
world need fall down and worship" (*Liberty, Equality, Fraternity*, 1873, 254).

[39] *CL*, 41.

cepted, no rule founded on a theory of absolute unselfishness can be laid down without a breach between law and working beliefs." [40]

Holmes did not, I think, advocate the law's responsiveness to the felt necessities of a society merely because it would provide egoism with legal sanctions. He found that the principle of responsiveness provided a helpful guide in the interpretation of legal history. It cast light, for instance, on the law's decision to meet the clamor for vengeance by affording public processes of prosecution. The policy also served the larger end of reducing the law's responsibility for creating an authoritative body of public and private morals. One who had come to question the sanctity and fixity of moral principles inclined naturally towards a philosophy of law which would deny to judges the prerogative of enforcing an imagined categorical imperative of ethics and assign to them, instead, the more limited office of translating a society's demands into its rules of law. Finally, it is not a distortion, I think, to suggest that Holmes's emphasis on the necessity that rules of law be responsive to the public will bespoke that same dissatisfaction with the Austinian concept of the unhampered sovereign which he had expressed as Harvard lecturer in 1872.[41] The judge and his sovereign, if they are to retain an effective authority, are compelled to respect and enforce the wishes of those groups in society which have effective power to disrupt the going order if their expectations are not fulfilled.

This insistence that "the first requirement" (not, it should be noted, the sole necessity) of a sound body of law is its correspondence with the demands of the community bore a close relationship with Holmes's often reiterated "shocker" that "truth [is] the majority vote of that nation that could lick all others." [42] In private correspondence he once added a significant explication of that aphorism. The vote which he had in mind, he said, was the majority

[40] *Id.,* 44.
[41] *See supra,* p. 72 *et seq.*
[42] See, e.g., "Natural Law," *CLP,* 310.

vote "in the long run—and as to that we have to rely for consolation upon a few, at times." [43] One may, I take it, apply that qualification to the analogous pronouncement in *The Common Law*, and thus consider that the desired correspondence between the law and the demands of the community was accompanied by the assumption that judges and legislators must exercise an appreciable degree of judgment in assessing the vitality both in time and in wisdom of the community's requirement. Holmes's fatalistic analysis of legal history, even with this qualification added, would not, of course, have pleased the Kantians with their categorical imperative. To others, however, the qualification may indicate that he did not mean to subordinate the law and the judges to the rule of public whim. Yet it is clear that Holmes's definition of the first requirement of a sound body of law went far towards an elimination of fixed moral principles from its inner substance.

Having defined his ethical and juristic assumptions—that self-preference is a desirable principle of conduct, and that the law must satisfy the dominant needs of a society—Holmes turned to his descriptive or scientific task. In its broadest terms, that task was to ascertain whether the criminal law respects the Kantian hypothesis of equality: the dogma that each man is always to be looked upon as an end, and never to be treated as a means. Holmes's first response was a reminder that the rule or dogma of equality

makes an equation between individuals only, not between an individual and the community. No society has ever admitted that it could not sacrifice individual welfare to its own existence. If conscripts are necessary for its army, it seizes them, and marches them, with bayonets in their rear, to death. It runs highways and railroads through old family places in spite of the owner's protest, paying in this instance the market value, to be sure, because no civilized government sacrifices the citizen more than it can help, but still sacrificing his will and welfare to that of the rest . . . If a man is on a plank in the deep sea which will only float one, and a stranger lays hold of it, he will thrust him off if he can.

43 To Charles Owen, February 5, 1912 (copy HLS).

When the state finds itself in a similar position, it does the same thing.[44]

To the extent that Holmes emphasized the subordination of personal freedom to the power and authority of the state he suggested that nothing in the order of nature compelled respect for individualism. Upon such a self-preferring ethics as that which he outlined there could be built a new social order—a collective, in place of an individualized, society. This is not to say that he was preaching socialism or advocating an extension of public power. It is not surprising, however, that when the jurist who had formulated this philosophy of law later found himself a judge, he tended to permit the public authority to prevail over private interest. It may fairly be said, I think, that Holmes molded from the fierce individualism of a self-preferring ethic a philosophy of law which strengthened the foundations upon which collectivism was building. In 1898 his friend Dicey delivered his Harvard Lectures, *Law and Public Opinion in England During the Nineteenth Century,* in which he traced the movement of English law towards collectivism. Holmes's philosophic effort of 1880 was not, I suggest, entirely unrelated to Dicey's historical endeavor.

Holmes had cited instances of self-preference to show that neither public nor private conduct in actuality reveals an appreciable respect for Kant's categorical imperative. Does an acknowledgment that Holmes had routed Kant mean that he had also succeeded in eliminating all ethical considerations (other than self-preference) from the criminal law? Perhaps some moral elements, neither categorical nor imperative, might still deserve recognition and respect. There was still to be considered the oft-repeated maxim that *mens rea*—the evil mind—is an essential element in criminal liability. The maxim was born long before Kant's metaphysics were

[44] *CL,* 43-44. Compare Kant's consideration of the case of the shipwrecked sailors and the surviving plank (Caird, *The Critical Philosophy of Kant,* II, 323). With Holmes's recognition of society's "right" to sacrifice individual lives and interests to the general welfare, it is interesting to compare his father's observation: "We hang men for our convenience and safety; sometimes shoot them for revenge" ("Mechanism in Thought and Morals," *Collected Writings,* VIII, 306).

conceived, and many philosophers who were not Kantians had accepted the maxim's policy as sound and valid. Bentham, Austin, and Mill—even, for a time at least, the savage Stephen—had considered wickedness to be a required ingredient of criminality.[45] The standard textbooks on criminal law kept the maxim aglow with the kindling of piety.

The doctrine which requires an evil intent lies at the foundation of public justice . . . [N]either in philosophical speculation, nor in religious or moral sentiment, would any people in any age allow, that a man should be deemed guilty unless his mind was so . . . The calm judgment of mankind keeps the doctrine among its jewels. In times of excitement, when vengeance takes the place of justice, every guard against the innocent is cast down. But with the return of reason comes the public voice, that, where the mind is pure, he who differs in act from his neighbors does not offend." [46]

When Holmes prepared his lecture on criminal law he had already, in the essay on Primitive Notions, committed himself to the historical proposition that in primitive and early systems of law moral blame had been conceived to be an essential element of criminal liability. That reading of history, however questionable it may be, might seem to give some support to the traditional doctrine with respect to *mens rea*. In his essays on the Theory of Torts and on Trespass and Negligence—both of which were to be incorporated in the third and fourth lectures—Holmes's principal effort had been to show that civil liability, though often defined in the language of morals, had in fact discarded the requirement of personal culpability and had established an external standard of fault. The two theses might thus seem to converge in confirmation of the traditional doctrine that although the *quo animo* with

[45] Holmes called attention to apparent change in Stephen's opinion between the time when he said in *A General View of the Criminal Law of England* that "wickedness" is essential to guilt in murder and the time when he prepared his *Digest of Criminal Law*, when he seemed to cast out *mens rea* even in cases of murder (*CL*, 51–52).

[46] Joel Prentiss Bishop, *Commentaries on the Criminal Law* (6th ed., Boston, 1877), I, 161, 162.

which an act is done is not always relevant to liability in tort, *mens
rea* is always an essential element of criminal liability.

Other considerations than the high improbability that Holmes,
with his longing for originality, should endeavor to confirm traditional doctrine made it clear at the very outset that the lecture on
criminal law was not going to endorse the conventional dogma
about *mens rea*. It was highly unlikely that one who saw the state's
self-preference as a legitimate and dominant interest secured by
the criminal law should let that interest be endangered by the actions of high-minded and pure-hearted defendants. Furthermore,
the preventive as contrasted with the reforming and retributive
purposes of punishment suggests, if it does not necessitate, a considerable public indifference to the temper of an offender's mind.
As soon as Holmes made it clear that the predominant if not the
single purpose served by punishment was prevention of dangerous
conduct,[47] he had taken a long step towards the repudiation of
mens rea as it had traditionally been conceived. The renunciation
became explicit when he asserted that he believed that the essentials of liability were the same in the criminal law as they were in
the law of tort.

As we have seen, he had announced that conviction in his first
lecture. Its justification, however, was postponed until the second.
Two considerations led Holmes towards his iconoclastic thesis.
The first was an aspect of the law which even Kant, despite his
categorical imperative, had emphasized.[48] The purpose of the criminal law, "for the most part," is

only to induce external conformity to rule . . . In directing itself
against robbery or murder, for instance, its purpose is to put a stop to
the actual physical taking and keeping of other men's goods, or the actual poisoning, shooting, stabbing, and otherwise putting to death of

[47] "Prevention would accordingly seem to be the chief and only universal purpose of punishment" (*CL*, 46).
[48] In notes which Holmes had made when he was reading Barni's French translation of Kant's *Metaphysics of Law* in 1872 there appears the following entry:
"44. *Concerned only with external acts*. 46."

other men. If those things are not done, the law forbidding them is equally satisfied, whatever the motive.[49]

Coupled with this externality of the law's purpose is its readiness to sacrifice the individual for the securing of public order. Each of these considerations made it seem to Holmes improbable that the criminal law should be available only against those men who are guilty of personal moral fault. As essayist, though not yet as lecturer, he had made a persuasive argument in support of an external standard of tort liability. It seemed to him that if that argument were accepted it would be easy to sustain the thesis that the same standard must control the criminal law. Civil liability "in its immediate working, is simply a redistribution of an existing loss between two individuals . . . [S]ound policy lets losses lie where they fall, except where a special reason can be shown for interference. The most frequent of such reasons is, that the party who is charged has been to blame." [50] Yet the defendant in tort who is guilty of no moral wrong may be compelled to make good another's loss merely because he was the actor responsible for the injury. All this being true, does it not follow, almost *a fortiori*, that the criminal law, which is concerned neither with the redistribution of loss nor the retribution of sin, should show the same indifference to moral blame? "When we are dealing with that part of the law which aims more directly than any other at establishing standards of conduct, we should expect there more than elsewhere to find that the tests of liability are external, and independent of the degree of evil in the particular person's motives or intentions." [51]

Surely there is considerable force in the logic of this argument. It is not, of course, appealing to those who reject the moral (or immoral) implications in Holmes's premise that "public policy sacrifices the individual to the general good." [52] If, however, that descriptive premise with its approving implication be accepted,

[49] *CL,* 49.
[51] *Id.*
[50] *Id.,* 50.
[52] *Id.,* 48.

Holmes's contention that an external standard is more to be expected in criminal than in civil matters has considerable strength. It must not be forgotten, furthermore, that when Holmes urged the propriety of an external or objective standard of criminal liability he was not demanding the entire exclusion of moral elements from that standard. He followed his defense of externality with an explicit reminder of the limits of his thesis. "It is not intended to deny that criminal liability, as well as civil, is founded on blameworthiness." [53] This was not simply a reminder of the historical thesis which Holmes had developed—that the primitive passion for vengeance was accompanied by imputations of blame. He spoke of and for his own times when he went on to say that the denial that criminal liability is founded on fault "would shock the moral sense of any civilized community." To put it another way, as he did, "a law which punished conduct which would not be blameworthy in the average member of the community would be too severe for that community to bear." [54] What our society demands is that each mature person not disabled by insanity must, in his conduct affecting others, attain that standard of responsibility which measures the capacity of the average man. Our society considers that a person who possesses that capacity and yet engages in forbidden conduct is morally culpable. *Mens rea,* in that objective sense, is an element in his crime. The enforcement of the objective standard means, of course, that in some circumstances we condemn men for their offenses though we cannot fairly assert that they also are guilty of personal moral fault. A sane offender may be punished for his forbidden action though his intelligence and understanding, being less than average, do not tell him what a wiser man would know. He is not a sinner, yet we may condemn him for his crime.

This analysis of the criminal law was obviously affected, as we have seen, by Holmes's ethical presuppositions. Had he been less confident than he was that society properly prefers its own security and welfare to the freedom and equality of individual persons, he

[53] *Id.,* 50. [54] *Id.*

would surely have felt less impelled than he did to identify—perhaps to overstress—the exceptional cases in which a morally blameless man may be condemned for crime. Yet one should not treat that identification and emphasis as the total repudiation of morality in law. Those who find self-preference an inadequate standard for private and public morals have tended, I think, to exaggerate the radicalism of Holmes's related thesis that liability, whether civil or criminal, is measured by an external standard. It has been stated, for instance, that Holmes argued that liability rests on "an objective non-moral foundation." [55] Surely the assertion that an individual must, at his peril, take no action which would be morally blameworthy in the average man is not to remove the moral foundations of the legal system. Perhaps another theory of liability than Holmes's is to be preferred. Perhaps no man should be convicted of crime who has not wittingly committed a moral fault. It is, however, a grave distortion of Holmes's argument to suggest that because he substituted an objective for a personal standard of blame he rested liability on a nonmoral foundation. The insistence that criminal law demands the observance of a standard of responsible conduct higher than some individuals are capable of achieving may violate the canons of Christian mercy and may be an unsound principle of criminal law, but it surely is not a repudiation of morality. In the end one cannot help feeling that those who

[55] Jerome Hall, "Interrelations of Criminal Law and Torts," *Columbia Law Review*, 13:762 (September 1943). For this misinterpretation of his thesis Holmes may not have been wholly blameless. Though I find it virtually impossible to see in the lecture on criminal law any suggestion that the substitution of an objective for a personal standard of fault amounts to the exclusion of morality from the concept of liability, there is a passage in the fourth lecture which would suggest that Holmes saw a moral standard and an external standard as opposites. He there stated that "it will aid in the general object of showing that the tendency of the law everywhere is to transcend moral and reach external standards . . ." (*CL*, 135). It seems quite clear, I think, that what Holmes referred to here, as in the lecture on criminal law, was the contrast between a personal and an objective, or social, standard of fault. In Holmes's own copy of *The Common Law* there is a penciled comment, in his hand, concerning the phrase I have quoted. Over the word "transcend" is written "laudatory word," and in the margin the suggested rephrasing is as follows: "pass over from moral to external standards."

have protested against Holmes's objective standard of criminal liability have not been so much troubled by the objectivity of the standard as they have by the relativism of the standard which he objectified.

It is not necessary, I think, to summarize the descriptive portion of Holmes's lecture on criminal law. His principal effort was to show that the philosophical analysis—supported by the historical interpretation to be developed in the lectures on tort—was consistent with the English and American decisions. It was not difficult to show that familiar words which in common speech connote personal fault often lose that connotation when they survive in the criminal law. The law in books tells us that when a defendant has committed homicide with malice aforethought he is guilty of murder. The decisions make it clear, however, that if the known state of things "is such that the act done will very certainly cause death, and the probability is a matter of common knowledge, one who does the act, knowing the present state of things, is guilty of murder . . ." [56] The traditional formula encourages the illusion that a killer is a murderer only when he is moved by personal malevolence. It thus suggests that criminal liability is measured by an internal or personal standard of fault. The law as enforced, however, treats the offender as a murderer if a man of reasonable prudence would have seen death as the probable consequence of his action.

It should be especially noted, perhaps, that Holmes at one stage in his lecture went beyond his defense of the objective standard of criminal liability to indicate that there have been occasions on which the legislature has seen fit to impose an even more rigorous standard. Occasionally the lawmaker has been persuaded that conduct not seen by the man of ordinary prudence to involve danger of social harm does in fact offer serious risks. It has, accordingly, made the doing of such acts criminal. Such statutory offenses establishing strict criminal liability do not rest upon those principles which justify the prosecution of crimes committed with wilfulness or negligence. "The law," he said, "may . . . throw on

[56] CL, 53-54.

the actor the peril, not only of the consequences foreseen by him, but also of consequences which, although not predicted by common experience, the legislator apprehends." [57] He went on to say that he was not suggesting that this exceptional type of criminal liability was derived in any way from the principle of objectivity which governed most of the criminal law. He saw the liability as exceptional and suggested that it might not be "right." As judge he later found himself enforcing that type of liability,[58] but so far as one can see he never came to look upon it as the by-product of his basic thesis.

In his effort to give the objective standard generally controlling force throughout the criminal law, Holmes had obviously been troubled by those crimes in which a defendant's guilt is dependent upon a showing that his actual personal intention was of a certain sort. For Holmes was forced to acknowledge that in the criminal law of attempts, as in that of larceny and burglary, it is essential for the state to show that the accused in fact intended that his act should have certain consequences. Did those cases indicate that the criminal law is, on some occasions at least, seeking to measure liability by a personal or internal standard of blame? Admitting that the standard is, in some cases, personal and not objective, Holmes was nonetheless satisfied that the law's occasional concern for the actual intent which motivated conduct was not the reflection of its disapproval of a sinful mind but of its recognition that the probability of injury is increased when the offender intends to do harm. "The importance of the intent is not to show that the act was wicked, but to show that it was likely to be followed by hurtful consequences." [59]

[57] *Id.*, 59. Such offenses have, since Holmes's day, secured frequent recognition—even by those who see *mens rea*, as traditionally defined, as an essential element of criminality. See, e.g. Hall, *General Principles of Criminal Law* (2nd ed., Indianapolis, 1960), chapter x.

[58] See, e.g., *Commonwealth* v. *Smith*, 166 Mass. 370 (1896).

[59] *CL*, 68.

7

A Theory of Torts

Before turning to Holmes's two lectures on Torts it may be well to remind the reader of attitudes which Holmes had taken with respect to that field of law in his earlier writings. Although he had once expressed a serious doubt whether torts was a fit subject for a law book, by 1873 he had come to recognize that there were satisfactory reasons, both historical and analytical, for including the subject in the *corpus juris*.[1] Having reached that conclusion, he then looked for a theory of torts. In the essay bearing that title, he opened his discussion with the reiteration of his disagreement with Austin's assumption that civil liability, whether in contract or tort, always imports culpability.[2] Before turning to an analysis of the concept of negligence in civil cases he indicated, very clearly, that some common-law liabilities for tort are imposed upon defendants who are guiltless of any personal wrong. "The old writs in trespass," he said, "did not allege, nor was it necessary to show, any thing savoring of culpability. It was enough that a certain event had happened, and it was not even necessary that the act should be done intentionally, though innocently." He concluded this historical rejection of Austin's thesis with the statement that a treatise on torts should, at the one extreme, include a class of cases "in which the cause of action is determined by certain

1 See *supra*, pp. 64–65, 82.
2 *Am. L. Rev.* 7:652. The essay contained no indication that Holmes then questioned Austin's thesis that *mens rea* is essential to criminal liability.

184

overt acts or events alone, irrespective of culpability." [3] At the other end of the spectrum would be "those liabilities in which culpability is in general an essential element. Such are frauds, or malicious or wilful injuries; perhaps, also, certain negligent acts (*stricto sensu*) , where the negligence referred to is the actual condition of the defendant's consciousness." [4] The balance of the essay was devoted to an analysis of the large group of cases lying between these extremes—the cases, that is, in which negligence was the gist of the action. It was in connection with that body of cases that he proposed the substitution of an external for the traditional standard of liability.

The argument for externality in the law of negligence was built to a considerable extent around an analysis of the jury's role —an analysis which was related to Holmes's criticism of the Austinian thesis that law may always be identified as the command of the sovereign. Holmes argued that the judges in some cases, and the juries in others, take notice of prevailing standards of conduct, and measure questioned behavior against their requirements. Courts and juries are thus constantly engaged in the task of converting the community's standards into binding rules of law. These criteria, despite Austin, are as much law as are the statutes and other orders promulgated by the sovereign. Once they are recognized they become authoritative rules of conduct with which each person must comply. Their externality consists in the fact that, known or unknown, they are binding upon virtually every person in the community. Each man acts at peril of liability when his action causes damage and is found by judge or jury to have fallen below the prevailing standard of due care. In "The Theory of Torts" Holmes did not question the validity of orthodox decisional doctrine with respect to liabilities at the two extremes of the spectrum. He assumed that the English law traditionally recognized some absolute liabilities in tort—liabilities, in other words, in which fault, whether measured by a personal or an objective standard, was not required. He also took it for granted that

[3] *Id.,* 652–653.
[4] *Id.,* 653.

the torts involving malice, fraud, and intent required proof that the offender was moved to action by one or the other of those impulses. In accepting these orthodoxies of case law, Holmes realized, as we have seen, that with respect to absolute liabilities he was repudiating Austinian theory.[5] One may suppose that with respect to the liabilities at the other end of the spectrum he saw his own view as consistent with Austin's. With respect to the cases involving the external standard—cases of negligence, that is—he asked for a radical modification of Austin's theory.

Though the first two lectures in *The Common Law* were not directly concerned with a theory of torts they obviously had implications quite at odds with the theory which Holmes had offered in 1873. He had, in the first place, come to believe that one theory governed both criminal and civil liability—a belief which he may not have formed until shortly before the lectures were prepared for delivery.[6] With that as the premise of the first two lectures, it was clear that when Holmes asserted in the first that a defendant's culpability had been an inherent element in primitive systems of law he repudiated his earlier opinion that some liabilities in tort had always been absolute. When he went on, in the second lecture, to argue that in the criminal law the objective standard determines whether intent, malice, and negligence are criminal, he also indicated—at least by implication—that he had come to believe that objectivity must govern those cases in tort which he had earlier classified as involving personal culpability. This second implication was not a surprise to those who had read the essay on Trespass and Negligence in the *American Law Review* for January 1880, for Holmes had there carried his historical and analytic argument to its all-inclusive dimensions—dimensions which made

[5] Austin's eminent disciple, Sir John Salmond, was not far wrong, probably, in supposing that Austinian logic required *mens rea* in civil as in criminal cases. It was as a committed Austinian that Salmond expressed vigorous hostility to those English decisions, including *Rylands* v. *Fletcher,* in which liability without culpability had been recognized. See Salmond, "The Principles of Civil Liability" in his *Essays in Jurisprudence and Legal History* (London, 1891), 123; Salmond, *The Law of Torts* (11th ed., by F. V. Heuston, London, 1953), 21–27.

[6] See *supra,* p. 164.

the objective standard of controlling significance in the whole field of tort.[7] That essay, slightly revised, constituted his third lecture in the Lowell Institute series.

That Holmes's opinions with respect to the fundamentals of liability in tort were altering and developing during the years in question is not surprising. The issues had not yet been seriously or systematically considered by English or American scholars. There was little, if any, awareness that a philosophy of law could not easily accept both the Austinian thesis that all liabilities are grounded in personal fault and the traditional case law which recognized absolute liabilities in tort. Holmes was probably the first lawyer squarely to face the issues thus posed by philosophy and decisions. He had made a beginning in the essay of 1873. He carried his inquiry much farther in the paper of 1880; and the conclusions reached in the second paper were repeated and refined in the third and fourth lectures of *The Common Law.*

Beyond these questions of theory and of fact lay questions of policy to which courts and scholars had begun to give increased attention.[8] Without undue oversimplification it may be said that American judges of the nineteenth century had been showing an increased reluctance to enforce the English doctrine that liability in tort might be imposed upon a person who was personally guiltless of fault. The American unwillingness to impose such liability doubtless had many sources. It is, perhaps, fair to suggest that the judges saw social advantage in imposing no penalties on enterprising people who had gone forward to their own gain at the expense of others. The moral platitudes which Bishop had uttered with respect to *mens rea* in the criminal law [9] did not lose all their force when civil liability was in issue. And John Austin, after all, had supported the thesis that civil and criminal liability were both imposed for punitive purposes. It was not unnatural, certainly,

7 *Am. L. Rev.,* 14:1.

8 Melville M. Bigelow's *Leading Cases on the Law of Torts* (Boston, 1875) at 487 *et seq.* contained a discerning note on some phases of the basic problems. It is not unlikely that this discussion of history and policy may have stimulated Holmes's interest to a new curiosity.

9 *Supra,* p. 177.

that there should be some reluctance to transpose a rule of the old English law not justified by utilitarian morality to the enterprising air of the United States. On the other side of the Atlantic, despite the views of Austin, there were considerations working in favor of absolute liability. First, of course, there were the rather clear precedents enforcing it. Furthermore, a certain brand of liberalism might fairly find justice, if not morality, in the traditional doctrine that the innocent bystander should be able to secure some compensation from those men of action who inflict injury, even if they are not guilty of wilful or negligent wrong. The conservatism of many lawyers thus combined with the progressivism of some reformers to give support to the recognition of absolute liability in tort.[10]

Whether or not it is legitimate to discover a conflict between English and American doctrine, it is, I think, wholly clear that two theories of tort liability were struggling for dominance at the time when Holmes wrote and spoke of the issue. The one view, perhaps to be described as American, asserted that liability in tort is to be imposed only when the defendant is guilty of some personal fault. The other, apparently supported by English decisions, recognized that some liabilities in tort may be imposed on defendants who are personally quite blameless. What Holmes offered as an alternative to these two conflicting theories was essentially a compromise. Though he recognized, in favor of English doctrine, that there are some cases in which the law has seen fit to impose liability on wholly guiltless persons, he urged that tort liability in the generality of cases was imposed only if the defendant had done injury in circumstances which would be culpable in an average man.[11] He urged, in other words, that legal liability for tort was

[10] In Thomas Beven's *Principles of the Law of Negligence* (2nd ed., London, 1895), I, 663 *et seq.*, may be found an interesting discussion of the differing views of the English and the American courts. Beven looked with some hostility upon the American tendency, as he saw it, to adopt a rule by which "the quiet citizen must keep out of the way of the exuberantly active one" (*id.* 679).

[11] "It is undoubtedly possible that those who have the making of the law should deem it wise to put the mark higher in some cases than the point established by common practice at which blameworthiness begins" (*CL*, 115). Holmes went on to

generally imposed when, and only when, the defendant's conduct did not satisfy the objective standard established by current morality. This theory he had already suggested, in so far as the case-law of negligence was concerned. In his first lecture on torts, that on Trespass and Negligence, he endeavored by an analysis of decisions to justify that earlier thesis. In the second, that on Fraud, Malice, and Intent, he extended his thesis to include the contention that even when those "vituperative epithets" seem descriptive of a defendant's wrong the law is in fact using the objective, and not the personal, standard of blame.[12]

It will not be necessary, I think, closely to follow the course of Holmes's argument through the two lectures. His argumentative achievements, whether as logician or as historian, are less interesting and important than the spirit which moved him. He was compelled, of course, to recognize that many traditions of thought and phrasing stood in his way. At the one extreme there were the frequent assertions of English judges, particularly in cases involving trespass to real estate, that a man is responsible civilly for all damage flowing directly from his acts, however blameless they may have been. At the other extreme there were the numerous dicta, both English and American, that in actions involving negligence, fraud, intent, and malice—generally actions stemming from trespass on the case—only a personally culpable defendant could be charged. Many of the scholars and lawyers who had sought for a reconciling general principle had abandoned the search, satisfied that the two streams of doctrine, flowing as they did from different forms of action, quite naturally carried different waters of theory. Holmes refused, in this matter, to let substantive theory become the slave of procedural history. "Since the ancient forms of action

---

suggest that *Rylands* v. *Fletcher* might find its best explanation in such considerations as these.

12 *Id.*, 120. Just as he recognized that at one extreme liability might on grounds of policy be imposed though blame, measured by the objective standard, was lacking, so he acknowledged that there might be a few liabilities in tort dependent entirely upon the existence of personal fault in the defendant's part. Liability for malicious prosecution and for conspiracy he thought might be of that sort. See *CL*, 142, 143.

have disappeared, a broader treatment of the subject ought to be possible." [13] It was no longer fitting that jurists should confine themselves to technical reasoning.

The philosophical habit of the day, the frequency of legislation, and the ease with which the law may be changed to meet the opinions and wishes of the public, all make it natural and unavoidable that the judges as well as others should openly discuss the legislative principles upon which their decisions must always rest in the end, and should base their judgments upon broad considerations of policy to which the traditions of the bench would hardly have tolerated a reference fifty years ago.[14]

To call off a search for general principle because history leads one down procedural *culs de sac* would be to betray the responsibilities of thoughtful scholarship.

One link in Holmes's chain of argument deserves special attention. His definition of the "act" essential to criminal liability has often been cited and discussed. It is significant, however, that he had first offered the definition in the essay on Trespass and Negligence, thus making it clear that the definition was of critical, if not crucial importance to his objective theory of liability.[15] His persuasion that the essential elements of criminal and tort liability were the same led him, in his lecture on criminal law, to repeat the definition of "act" which he had already formulated when developing his objective theory of liability in tort.[16]

Holmes's definition of "act"—as the law uses the word—was not significantly different from Austin's. The father of analytic jurisprudence had defined acts as the bodily movements which immediately follow our desires of them.[17] James Fitzjames Stephen, despite his Austinian bias, found that definition inadequate, at least for the purposes of the criminal law, for in his *General View*

[13] *Id.*, 78.

[14] *Id.*

[15] *Am. L. Rev.*, 14:9. The passage reappeared, with very slight changes, in the second lecture (*CL*, 91).

[16] *CL*, 54 *et seq.*

[17] Austin, *Jurisprudence* (4th ed., London, 1873), I, 427, 433.

he had stated that an act—or what he called an "action"—"consists of voluntary bodily motions combined by the mind towards a common object." [18] He had thus made the actor's intention an element which the criminal law must embrace within its concept of the act. Though Holmes may have had principles of psychology in mind when he chose Austin's over Stephen's definition, it is clear, I think, that his fundamental dissatisfaction with Stephen's lax analysis was that it encouraged the use of personal or internal standards of liability. Stephen's definition had been introductory to his assertion that *mens rea* is an essential of criminal liability. Though Austin, as we have seen, had also made personal fault an essential element of criminality (and of civil liability as well), he had brought culpability in, not through his definition of an act, but by an independent analytic effort.[19] Holmes evidently saw that if he accepted Stephen's definition he would have a hard, if not a hopeless, task in sustaining his basic thesis with respect to the objectivity of standards. The law, in his judgment, was concerned with intent only at its very initial stage—"the contraction of the muscles must be willed." [20] That concern it must preserve, since "the reason for requiring the act is, that an act implies a choice, and that it is felt to be impolitic and unjust to make a man answerable for harm, unless he might have chosen otherwise." [21] Holmes did not go so far, however, as to assert that whenever a man has voluntarily contracted his muscles and the proximate result is harm to another, the actor is liable. That assertion would have tended towards recognition of absolute liability. The choice of action "must be made with a chance of contemplating the consequences complained of . . . An act cannot be wrong, even when done under circumstances in which it will be hurtful, unless those circumstances are or ought to be known." [22]

It has been urged that psychological misconceptions and arbitrary exclusions impair the definition which Austin and Holmes

18 *A General View of the Criminal Law of England* (London, 1863), 81.
19 See his Twenty-fourth Lecture; *Jurisprudence*, I, 472 *et seq.*
20 *CL*, 54.
21 *Id.*
22 *Id.*, 54, 55.

supported.[23] One can easily see, however, why Holmes seized upon it, in preference to Stephen's alternative, with such enthusiasm. It provided a logical, as distinguished from a historical, justification for that portion of his objective theory which cast *mens rea* aside in both civil and criminal cases. As I have indicated, it did not, as a matter of logic, exclude the possibility of absolute liability, either criminal or civil, being imposed upon those whose acts had done damage. That exclusion Holmes had justified partly through a reading of history which found fault lying at the root of all liabilities and partly by considerations of justice and policy—the prevailing moral judgments of the community. Though his definition of "act" did not, therefore, contain within its own four corners the entire theory that the law's standards are objective, it contributed persuasive logic to Holmes's fundamental thesis. This eagerness to find not simply historical, but logical justifications for the objective theory reflected, I think, a most important aspect of Holmes's intellectual inclination.

Had Holmes been writing merely as historian of the common law, it is hard to believe that he would have discovered a uniform theory of liability in tort. He acknowledged as much when he stated that that body of law had neither begun with, nor worked out, a general theory.[24] He recognized that while the forms of action had controlled the shape of doctrine no substantive theory which governed in one procedural domain could claim authority in another. He admitted, in other words, that the objective theory of liability was the child of a jurist and not the offspring of a historian. Yet being himself a man bred in the common law he took it for granted that no philosophy for that law could be respected if it showed too cold a disdain for history. The "cross-lights of tradition" [25] might not expose a single strand of theory, binding decisions and doctrine into rational shape, but they could not be

---

[23] See, e.g., P. J. Fitzgerald, "Voluntary and Involuntary Acts," in *Oxford Essays in Jurisprudence* (Hart, ed., London, 1961), 12 *et seq*.

[24] *CL*, 77.

[25] *Id.*, 153.

turned off as merely distracting illuminations. As Holmes saw his task, it was that of formulating a theory of torts which would be both useful in a legal order no longer crippled by procedural deformities and not inconsistent with historic tendencies of the common law.

In the lectures on torts, Holmes repeatedly made it clear that he realized that the philosophic implications which he discovered in decisions had not been recognized before, not even by the judges who had reached those decisions. They had seldom felt the need which he felt so intensely—that of discovering a single principle of liability in tort. "It can hardly be supposed," he said, "that a man's responsibility for the consequences of his acts varies as the remedy happened to fall on one side or the other of the penumbra which separates trespass from the action on the case." [26] Yet many generations of lawyers and judges had lived contented professional lives wedded to the supposition which Holmes renounced. He rejected the proposition that "trespass is for acts alone, and case for consequences of those acts," not by showing that the statement was historically false, but by reminding his audience that under his definition of acts all suits in trespass are for consequences of acts.[27] It was logic, therefore, which called for a single standard of liability.

In suggesting an interpretation of history which could consist with the objective theory, Holmes, of course, ran the risk of antagonizing some historians and some philosophers. The historians, purporting indifference to the philosophical problem, could urge, with some justification, that Holmes had shown such a dominating eagerness to sustain his philosophical thesis that he had distorted and misinterpreted the legal past.[28] Jurists who favored the recognition or extension of absolute liabilities could complain that Holmes, through his objective standard, proposed an exaggeration

26 *Id.*, 80. "[Holmes] spoke here as the rationalist, not as the historian." C. H. S. Fifoot, *History and Sources of the Common Law: Tort and Contract* (London, 1949) , 187, note 19.

27 *Id.*, 91.

28 See, e.g., Fifoot, *History and Sources*, 184 *et seq.*

of moral elements in the law.[29] Others who thought that personal culpability should be essential to legal liability could protest that he was urging an unnatural and undesirable separation of law from morals.[30] Not at all surprisingly, each line of criticism has been followed.

With respect to the historical criticism, Holmes would have acknowledged, I take it, that he had pressed decisions into a philosophically favorable shape. Persuaded, like other thoughtful lawyers, that there was sore need for a coherent theory of liability in tort, he formulated such a theory and then endeavored to show that the theory which he favored was not precluded from acceptance by a stream of opposing decisions. In dealing with the classic cases of liability in tort he never suggested that his reading of the cases was either orthodox or incontestable. His interpretations seemed possible, and if defensible had the great merit of allowing a unifying theory to take effect. His preparatory quotation from Lehuërou was peculiarly applicable to his theory of torts: "Nous faisons une théorie et non un spicilège." [31] Dialectical skill combined with generalizing boldness to produce an analysis which enormously affected the development of the law of torts on both sides of the Atlantic. It may be thought that Holmes was too ambitious in his search for a single principle which would govern all cases from one end of the spectrum of liabilities to the other. Perhaps both history and policy give more support for a set of principles than for a single standard of liability. Yet his effort, if not completely successful, was of imposing consequence in jurisprudence. He had provided a structure of theory which shaped the common law of torts for many generations.

Taking the first four lectures as an entity, the most question-

[29] See Thomas Beven, *Negligence* (3rd ed., London, 1908), I, 593 *et seq.*; P. A. Landon in Pollock, *Torts* (14th ed., London, 1939), 140.

[30] James Barr Ames, "Law and Morals," *Harv. L. Rev.*, 22:97 (December 1908); reprinted in Ames, *Lectures in Legal History* (Cambridge, Mass., 1913), 435. See also Brooks Adams, "The Modern Conception of Animus," *Green Bag*, 19:12 (January 1907).

[31] The quoted phrase is in *Histoire des institutions Carolingiennes* (Paris 1843), 118.

able aspect of the achievement concerns, I think, the central thesis
as it relates to the criminal law. Did Holmes's judgment that the
standard suggested for the unification of the law of torts should
also embrace the criminal law have historical or analytic justification? By pressing for all-inclusive unity of principle Holmes obviously went beyond the insistent need for clarification of doctrine
in one area of law in order to establish a single standard throughout the entire domain. He had himself acknowledged that the purpose of the civil law—providing for the fair distribution of losses
between two litigants—is critically different from the preventive
ends of the criminal law.[32] Yet he was quick to assume, rather than
careful to establish, that the two systems of law should be ruled by
a common objective standard of liability. An effective case for such
unification might, perhaps, be made, but one searches *The Common Law* in vain for a persuasive argument—save that of symmetry—in favor of the single standard.[33] One tends, accordingly,
to wonder whether Holmes did not too quickly leap to the conclusion that the arguments for objectivity which he had first applied to negligence and then to the whole of the law of torts could
easily and properly be extended to include the whole of the criminal law as well. He had once spoken with slight disdain of the English judge who believed an ounce of precedent to be worth a
pound of principle.[34] Did he, perhaps, show an excess of that same
disdain when he urged that a unifying principle should embrace
at once the law of torts and the criminal law?

It would not be a fruitful enterprise, I think, to search out those
traits of character and mind which led Holmes to seek a single
standard of liability, by which the civil and the criminal law might

[32] It is noticeable that Holmes never asserted, as did Austin and Salmond, that
civil, like criminal, liability is imposed for preventive purposes. He went no farther
than to indicate that prevention might be one of the ends sought by the law of
torts. "The purpose of the law is to prevent or secure a man indemnity from harm
at the hands of his neighbors, so far as consistent with other considerations which
have been mentioned, and excepting, of course, such harm as it permits to be intentionally inflicted" (*CL*, 146). Cf. *id.*, 145.

[33] See *supra*, p. 164.

[34] In an unsigned review of Bennett and Holland's *Massachusetts Digest, Am.
L. Rev.*, 6:734 (July 1872).

be governed. That he made this endeavor in *The Common Law* indicates, of course, that he had not wholly lost his first philosophical enthusiasm for discovering a scientific order in the law. More significant perhaps than the survival of that enthusiasm is the manifest conviction that the law's greatest need was for certainty. Among the most important theses in *The Common Law* was that which emphasized the desirability of hastening the transfer of recurring questions of negligence from the hands of the jury to those of the court.[35] In 1873, in the essay on the Theory of Torts, Holmes had said that "it is little better than lawlessness" to allow recurrent questions, when they are virtually identical, to be answered by different juries in differing and conflicting ways.[36] In *The Common Law* he spoke with some bitterness of the limitations which the legislature of Massachusetts had put upon the judges in their relationships with juries.[37] Believing that law was prediction, Holmes naturally took unpredictability to be lawlessness. The acceptance of the objective standard of liability in tort and crime would, in his eyes, accelerate certainty, for it would permit and encourage the judges to apply a known standard with foreseeable regularity. "A judge who has long sat at *nisi prius* ought gradually to acquire a fund of experience which enables him to represent the common sense of the community in ordinary instances far better than an average jury . . . [T]he sphere in

35 *CL*, 122 *et seq.*

36 *Am. L. Rev.*, 7:659.

37 "When judges are forbidden by statute to charge the jury with respect to matters of fact, and when the court *in banc* will never hear a case calling for inferences of fact, it becomes of vital importance to understand that, when standards of conduct are left to the jury, it is a temporary surrender of a judicial function which may be resumed at any moment in any case when the court feels competent to do so. Were this not so, the almost universal acceptance of the first proposition in this Lecture, that the general foundation of liability for unintentional wrongs is conduct different from that of a prudent man under the circumstances, would leave all our rights and duties throughout a great part of the law to the necessarily more or less accidental feelings of a jury" (*CL*, 126). This same passage, as it first appeared in the essay "Trespass and Negligence," was followed by a supplementary comment: "And this is the fact to-day to a greater extent than some at least can contemplate with pleasure" (*Am. L. Rev.*, 14:35).

which he is able to rule without taking their opinion at all should be continually growing . . . [T]he tendency of the law must always be to narrow the field of uncertainty." [38]

If the key to the first four lectures was Holmes's desire for certainty in law, one may see his effort to extend the objective standard of culpability to the criminal law as something more significant than an attempt to impose a logical and scientific symmetry upon the common law. Nor was it merely because the law of torts and the law of crimes share a common language, much colored by overtones of morality, that a single and external standard of culpability seemed to Holmes to be appropriate. Every reduction in the jury's lawmaking role tends to replace capriciousness with stability. If certainty is a fitting element in any portion of the law, it has its highest claim to emphasis in the criminal law, for it is there, above all, that predictive warnings are desirable. To recognize that the enforcement of an objective standard in the law of torts would be to increase the certainties in that portion of the law is to acknowledge that if the same standard were to prevail in the criminal law the consequence would be the same. Though Holmes chose to discuss the relationship between the objective standard and the goal of certainty in his essay and lecture on Trespass and Negligence, rather than in his reflections on the criminal law, it is wholly clear, I think, that he believed that the relationship gave special strength to his theory of objectivity as it relates to criminal liability. Those who have found the lecture on criminal law unsatisfactory and unpersuasive have not, I think, given sufficient attention to this aspect of Holmes's effort.

The suggestion that a desire for certainty in law pervades the first four lectures intimates that the lectures may be best understood if they are read neither as the analysis of a philosopher nor as the diagnosis of a historian, but as the proposals of a reformer. Remembering Holmes's frequent expressions of distaste for the "upward and onward twaddle of the day," [39] and recalling his asser-

[38] *CL,* 124, 127.
[39] To Clara Sherwood Stevens, Aug. 12, 1914 (HLS).

197

tion that "I don't believe much in anything that is, but I believe a damned sight less in anything that isn't," [40] one may feel that it is highly improbable that a reforming spirit infused his lectures. One should not forget, however, that in one of his very first published comments on the law he had lightly touched one of the themes which received his attention as Lowell Lecturer. That earlier comment had been quite explicit in its reforming temper. "No branch of knowledge," he had said,

affords more instances than the law, of what a blessing to mankind it is that men begin life ignorant. Every one knows that it often happens, that, from historical causes, analogous cases are governed by dissimilar rules, and that forms which have lost their significance by lapse of time remain as technicalities. One who is familiar with these nice distinctions has no interest in their reform, even if he does not become prejudiced in their favor. But when, after barely three years' study, a young man finds himself at once in active practice, to simplify rules, to destroy anomalies, to make partial analogies complete, is his only safeguard. [41]

In these reflections of 1869 nothing explicit was said, to be sure, of the merits of certainty in law. Yet it would be impossible, I think, to deny that the lectures on the common law had their originating impulse in the reforming spirit which the young Holmes had earlier expressed.

The dogma of one brand of liberalism may repudiate the suggestion that the man who seeks to confine the jury's role in civil and criminal litigation may be classified as a reformer. It tells us that no effort to reduce popular control of the administration of justice can be considered regenerate. If that dogma governs our understanding, then, of course, Holmes was not proposing reform. He was urging reaction. I should suppose, however, that we may give the language of reform, at least as it applies to law, a wider-ranging meaning than one tradition gives it in politics. It is quite

[40] To John H. Wigmore, Dec. 4, 1910 (HLS). Holmes informed Wigmore that he had uttered this thought to President Theodore Roosevelt.

[41] Unsigned review of 23 *Iowa Reports*, in *Am. L. Rev.*, 3:357 (January 1869). Cf. *CL*, 78.

clear, I take it, that neither at the beginning of his maturity nor in his later years did Holmes look upon the virtues of democracy as unqualified. As a Union soldier he had bluntly stated that he loathed "the thick-fingered clowns we call the people." [42] As a man of seventy-five he asserted that "there are some advantages . . . in having gentlemen at the top," for "you can't get the last curl of the moustache any other way." [43] These were not, of course, the reflections of a "do-gooder." Yet one who was skeptical about the possibilities of achieving social regeneration through the strict enforcement of the slogans and platitudes of democracy might still believe that the public welfare would be advanced by increasing the clarity and certainty of law. Perhaps some of Holmes's satisfaction with his theory of liability came from the speculative grace of its uniformity. Yet I suspect that in greater part it came from the conviction that he had formulated a theory which might increase the law's certainty and, therefore, the law's utility. This, I think, was the satisfaction of a reformer.

Those who remember some of the aphorisms of Holmes's later days—"certainty generally is illusion, and repose is not the destiny of man"; [44] "delusive exactness is a source of fallacy throughout the law" [45]—may find it hard to accept the suggestion that a longing for certainty significantly affected his early juristic efforts. It should not be forgotten, however, that the aphorisms of his later years were not endorsements of uncertainty. They were a realist's acknowledgment that some desired certainties are unobtainable and that some which have been obtained are undesirable. It is possible, furthermore, that the later reflections bespoke the disappointment of experience—a recognition that he had not been wholly successful in his effort to persuade his contemporaries that a pro-

[42] *Touched with Fire: Civil War Letters and Diary of Oliver Wendell Holmes, Jr.* (Howe, ed., Cambridge, Mass., 1946), 71.

[43] *HLL*, I, 42.

[44] "The Path of the Law," *CLP*, 167, 181. Cf. Lord Hardwicke in *Walton* v. *Tryon*, 1 Dick. 244, 245 (1753): "Certainty is the mother of repose, and therefore the law aims at certainty." See also Sergeant Carus in *Stowell* v. *Lord Zouch*, Plowden, 353, 368 (1568).

[45] Dissenting in *Truax* v. *Corrigan*, 257 U.S. 312, 342 (1921).

gressive reduction of the jury's responsibility would be desirable. And it will later be seen, I believe, that both on the Massachusetts court and on the Supreme Court of the United States, Holmes did what he could to transform a theory of jurisprudence into a fact of law.[46] He sought, in other words, to hasten the translation of adjudications of juries into rules of law. He did, on occasion, take an almost callous satisfaction in emphasizing the unpredictability of jury verdicts,[47] but his dominant concern as judge was, I think, the same as it had been as scholar—a desire to minimize uncertainty.

[46] See, e.g., *Commonwealth* v. *Sullivan*, 146 Mass. 142 (1888); *Baltimore & Ohio Railroad Co.* v. *Goodman*, 275 U.S. 66 (1927).

[47] *Nash* v. *United States*, 229 U.S. 373, 377 (1913); *Commonwealth* v. *Pierce*, 138 Mass. 165, 178 (1884).

8

Elements of Possession

T*he intense interest* of nineteenth-century jurists in problems of possession is somewhat mystifying to the lawyers of the
twentieth. Recognizing that problems of possession had been of
critical importance in the formulary system of the common law
and acknowledging that the law of larceny was an artful embroidery of nice distinctions between title, possession, and custody, today's lawyer more often sees problems of possession as whetstones
for the minds of law students than as significant issues of jurisprudence.[1] Is it an actionable wrong to the hunter in hot pursuit of
that "noxious and incorrigible beast, the fox," for another sports-
man to kill and take away the quarry?[2] Does the diminutive chim-
ney sweep have a better claim to the jewel which he finds than the
goldsmith to whom the sweep hands it over for appraisal?[3] And
what of the happy customer who finds a pocket-book on the floor
of the shop? Does he or the proprietor have the better right to the
treasure-trove?[4] Does the borrower or the owner of a safe keep
money which, unknown to the owner, was concealed in its lining,
and which was uncovered by the borrower?[5] The student has a

---

[1] See the discerning and clarifying discussion of these matters in C. H. S. Fifoot, *Judge and Jurist in the Reign of Victoria* (London, 1959) , chapter four.

[2] *Pierson* v. *Post,* 3 Caines (N.Y.) 175 (1805) .

[3] *Armory* v. *Delamirie,* 1 Strange 505 (1722) .

[4] *Bridges* v. *Hawkesworth,* 21 L.J., Q.B. 75 (1852) .

[5] *Durfee* v. *Jones,* 11 R.I. 1 (1877) .

good chance of giving an intelligible if not a "right" answer to each of these questions if he is able to analyze and define the concept of possession. It is not today assumed, however, that he needs the insight of a philosopher to comprehend the matters in issue. It is realized, of course, that the historian of the common law must not only trace the sequence of legal events, but analyze the development of legal concepts, and, accordingly, do his best to grasp the concept of possession. To acknowledge this is not, however, to assert that the concept presents issues of absorbing moment. Today's practitioner is apt to embark upon the waters of possession sharing the comfortable assumption of Blackstone that charts are not needed for the crossing. They know that the philosophers have made them, but they are not sure that those judges who have put them to use have landed safely on the other shore.

The jurists of the nineteenth century had been led by two interests to look upon questions of possession as deeply significant. First, of course, was the largest question: What considerations justify private interests in property? Second stood the historical issue: By what processes did man come to assume dominion over things and then validate dominion by the authority of law? Holmes, as we have already seen, had followed with considerable attentiveness the course of inquiry into the historical problem, and had been led by anthropologists and institutional historians to recognize that private, personal rights in property had a relatively late origin in social institutions.[6] It is not unlikely, I think, that this interpretation of institutional history reinforced that philosophical skepticism which questioned the existence of transcendental foundations of possessory and proprietary interests. Yet when Holmes turned to those philosophers who had exercised the greatest influence on juristic analysis of possession and ownership—Kant and Hegel—he found that they had laboriously and ingeniously sustained rights of property with the flying buttresses of metaphysics. By the Kantian analysis each man's personality dominates a certain ring or circle of things—objects which he has brought within the reach of his will—and, through the safeguarding of

[6] See *supra*, p. 150.

this material aura, society secures the freedom and equality of each of its members.[7] Hegel pushed these suggestions to a level of higher abstraction, insisting that property is a necessity of reason.

Free-will must realize itself; that is, necessarily in an outer as outer. "Seizure is the enunciation of the judgment that a thing is mine. My will has subsumed it—given it that predicate of mine. It is the right of will so to subsume in itself all external things whatever, for it is in itself the universal; while they, not referent of themselves, are only under necessity and not free." [8]

Such speculations as these were more philosophic than juristic, and Holmes, quite naturally, had turned from the abstractions of Kant and Hegel to what he hoped might be the more pedestrian efforts of the jurists. The times, as we have already seen, were such as to make it of great importance to the structure of the common law that a theory of possession built on other foundations than those established by the forms of action should be formulated. Unhappily it was still the fact, as Nathaniel Lindley (later Lord Lindley) had stated in 1855, that "upon the English law of possession there is not . . . any work, good, bad, or indifferent." [9] Even John Austin had failed to formulate a theory of possession. Just as he was to lecture on that topic his health gave way and whatever theory he had intended to set forth remained unpublished. Of theories of possession he had said little more than was implied in his generous, if less than expansive, words spoken of Savigny's classic work on Possession: "Of all books which I pretend to know accurately [it is] the least alloyed with error and imperfection." [10] With no domestic theory to build upon, it was no wonder that the quest for a theory of possession led English and American scholars to the writings of Savigny and the German Pandectists.

7 See Edward Caird, *The Critical Philosophy of Kant* (Glasgow, 1889) , II, 325.

8 James Hutchison Stirling, *The Philosophy of Law* (St. Louis, 1874) , 55, quoting Hegel.

9 *An Introduction to the Study of Jurisprudence; Being a Translation of the General Part of Thibaut's System des Pandekten Rechts* (London, 1855) , Appendix, cxvii. Holmes had read Lindley's volume in 1870.

10 See Fifoot, *supra*, note 1, 85–87.

When Holmes turned his attention to the work of the German jurists he went first, of course, to Savigny. Thereafter he plowed his way through the pages of Bruns, Gans, Puchta, and Jhering.[11] Wherever these jurists marched they seemed to Holmes to follow in the ponderous footsteps of Kant and Hegel. The concepts of freedom, equality, and will had so dominated the minds of the Pandectists that they had forced their analysis of possession into a mold shaped by the abstractions of philosophers. The metaphysics of freedom, equality, and will could not allow the possibility that one who held property, not for himself but for another, might secure the law's protection for his holding. If he had not made, or did not seek to make, a piece of property his own, what imperative of freedom and will could sustain his claim that his non-self-regarding interest was entitled to protection? Obviously one who held for another—a bailee, for example—could not be a possessor, for he did not have that self-regarding *animus* which the metaphysics of will requires. For that metaphysics of will tells us that no one who is not an owner, or, at least, on his way to becoming an owner, can be recognized by law to be a possessor.

Holmes's search had led him beyond a theory, through a philosophy, to a metaphysics of possession. He was quick to see that some of the most fundamental doctrines of the common law were not only at odds with Kantian and Hegelian principles but were wholly different from the rules of the Roman law. He, therefore, set himself the task of seeking as historian the sources and defining as analyst the structure of the common law's theory of possession. The first fruit of that effort was an essay on Possession and a briefer sequel on Common Carriers and Common Law. These two essays —with their order reversed—became the fifth and sixth lectures in *The Common Law*. After the essays appeared in the *American*

11 Holmes's "Black Book" contains detailed notes on Savigny's treatise, on Bruns's *Das Recht des Besitzes* (Tubingen, 1848), on the sections of Windscheid's *Lehrbuch des Pandekten Rechts* (Dusseldorf, 1875) which dealt with possession, and on Puchta's essay on possession in the second volume of Weiske's *Rechtslexicon* (Leipzig, 1844). Though his reading list and his references in *The Common Law* indicate that he had read Jhering's comments on possession, notes on that reading do not seem to survive.

Law Review Holmes wrote to Arthur G. Sedgwick and described the impulse and objective which had moved him to write the two papers.

I consider that the test of the theory of possession was the way in which the law deals with bailees. I found the Englishmen Fitzjames Stephen in his Criminal Law (appendix), Markby, etc. were following the theories of Savigny, which are those of a Romanist inspired by the Kantian philosophy.[12] My first point, therefore, was to show by the way our law dealt with bailees that theories based on the Roman law *as the Germans understand it* (it is immaterial whether they have distorted it or not), would not fit our law and that our law was in this respect truly national—Teutonic & not borrowed from Rome. Backed in this way, it is easier to maintain that what has been put out by the German jurists, who are all Kantians or Hegelians, as the theory of possession in all possible systems, is in truth only a theory carefully adapted to the facts of the only system known to the writers—although stated as if it were developed *a priori*. I think the theory which I state and which is simply that which would occur to the unregenerate mind as the only natural one is much more advanced than Hegel's rot on the subject. But if I am right it makes a pretty big hole in his philosophy.[13]

It is not unlikely, I think, that those persons who had attended the first four of the Lowell Lectures thought, for a time at least, that the fifth, on bailment, had at its core the same problem which had unified the earlier lectures—the problem, that is, of whether culpability is an essential element of legal liability. For the problem with which the largest portion of the fifth lecture was concerned was to trace the absolute liability of common carriers to a forgotten, yet critically important source. Seven years before the lecture was delivered, Holmes had evidently not recognized that

12 Stephen's discussion of possession was in his *Digest of the Criminal Law* (London, 1877), 376 *et seq*. He had explicitly acknowledged his indebtedness to Savigny and had asserted that possession means, "in the common use of language, a power to act as the owner of a thing" (*id.*, 380). Markby's discussion of possession was in his *Elements of Law* (Oxford, 1871), 165 *et seq*. He also had built his analysis on Savigny's. He, like Holmes, assumed that Savigny had not merely given an historical explanation of the Roman law on possession, but had formulated a universal conception.

13 Holmes to Sedgwick, July 12, 1879 (copy, HLS).

source as important. As editor of the 12th edition of Kent's *Commentaries*, he had allowed the Chancellor's comments on the liability of common carriers to stand unquestioned. Chancellor Kent had spoken of the "extraordinary responsibility" of common carriers and had accounted for it in the way usual among the commentators who had gone before him. Pointing out that the common carrier is "in the nature of an insurer, and is answerable for accidents and thefts, and even for loss by robbery," the Chancellor had then repeated conventional doctrine when he asserted that this unusual liability "was taken from the edict of the praetor in the Roman law." [14] Though, as I say, Holmes as editor had allowed this passage to pass unnoted, in his own copy of that edition there is a marginal comment in his handwriting stating bluntly: "This is not so," and making a reference to 12 *American Law Review* 692 —his own article on Common Carriers and the Common Law.

The repudiation of Kent's reflections on common carriers was not the rejection of his description of the carrier's liability as absolute. Rather, it was the denial of the Chancellor's assertion that the rule of strict liability had been imported into England from Rome. He was not, in other words, examining or refining the legal concept of fault. He was tracing the liability of common carriers to its true source. The tracing produced two important and closely related historical theses: first, that the strict liability of common carriers was the surviving remnant of an absolute liability imposed by the common law on all bailees; second, that this ancient doctrine of the common law was derived from Teutonic procedures which gave protection to the possessory rights of bailees. Of these two insights the second was the more important, for it provided the historical foundations for the theory of possession which Holmes outlined in his sixth lecture.

The interpretation of legal history which Holmes presented in his essay on Common Carriers and the Common Law and the lecture on bailments had not, I believe, been suggested by any earlier student of the common law. In summary it came to this. In the primitive Teutonic legal order the possessor, rather than the

[14] *Commentaries*, II, *597–*598.

owner of goods—the bailee, that is, rather than the bailor—had all the remedies for injuries which may be done to the bailed property. This safeguarding of the bailee was first revealed in the early German law providing remedies for cattle-stealing. "The natural redress for the wrong was to follow the trail with one's friends and take back the plunder with the strong arm. The Salic law mirrors nature and prescribes following the trail, and the Anglo-Saxon laws are very full upon the same matter." Because of the "executive" nature of the procedure for the recovery of property lost against one's will,

it could hardly have been started by any other than the person on the spot in whose keeping the cattle were, and the texts . . . show that the only point to be sworn to was touching the plaintiff's unwilling loss of possession. Hence it is concluded that possession was the foundation of the action, and that no other than the possessor could avail himself of this only known remedy.[15]

Since the law had not yet made any remedy available to bailors against third persons, whether they were thieves, finders, or purchasers in good faith from the bailee, the only relief which bailors could secure was against the persons to whom they had entrusted the goods—the bailees. Because only the bailee could recover from a thief it seemed fitting that he should be accountable to his bailor, though the theft had occurred without his privity or fault. The absolute liability of the bailee at common law, accordingly, is traceable to the combination of circumstances which made remedies available to him against third persons and denied them to the bailor.

From this Teutonic point of origin Holmes moved forward in time, still following the trail of the bailee's liability. He called attention to the processes by which the early strictness of that liability had been qualified, showing that it had been brought about, not through acknowledged considerations of policy, but by collateral, procedural developments, particularly those which permitted

15 "Possession," *Am. L. Rev.*, 12:688–689. The same description, in a somewhat abbreviated form, appeared in "Common Carriers and the Common Law," *id.*, 13:611, and in *CL*, 165.

the bailor, in some circumstances at least, to have his remedies against the third party. Yet in the seventeenth century there were still instances in which a bailee was held absolutely responsible for the safety of goods put in his charge, and among the bailees so held strictly liable were common carriers. When in the next century, and in the nineteenth as well, the judges and scholars found that the absolute liability of carriers was an exception grafted onto the common law of bailments, either from Roman sources or from special custom, they had misinterpreted legal history and, in the process, evaded the responsibility which properly was theirs—the responsibility, that is, of determining whether it is sound policy to keep alive the strict liability of carriers when the liability of all other bailees, originally absolute, had been mitigated by requirements of culpability.[16] Though Holmes did not specifically either favor or condemn the ancient principle that all bailees are subject to an absolute liability, the temper of his discussion made it quite clear, I think, that in the modern world such liability should be the exception, not the rule.

In a suit in admiralty which Holmes argued before Mr. Justice Clifford in 1879, he sought to persuade the Court that the liability of a carrying vessel for damage done to cargo should not be measured by the misleading dogma of the common law, by which all common carriers are insurers, but should be determined by that analysis of history and those considerations of policy which he had outlined in his essay on Common Carriers and the Common Law.[17] Holmes represented the owner of a steam vessel, the *Svend*, which had been seized on *in rem* process. In a trans-Atlantic crossing, sheet iron, carried on the *Svend*, had been greatly damaged by rust. After a hearing in the District Court, the libel had been dismissed, either on the ground that the loss was within the excepted peril: "not answerable for leakage, breakage or rust," or that the

[16] In the essay on Common Carriers, Holmes had made these points in criticism of the opinions of Mr. Justice Brett and Sir Alexander Cockburn in *Nugent* v. *Smith*, 1 C.P.D. 19 (1875); *id.* 423 (1876).

[17] *The Svend*, 1 Fed. 54 (1879). The names of the proctors do not appear in the reports. The record and briefs are preserved, however, in Holmes's library at the Library of Congress and contain many annotations in Holmes's hand.

rust had been caused by wetting consequent upon extraordinary gales. On appeal to the Circuit Court, where the testimony of sixty witnesses was received, the decree was reversed. Holmes's unsuccessful argument dealt not only with the issues of fact with respect to the cause of the rusting, but with the question of law relating to the status of carriers by sea. Holmes called Justice Clifford's attention to his article on Common Carriers and the Common Law. "It is believed," he said, "that some new light has been thrown on these [precedents] by an article in the *American Law Review* for last July (Vol. 13, p. 609)." [18] Acknowledging that the inequality of bargaining power between railroads and shippers might justify the rule which makes carriers by rail insurers, he urged, as he had in his essay, that the liability of other carriers should not be grounded on the false dogma and the misleading history of Holt and Story, but should be measured by considerations of policy. A bailee's liability should be that of an insurer only when special considerations, such as inequality of bargaining power, provide a justification. In the absence of some showing that carriers by sea have a stranglehold on shippers, making suspect all contractual limitations of the vessel's liability, provisions excepting liability for certain perils should be given their natural meaning and effect. He repeated, in substance, the concluding thesis of his essay:

> If there is a sound rule of public policy which ought to impose a special responsibility upon common carriers, as these words are now understood, and upon no others, it has never yet been stated. If, on the other hand, there are considerations which apply to a particular class among those so designated,—for instance, to railroads, who may have a private individual at their mercy, or exercise a power too vast for the common welfare—we do not prove that the reasoning extends to a general ship or a public cab by calling all three common carriers.[19]

Not surprisingly, Justice Clifford refused to follow the radical course which Holmes urged him to take. Citing Story on *Bailments,* the Justice reiterated the two familiar propositions—first, that "carriers of goods, if common carriers . . . are insurers of

18 Brief for the Claimant, 28.   19 *Am. L. Rev.*, 13:630. Cf. *CL*, 204–205.

the goods" and, second, that "ship-owners and masters of ships employed as general ships in the coasting or foreign trade, or in general freighting business, are deemed common carriers by water, and as such are as much insurers of the goods they transport as common carriers by land . . ." [20] Quite probably such hopes as Holmes may have had that he could secure a favorable decision from Justice Clifford were based upon the possibility that on the issues of fact the Court would find in his favor. Perhaps he also saw some remote possibility that the Justice would find the fresh interpretation of history and the original analysis of policy so persuasive that he would repudiate accepted dogma. If there was a touch of academic innocence in this hope, there was courage in the effort to lead Justice Clifford towards those ends which Holmes had defined in the essay on common carriers and which became, as it were, the central theme of *The Common Law*.

Every important principle which is developed by litigation is in fact and at bottom the result of more or less definitely understood views of public policy; most generally, to be sure, under our practice and traditions, the unconscious result of instinctive preferences and inarticulate convictions, but none the less traceable to public policy in the last analysis . . . The importance of tracing the process lies in the fact that it is unconscious, and involves the attempt to follow precedents, as well as to give a good reason for them, and that hence, if it can be shown that one half of the effort has failed, we are at liberty to consider the question of policy with a freedom that was not possible before.[21]

Holmes had endeavored to give Clifford his freedom. The Justice rejected the offer. Did this rejection, perhaps, give a special zest to Holmes's comment on the qualities of Justice Clifford once expressed to Felix Frankfurter: "He crawled over a case like a worm, but just as I expected him to reach the crucial point he stopped"?

Though the essentials of Holmes's historical argument with respect to the roots of the carrier's absolute liability have been accepted by learned scholars, they have been persuasively criticized

[20] 1 Fed. 54.   [21] *Am. L. Rev.*, 13:631.

by others.[22] It is quite apparent that in the lecture on bailments, as in those on criminal law and torts, Holmes was seeking to support a philosophical thesis or point of view by an original interpretation of history. He did not make it as clear in the lecture as he had in the essay on common carriers that his interest in their liability was more philosophical than historical. Yet a careful reading of the lecture shows one clearly that his ultimate concern when he spoke of common carriers was not that of tracing their absolute liability to its common law source. That effort seemed to him worth making because it led him to the common law's theory of possession, a theory which, if accepted, might overthrow the deforming tyranny that German metaphysics had exercised over legal philosophy.

In his consideration of the history of carriers' liability, Holmes did not hesitate to expose two aspects of conviction—perhaps of prejudice—which led him to see the search for a theory of possession as an endeavor of very large importance. The first bias which Holmes revealed in his discussion of the liability of carriers had been encouraged, if not initiated by the studies of Henry Adams and his Harvard associates. It was the somewhat romantic persuasion that the clearest waters of the common law were traceable to "an original reservoir of Teutonic law." [23] In the essay, though not in the lecture on Bailment, Holmes had stated quite explicitly that "the responsibility of common carriers is of pure Teutonic origin." [24] This dictum did not mean, of course, that Holmes or the archaeologists had discovered the tracks of common carriers beneath the pine needles of the Black Forest. What it meant was that

22 Sir William Holdsworth was, perhaps, the most distinguished scholar to defend Holmes's interpretation of history (*History of English Law,* 3rd ed., London, 1923, III, 336–350). Professor Plucknett, Professor Beale, and Dr. Fletcher have criticized Holmes's thesis: Theodore F. T. Plucknett, *A Concise History of the Common Law* (5th ed., Boston, 1956) 476–482; Joseph H. Beale, "Carrier's Liability," *Select Essays in Anglo-American Legal History* (Boston, 1909), III, 152; Eric G. M. Fletcher, *The Carrier's Liability* (London, 1932), *passim*. For a very valuable recent survey see George W. Paton, *Bailment in the Common Law* (London, 1952).

23 Fifoot, *History and Sources of the Common Law: Tort and Contract* (London, 1949), 158, note 28.

24 *Am. L. Rev.,* 13:610.

the strict or absolute liability of carriers in the nineteenth century was traceable to the rights and responsibilities of possessors as they existed under the law of the Salian Franks. It is quite probable, I think, that it was the paper of one of Adams's students in the *Essays in Anglo-Saxon Law* which first called Holmes's attention to the fact that Teutonic and Anglo-Saxon laws had given the possessor of cattle and other personal property effective remedies against thieves and other wrongdoers. In his unsigned review of the *Essays,* Holmes had given particular attention to the paper on Anglo-Saxon procedure which J. Laurence Laughlin had contributed to the volume. In the course of his comment, Holmes had noted that in the procedures described by Laughlin

the action for movables involuntarily parted with was deemed so indivisibly connected with the trespass of the taking, that it was only allowed to the person deprived of possession. The owner who had intrusted his property to a bailee could not sue, but the bailee was the proper plaintiff.[25]

When Holmes came to tell the story of the carriers' liability and to correct the conventional interpretation of that history, his starting point in time and doctrine was that which Laughlin had emphasized. Holmes, like Adams's young associate, took his Teutonic law from Laband's *Die vermögensrechtlichen Klagen nach den sächsischen Rechtsquellen des Mittelalters* and Heusler's *Die Gewere,* and added a reference to unsigned reviews by Henry Adams in the pages of the *North American Review.*[26]

In the preface to the third edition of his *Principles of Contract,* Pollock, discussing *The Common Law,* saw its leading idea to be "that our procedure, and our legal theory so far as thereon founded or therein involved, are of native Germanic origin, and the resemblances to Roman law, save so far as they consist of features common to all archaic law may be regarded as superficial." Doubtless with Adams, perhaps with Melville Bigelow in mind, Pollock went on to say that this view of the origins of English law

[25] *Id.,* 11:327, 330 (January 1877). For the identification of Holmes as the author of this review see *supra,* p. 147, note 28.

[26] See *CL,* 166, note 1.

"is characteristic of what may by this time be called the American school of historical criticism," and that though it was liable to exaggeration in details, it is "in the main a sound one." [27] Some members of the American school were, doubtless, led by a romanticism characteristic of their time to seek for wholesome simplicities, both political and social, in the Teutonic shadows. Possibly this influence played its part upon the mind of Holmes. It is abundantly clear, however, that this romanticism would not have carried him into "the American school of historical criticism" had not a deeper impulse moved him. The character and strength of that impulse were not fully revealed in the lecture on bailments but were exposed with candor and feeling in the lecture on possession.

Holmes had searched for a theory of possession. What the German jurists offered him was a metaphysics of will, equality, and freedom—a metaphysics so arrogant in its abstraction that it was wholly indifferent to the fact that a vast system of law, the common law of England, had always recognized that a self-regarding *animus* is not essential to possession.[28] When Holmes found that the romantic school of American historians had uncovered Teutonic procedures by which non-self-regarding possessors were protected, it is small wonder that he seized upon their history with enthusiasm and made it his own. As lecturer on criminal law he had revealed one aspect of his distrust of any legal theory which was built upon Kant's imperatives. He had there used the materials of history to show that equality and freedom have not been the ultimate values in the criminal law. The essay and lecture on bailments were Holmes's attempt to show that the common law's theory of possession, like its theory of criminal liability, was not responsive to Kantian imperatives.

27 Page xi. The preface to this edition, which was published in 1881, commented at length, as we shall later see, on Holmes's theories of contract as stated in the seventh, eighth, and ninth lectures in *The Common Law*.

28 Like J. Laurence Laughlin before him, but perhaps with more malicious satisfaction, Holmes called attention to the fact that the German analyst of possession, Bruns, true to Hegel, had misrepresented the Lex Salica when he asserted that under its provisions the basis of an action for loss or recovery of personal property "was the ownership of the plaintiff." See *Essays in Anglo-Saxon Law*, 212; *CL*, 166, note 1.

Neither in the essays nor in the lectures did Holmes conceal what might perhaps be called his chauvinistic bias. The essay on possession had opened with a protest that in relationship to theories of possession "the Germans have long had it all their own way with the subject." He pointed out that "those German philosophers who have written upon law have known no other system than the Roman" and that they have been wholly unaware that English law enforces without hesitation some rules of possession which "are against what the German civilians would regard as first principles." He then went on to say that he would seek to show that the differences between the English and the Roman law are, in large part, "due to the sturdy persistence of the early traditions of our race . . ." [29] As lecturer he spoke even more vigorously when he insisted that "it is important to show that a far more developed, more rational, and mightier body of law than the Roman, gives no sanction to either premise or conclusion as held by Kant and his successors." [30] His reading of the German jurists had already led him, perhaps, to the conviction which he expressed many years later: "In general if a learned German has maintained a proposition it is pretty safe to contradict it, with a very smug and unpolemical air." [31] His essay and his lecture were efforts in contradiction.

Beyond the slightly chauvinistic impulse to defend the good sense of English law lay considerations of deeper significance. Holmes was outraged by a Kantian's condemnation of contemporary German statutes allowing tenants to have possessory remedies for their "sacrifice of principle to convenience." In Holmes's eyes, "the first call of a theory of law is that it should fit the facts." "What is left," he asked, "of a principle which avows itself inconsistent with convenience and the actual course of legislation?" [32] In connection with problems of possession he emphasized the same consideration which had moved him towards his central conclusions with respect to criminal law—the necessity, as he saw it, that the law accept human nature as it finds it. One of the primary pur-

29 *Am. L. Rev.*, 12:688.
30 *CL*, 210.

31 *HPL*, II, 187.
32 *CL*, 211.

poses of making possessory remedies available to persons who have some lesser interest in property than title is to provide an orderly alternative to private warfare. "Those who see in the history of law the formal expression of the development of society will be apt to think that the proximate ground of law must be empirical, even when that ground is the fact that a certain ideal or theory of government is generally entertained. Law, being a practical thing, must found itself on actual forces. It is quite enough, therefore, for the law, that man, by an instinct which he shares with the domestic dog, and of which the seal gives a most striking example, will not allow himself to be dispossessed, either by force or fraud, of what he holds, without trying to get it back again. Philosophy may find a hundred reasons to justify the instinct, but it would be totally immaterial if it should condemn it and bid us surrender without a murmur. As long as the instinct remains, it will be more comfortable for the law to satisfy it in an orderly manner, than to leave people to themselves. If it should do otherwise, it would become a matter for pedagogues, wholly devoid of reality." [33] This contention was the reiteration of a thesis which Holmes had emphasized in his unsigned review of the *Essays in Anglo-Saxon Law*. "It must not be forgotten that there is a limit to historical explanation as it is called. Some things (the origin of the notion of property, for instance) receive more light from an analysis of human nature." [34]

The common law and its judges had the good sense to accept man's nature as possessive. Despite the German jurists, the common law had, from the first, recognized that one need not be an owner of property to be entitled to the law's protection of his holding. The task confronting the jurist and the historian is to analyze the situations in which law has made its remedies available to persons not owning, but otherwise controlling property. One should not let himself be drawn away from this homely task by speculative disputation over "a preliminary question which has been debated with much zeal in Germany. Is possession a fact or a right?" [35] That distinction has no larger significance in relationship to possession

---

[33] *Id.*, 213.   [34] *Am. L. Rev.*, 11:330.   [35] *CL*, 213.

than it does with respect to other fundamental legal concepts such as property and contract.

A legal right is nothing but a permission to exercise certain natural powers, and upon certain conditions to obtain protection, restitution, or compensation by the aid of the public force . . . Just so far as possession is protected, it is as much a source of legal rights as ownership is when it secures the same protection.

Every right is a consequence attached by the law to one or more facts which the law defines, and wherever the law gives any one special rights not shared by the body of the people, it does so on the ground that certain special facts, not true of the rest of the world, are true of him. When a group of facts thus singled out by the law exists in the case of a given person, he is said to be entitled to the corresponding rights; meaning, thereby, that the law helps him to constrain his neighbors, or some of them, in a way in which it would not, if all the facts in question were not true of him . . .

The word "possession" denotes such a group of facts. Hence, when we say of a man that he has possession, we affirm directly that all the facts of a certain group are true of him, and we convey indirectly or by implication that the law will give him the advantage of the situation. Contract, or property, or any other substantive notion of the law, may be analyzed in the same way, and should be treated in the same order.[36]

By laying these foundations of analysis Holmes eliminated a range of problems which other theorists had considered. He nonetheless felt himself compelled to take the framework of further inquiry as it had been shaped by others. Civilian tradition identified two elements in possession, *corpus* and *animus,* the physical power to exclude others from control and a corresponding will to effect the exclusion. It was, of course, in relationship to the problems of *animus* that Kantian and Hegelian concepts had had their most exuberant influence. The philosophy of the German lawyers had taught them

that a man's physical power over an object is protected because he has the will to make it his, and it has thus become a part of his very self, the external manifestation of his freedom. The will of the possessor being

36 *Id.,* 214.

thus conceived as self-regarding, the intent with which he must hold is pretty clear: he must hold for his own benefit. Furthermore, the self-regarding intent must go to the height of an intent to appropriate; for otherwise, it seems to be implied, the object would not truly be brought under the personality of the possessor.[37]

Whether or not the German jurists had dealt fairly or accurately with the Roman law, Holmes did not bother himself to consider. What aroused his indignation was their misconception of the jurist's task. As Holmes conceived it, it is to find the theory which lies behind or has been inherent in the actuality of law. It is not that of formulating a theory which will consist with a metaphysics of will, of freedom, and of equality. "The business of the jurist is to make known the content of the law; that is, to work upon it from within, or logically, arranging and distributing it, in order, from its *summum genus* to its *infima species,* so far as practicable." [38] In fulfilling that task, as it applies to the problem of possession, Holmes did not go so far as to repudiate the traditional assumption that the basic elements in possession are *corpus* and *animus.* He did not take the position which skepticism might seem to support—the view that it is impossible, without excessive distortion of cases, to discover an all-embracing definition of the *animus* required by English law of those who are to be classed as possessors.[39] He believed that all of the decisions on possession— whether they related to finders (and trover), to thefts (and larceny), to bailments (and detinue), or to leases (and ejectment) —could be brought within the reconciling terms of his suggested analysis of *animus.* "If what the law does is to exclude others from interfering with the object, it would seem that the intent which the law should require is an intent to exclude others. I believe that such an intent is all that the common law deems needful, and that on principle no more should be required." [40]

[37] *Id.,* 219.
[38] *Id.*
[39] This doubting view has recently been taken in D. R. Harris's "The Concept of Possession in English Law," *Oxford Essays in Jurisprudence* (Guest, ed., Oxford, 1961), 69.
[40] *CL,* 220.

It would seem that in Holmes's eyes the greatest merit of his analysis of the *animus* behind possession was its elimination of that self-regarding element which the Germans had considered so essential. By casting that aside Holmes had made ample room for the English concept of bailment and the common-law possessory remedies of bailees. He realized, of course, that it would not be easy to bring some of the English decisions—particularly those concerning finders and those which denied to servants possession of their masters' goods—within the compass of *animus* as he conceived it. He dealt a little roughly, perhaps, with the cases on finders, but he was surely not the first or last jurist to ascribe to judges *rationes decidendi* which never ruffled their minds.[41] With respect to the fact that though the servant holding his master's goods has "as much intent to exclude the world at large as a borrower" the English law does not consider him a possessor, Holmes acknowledged that his test of *animus* broke down. He saw this exception to a unifying theory of possession as but one more indication that our law of master and servant "maintains many marks of the time when [the servant] was a slave . . . A slave's possession was his owner's possession on the practical ground of the owner's power over him, and from the fact that the slave had no standing before the law. The notion that his personality was merged in that of his family head survived the era of emancipation."[42]

One other aspect of the lecture on possession deserves emphasis. As we have seen, Holmes was not such a rebel against German dogma as to assert that the problem of *animus* in possession is illusory. He acknowledged, moreover, that the principle of externality which he favored for the criminal law and for liability in tort, should not be extended to the field of possession. "The intent inquired into here must be overtly manifested, perhaps, but all theories of the grounds on which possession is protected would

41 A number of scholars who are generally sympathetic with Holmes's theory of possession have concurred in the belief that his reading of English cases on finders was somewhat distorting. See, e.g., Arthur L. Goodhart, "Three Cases on Possession," in *Essays in Jurisprudence and the Common Law* (Cambridge, England, 1937), 75, 79.

42 *CL*, 227, 228.

seem to agree in leading to the requirement that it should be actual, subject, of course, to the necessary limits of legal investigation." [43] Yet Holmes was willing to give more effect to a generalized actual intent than were Savigny and his disciples. In Holmes's judgment the possessor of land or other property on which, without the possessor's knowledge, there lies concealed some lost or abandoned object, may properly be considered to be in possession of that object if he has the "general intent . . . to exclude the public" from the larger unit.[44] Doubtless it was the logic of his own concept of possession which led Holmes to take this view, but one suspects that it was attractive for the further reason that it involved a very specific rejection of Savigny's Kantian thesis that the possessor is protected "because he has that will to make [the object] his, and it has thus become a part of his very self, the external manifestation of his freedom." [45]

There was one phase of the problem as to which Holmes thought that a rule of externality should be controlling. It had been a thesis of Savigny that for possession once acquired to be continued "there must be always the same *animus* as at the moment of acquisition, and a constant power to reproduce at will the original physical relation to the object." [46] Holmes, by contrast, urged that "when certain facts have once been made manifest which confer a right, there is no general ground on which the law need hold the right at an end except the manifestation of some

[43] *Id.,* 216.

[44] *Id.,* 224.

[45] *Id.,* 219.

[46] *Id.,* 236. It has been suggested that Holmes was not justified in this summary of Savigny's opinion. See Carl J. Friedrich, "Law and History," *Vanderbilt Law Review,* 14:1036, note 32. It is difficult, I think, to see in what way Holmes misstated Savigny's thesis. "As possession has been seen to consist in physical power, associated with consciousness, it follows that in every case of acquisition two things are necessary, a corporeal relation and *animus.* The same must also concur for continuance; and this, therefore, must depend upon the same association as the acquisition of Possession; should such association cease, i.e., should either the corporeal act alone, or the *animus* alone, or both together terminate, the continuance of Possession also ceases. For all the distinction which can be discovered between the conditions of acquisition and continuance, refers only to their extent, not to their essence . . ." (Savigny on *Possession,* Perry, tr., London, 1848, 246) .

fact inconsistent with its continuance . . ." [47] To illustrate his thesis Holmes supposed the case of a finder of a purse of gold who

has left it in his country-house, which is lonely and slightly barred, and he is a hundred miles away, in prison. The only person within twenty miles is a thoroughly equipped burglar at his front door, who has seen the purse through a window, and who intends forthwith to enter and take it. The finder's power to reproduce his former physical relation to the gold is rather limited, yet I believe that no one would say that his possession was at an end until the burglar, by an overt act, had manifested his power and intent to exclude others from the purse.

The principle which Holmes applied for the resolution of the imagined case was not unrelated to his familiar principle of externality.

The law deals, for the most part, with overt acts and facts which can be known by the senses. So long as the burglar has not taken the purse, he has not manifested his intent; and until he breaks through the barrier which measures the present possessor's power of excluding him, he has not manifested his power. [48]

In dealing with this problem Holmes was not, to be sure, saying that the law in dealing with this type of problem substitutes an external for a subjective test of intention. He did, however, reject once more the Kantian inclination of Savigny's theory—an inclination which would require a constancy of the will's power to make its possessory longing physically effective.

In June of 1880, while Holmes was devoting his days to "practise of our mixed sort" and his evenings to the preparation of his lectures on the common law, he wrote to Pollock of the pressure which these divided responsibilities put upon him. A special difficulty prompted this special lamentation: "The frame of mind needed for successful speculation is so different from that into which business puts one." [49] He went on, however, to tell of a case which he had recently argued before the Supreme Judicial Court in which he had dealt with Roman doctrine with respect to possession. The case in question was destined, in fact, to be argued a

[47] CL, 236. [48] Id., 237-238. [49] HPL, I, 14-15.

second time by Holmes and a third time by Shattuck and Munroe, and to be decided—in favor of opposing counsel—after Holmes was himself a member of the Court, he, of course, not participating in the decision.[50] The incident deserves mention, I think, because it indicates that despite Holmes's comments to Pollock he had found it possible as practitioner, at least in this one case, to carry argument to an impressively high, speculative level. The controversy seemed, on its face, to be a thoroughly pedestrian dispute—a Boston merchant suing a Boston banker for the conversion of 184 bags of wool. Holmes, representing the defendant, filed an extensive brief in the Supreme Judicial Court—a document in which he traversed much of the ground which he had covered in his essay on possession. As advocate he returned to the assault which he had carried on as essayist, and belabored Lord Holt, Kent, and Story for their incorporation of Roman doctrine in the common law of bailment. He again insisted that a sloppy confusion between the custody of servants and the possession of bailees had corrupted understanding, and endeavored to lead the Court through the Year Books to sound analysis. He did not, however, add the reasoning of a philosopher to the argument of a historian. His client's case depended, in large part, upon convincing the Court that one who had physical control of personal property, with the permission of the owner, should, if at all possible, be considered its possessor. Holmes's effort to lead the Court in this direction did not, as in theory it might have, take an analytic form. Instead, he emphasized those considerations of social and mercantile policy which favor that doctrine of possession which permits the public to rely on manifest control. "The public is to be protected by certain outward visible signs. If the owner does not keep up that protection, it is immaterial through what causes he has failed. The public is a stranger to his intentions, and is authorized to rely, as it must rely, on what is apparent." [51]

50 *Thacher* v. *Moors,* 134 Mass. 156. The case was argued in March 1880 by Holmes and Shattuck, was reargued by them in November 1881, and a third time by Shattuck and Munroe in January 1883, when Holmes was on the bench.

51 Brief for the defendant in *Thacher* v. *Moors,* 134 Mass. 6 (Social Law Library, Boston).

Holmes concluded his argument with a characteristic blending of learning and judgment. "The foregoing argument," he said,

is not merely a logical working out of strict principles with public policy. The whole tendency of the law . . . is to attribute increasing importance to possession as a badge of title, especially in commercial transactions. This policy has always proved a necessity wherever commerce has existed. Throughout the continent of Europe it long ago led to the rule that in the dealings of the market, if nowhere else, *possession vaut titre* (Casaregis, Disc. 123 pr. 124; § 2, 3). In England it was recognized by the law of market overt, and when markets overt ceased to be, as they had been, the center of trade, the Factor's Act adopted the commercial law of the rest of the world. "The law of the market," as Sir H. S. Maine calls it, the policy of protecting trade, was seen to be more important than the policy of protecting titles.[52]

Holmes's argument in *Thacher* v. *Moors* did not, as I have said, persuade the Court. Perhaps this last of his efforts as advocate, like his first, savored "a little . . . of experimental philosophy," [53] and, through that savor, antagonized the hardheaded judges. Doubtless Holmes was disappointed when his colleagues told him that the case had not gone his way. Yet one may be fairly sure, I think, that he was not disheartened by his failure in persuasion. He had put his views on bailment and possession into his lectures and from there they might move forward towards recognition and acceptance. It was, after all, in the hope that he would experience "the secret isolated joy of the thinker, who knows . . . the subtle rapture of a postponed power," [54] that Holmes had undertaken to deliver the Lowell Lectures. His concern was not so much with winning cases as it was with affecting thought. He lost his case on bailments and possession, but there can be no question that his lectures on those subjects had a far greater influence on the common law than did the decision in *Thacher* v. *Moors*.

[52] *Id.*, 14.

[53] This was the comment of Mr. Justice Hoar on Holmes's first argument before the Supreme Judicial Court—the argument in *Richardson* v. *New York Central Railroad*, 98 Mass. 85 (1867). See *Shaping Years*, 275–276.

[54] *OS*, 31.

9

The Obligation of Contracts

B$_y$ *the middle* of the nineteenth century, English and American lawyers had belatedly come to recognize that a theory of contract had a place not only in political and moral philosophy but in jurisprudence as well. It was, accordingly, quite natural that Holmes should see an obligation to include in the Lowell Lectures some consideration of the history and nature of contract liability in the common law. As editor, essayist, and teacher he had never given such close attention to those matters as he had to the problems of liability in tort and to the nature of possession. As a consequence the three lectures on contract were prepared for the Lowell Institute on order, so to speak, and were written during the summer and autumn months of 1880. This is not to say, of course, that in his earlier analytic efforts and historical inquiries problems of contract liability had not concerned him. His reading list and occasional comments in book notes and reviews indicate that theory discussed extensively in the lectures on contract had already taken general shape when he turned to their preparation.[1]

1 Holmes had contributed a brief comment on A. Brown's *Epitome and Analysis of Savigny on Obligations* (London, 1872) to the *American Law Review* (7:320; January 1873). The long notice of Langdell's *Summary of Contracts* from which I have already quoted at length (*supra*, p. 156) also contained a brief comment on Sir William R. Anson's *Principles of the English Law of Contract* (London, 1879). Though Holmes's reading list does not include the first edition of Pollock's *Principles of Contract* (London, 1876), it seems hardly conceivable that he did not read his friend's volume. His personal library, now in the Library of Congress, included

The very great importance of the three lectures on contract cannot be fully appreciated without recognition of the condition of doctrine at the time when Holmes gave his close attention to the problem. For many generations there had been much philosophical discussion of the ethical and legal foundations of contractual obligation. It had become a dogma of political theory that the sanctity of contracts lies at the core of a free society. Sir Henry Maine had recently buttressed political doctrine with the historical thesis that man's social relationships had progressed from those of status to those of contract. The thesis contained a built-in assumption—doubtless wholly accurate—that in early societies the realm of truly consensual obligation was confined within very narrow boundaries: that a man was most frequently held to the performance of his undertakings not because he had assumed a promissory obligation to another but because he had committed a formal, almost a ritualistic, act to which the law ascribed certain sanctioning consequences. The historians of the Roman law had told of the processes by which it came gradually and grudgingly to be recognized that some contractual obligations were enforceable not merely by virtue of formality but by virtue of consent—a meeting of the minds of the contractors. Informal contracts were enforced in the Roman law, however, only if the promise given were of a certain character and were sustained by what the jurists called *causa*—a mark or element signifying actionability.

Sir Henry Maine, like many other English jurists of his day, took his Roman law relating to contracts from Savigny,[2] and his concept of contractual obligation from Pothier. To take law and concepts from those sources was to receive philosophy as well. The theoretical underpinnings of Savigny's analysis of contractual obligation had been established by Pothier and were also sustained by the presuppositions which supported his theory of possession.

a copy of the first edition given to him by Pollock. Not only in the essay and lecture on bailment, but in his earlier comments in *Coggs* v. *Bernard* in "Misunderstandings of the Civil Law" (*Am. L. Rev.*, 6:37) he had included some important reflections on the nature of consideration.

[2] Maine's discussion of contract is in Chapter IX of *Ancient Law*.

The concepts of will, freedom, and equality shaped his theory of contract. By Savigny's analysis, in all contracts there is "a union of several wills to a single, whole and undivided will," and the law's responsibility is to discover the unified will and see that it is effectuated. His analysis identified four constituent elements in every contract: (1) several parties, (2) an agreement of their wills, (3) a mutual communication of the agreement, and (4) an intention to create a legal relation between the parties.[3] As in so much of Savigny's writing there was some difficulty in separating his historical description from his philosophical prescription, but it is not surprising that his English disciples—Pollock and Anson, in particular—took his analysis of contract obligation to be something more universal than a historian's account of Roman law. The treatises on contracts which Pollock and Anson had published before Holmes prepared his lectures expressed their unreserved respect for the value to English jurists of Savigny's analysis. In the preface to his first edition Pollock stated that on points of Roman law, "and to a considerable extent, indeed, on the principles it has in common with our own," he had "consulted and generally followed Savigny's great work."[4] In the dedicatory letter, addressed to Lord Lindley which prefaced his fourth edition in 1885, Pollock stated that it was owing to Lord Lindley and James Bryce that he had "turned from the formless confusion of text-books and the dry bones of students' manuals to the immortal work of Savigny; assuredly the greatest production of this age in the field of jurisprudence, nor one easily to be matched in any other branch of learning, if literary form as well as scientific genius be taken into account."[5] In the first edition of his *Elements of Jurisprudence,* Thomas Erskine Holland seemed also to accept as philosophically

[3] This summary is based upon T. E. Holland, *Elements of Jurisprudence* (Oxford, 1880), 173–174. A most valuable sketch of nineteenth-century attitudes towards contract is to be found in G. C. Cheshire and C. H. S. Fifoot, *The Law of Contract* (5th ed., London, 1960), 16–17. See also K. O. Shatwell, "The Doctrine of Consideration in the Modern Law," *Sydney Law Review,* 1:289 (December 1954).

[4] Pollock, *Principles of Contract* (London, 1876), viii. See also Sir William R. Anson, *Principles of the English Law of Contract* (Oxford, 1879), Introduction.

[5] At p. iv.

and therefore universally valid the theory of contract which Savigny had developed.[6]

It is in no way surprising that the English jurists of the nineteenth century made the German scholar their guide. The English legal inheritance, so far as it related to contracts, was cluttered with ambiguities, refinements, and subtleties. It was recognized that while the forms of action had governed the enforcement of contracts there had been no great call for the discovery of the common law's fundamental principle of contract obligation. For certain "formal" contracts—instruments under seal—the defendant's obligation had not historically been looked upon as consensual. As in the formal obligations of the Roman law their binding force was more related to ritual than to reason. Yet the remedy for breach of such an obligation, the action of covenant, was classed as an action of contract. With respect to obligations under "informal" contracts, it was assumed they were truly consensual. Yet it was recognized that they were valid and binding only if that vague something known as "consideration" were an element in the contract. For the common-law practitioner it was enough, perhaps, to know that an action of covenant would lie for breach of a promise under seal, an action of debt for breach of a promise given by the defendant in exchange for a *quid pro quo,* or benefit received, and an action of assumpsit for the nonperformance of a promise on which the plaintiff had relied to his detriment. If generalization were possible it could not go much farther than to assert that the consideration required for the validity of informal contracts might consist either in benefit to the promisor or detriment to the promisee. In the Court of Equity, however, where forms of action did not govern theory, a larger generalization was called for. It was not uncommon for the Chancellor and practitioners in equity to Romanize their principles and to assert that if the promise was supported by *causa*—the civilian's equivalent of consideration—it was enforceable.

The decline in the significance of the forms of action and the

[6] Holland, 173–174.

increasing assimilation of law to equity led, in this matter as in so many others, to the awareness that there was impelling need for an ordering theory. One historical tradition offered a tempting avenue to a reasoned scheme of things. Chancellor Kent had made the familiar English thesis an American orthodoxy when he suggested that English doctrine with respect to consideration was derived from the Roman law of *causa,* and was, in its essentials, no different.[7] As Kent's editor Holmes did not comment on this suggestion. The acceptance of this historical proposition, however questionable it might be, made it easy and natural for English and American lawyers to treat the theories formulated for explanation and clarification of contract liability in the Roman law applicable to the English law as well.[8] If English doctrine with respect to consideration was Roman in origin, if Savigny had provided not only an enlightening analysis of the Roman law of contract but a philosophy of contract valid for all societies, was it not the course of wisdom to follow in his footsteps? [9]

In none of his three lectures on contract did Holmes explicitly reiterate his earlier protests against allowing German interpretations of Roman law to distort understanding of the far mightier *corpus juris*—the English common law. It is entirely clear, however, that the impulse to set jurisprudence free of the Kantian clutch and of the Roman reins of German jurists inspired his lectures on contracts as it had those on crimes, torts, and possession.

---

7 *Commentaries,* II, *464 *et seq.*

8 Pollock, *supra,* note 4, 149; Anson, *supra,* note 4, 34.

9 See Edward Avery Harriman, *Elements of the Law of Contract* (Boston, 1896), 25–26: "It is clear . . . that there is no general theory of contracts to be found in the common law; which explains the zeal with which more than one writer has turned to the Roman law for a scientific and rational analysis of contract. The reason that there is no common law theory of contracts is simple enough, however. Our ancestors were familiar with debt and covenant and account and assumpsit, but in their legal reasoning their inquiry always was, 'Will debt lie? or covenant? or account? or assumpsit?' We have, therefore, a theory of debt, a theory of covenant, of account, of assumpsit; but we have no theory of contracts except what has been developed in very recent times from a combination of the different theories already existing."

Again he drove towards his objective first by the route of history and then by the way of analysis. The influence of the three lectures on contracts has been extraordinary and profound.

In the lecture on the history of contract in the common law, Holmes's primary effort was to refute the prevailing theory that the English doctrine of consideration was "borrowed from the Roman law by the Chancery, and, after undergoing some modification there, passed into the common law." [10] That historical thesis was not merely the facile orthodoxy of Kent and Blackstone; it was supported, if somewhat hesitantly, by the authority of such contemporary scholars as Pollock and Anson.[11] Surely it is not surprising that Holmes, already convinced that Teutonic procedure rather than Roman substance had given the common law its distinctive features, saw reason to suspect that English doctrines with respect to consideration could be shown to be "of pure German descent." [12] The historical endeavor in his first lecture on contracts was to establish that inheritance. The analysis, very briefly summarized, took this form. The modern law's principle that for the enforcement of sealed contracts no consideration is required, and its companion requirement that for simple contracts consideration is a necessity, are both traceable to procedural rules of the ancient Teutonic law. To maintain an action for money due— "except when the liability was simply to pay damages for a wrongful act" [13]—the plaintiff was required to produce either the defendant's writing or transaction witnesses, persons who could testify that the defendant had received some *quid pro quo* from the plaintiff. The substantive significance of the seal in later law was born of the procedural importance of the writing, and the substantive requirement of consideration was derived from the procedural necessity of witnesses to the defendant's beneficial receipt of a *quid pro quo*. Holmes also briefly told of the process by which the action of assumpsit, developing through a later period of legal

[10] *CL*, 253.
[11] Pollock, *Contracts* (2nd ed., London, 1878), 151–157; Anson, *supra*, note 4, 29–35.
[12] *CL*, 252.
[13] *Id.*, 270.

history, found room for the enforcement of those undertakings on which the plaintiff had relied to his detriment. He thus had taken account, without significant reference to Roman law, of the two recognized faces of consideration—that which finds its expression in benefit (derived from debt), and that which bears the aspect of detriment (derived from assumpsit). By this ingenious analysis of history Holmes not only succeeded in reducing the influence of Roman law to a minimum, but he also suggested a course of development which made the consensual, as distinguished from the formal, contract a late arrival on the stage of English legal history. To do that was, of course, to degrade prevailing dogma with respect to the philosophical centrality of consent and will.

Research and analysis by later legal historians have done much to undermine Holmes's interpretation of the history of consideration. He would not be surprised, perhaps, that this has been the case, for he prefaced his discussion of the historical problem with the explicit caution that he offered "the explanation . . . with great hesitation, and . . . with a full appreciation of the objections which might be urged." [14] First Pollock, then Pollock and Maitland, and later James Barr Ames at the Harvard Law School, called attention to occasional inaccuracies in Holmes's reading of the authorities, and to a somewhat impulsive eagerness to aggrandize the action of debt and de-Romanize the law of consideration.[15] The impulse, very surely, came from those same biases which had colored the earlier lectures—the persuasion that the roots of the common law were Teutonic, not Roman, and the mistrust, related to that persuasion, of the Kantian drift of most legal theory which sought to Romanize the common law. The historical analysis in

[14] *Id.*, 254.

[15] Pollock, *Contracts* (3rd ed., London, 1881), xi–xvii; Pollock and Maitland, *History of English Law Before the Time of Edward I* (Cambridge, England, 1898), II, 214, note 2; Ames, "Simple Contracts Prior to Assumpsit," *Lectures on Legal History* (Cambridge, Mass., 1913), 122. Other powerful criticisms of Holmes's historical analysis are to be found in Salmond, "The History of the Law of Contract," *Essays in Jurisprudence and Legal History* (London, 1891), 173; Fifoot, *History and Sources of the Common Law: Tort and Contract* (London, 1949), 395–396. See also W. T. Barbour, *The Early History of Contract* (Oxford Studies in Social and Legal History, Vinogradoff, ed., 1914, vol. IV), *passim.*

the first lecture on contracts was, doubtless, somewhat marred by Holmes's eagerness to sustain a philosophical thesis, yet the effort was such a powerful *tour de force* that it gave a new direction to all later inquiries into the history of contract and consideration in English law. Had Holmes never offered his hypothesis it is doubtful whether Ames, Barbour, Salmond, and Holdsworth would have moved towards that more eclectic resolution of the historical puzzle which today is generally preferred.

In 1888, after Ames had published his articles on the history of assumpsit, in which he questioned the sufficiency of Holmes's account of the history of consideration, Holmes wrote to Ames expressing a slight sense of injury. "I read your articles on assumpsit with much interest," he said:

[I] frankly admit that my account leaves something to be desired . . . but . . . I am pretty confident that the main course of my discussion is sound, and I think you exaggerate the importance of what I left out. I shall venture to complain to you of a slight note of asperity when you refer to me. I had to cover a great deal of ground in my book. My ideas on each subject so far as I know were new, and have been accepted as such. It would have been remarkable if in some matters of detail I did not err. I am as ready to accept a correction as another, but with a man whose opinion I value and whose learning I respect I cannot but feel hurt if his only public expressions sound as if written with a slightly irritated adverseness. I make too much of it by writing it down, but I like to be frank with an old colleague. I have recommended the articles all the same to one or two intelligent foreigners in search of light.[16]

Ames quickly replied:

What you say about the tone of my criticism, when alluding to your views, in my articles on assumpsit, came upon me as a painful surprise. You have certainly read into my remarks a spirit of which I was wholly unconscious. I must admit that when I differed from you or Mr. Salmond or Judge Hare or Prof. Langdell I expressed my dissent somewhat baldly. Much reading of German law books probably accounts in large measure for my doubtless too blunt manner of putting things. No one, I am sure, values your work in the field of legal history more than I do

16 Dec. 4, 1888 (HLS).

and it has been in my mind to dedicate to you my book on the "History of Tort and Contract," with your permission. The idea was suggested to me by the example of Bruns in dedicating to Jhering his book on "Possession" notwithstanding the many differences of opinion between the two.[17]

Mollified by this response, Holmes replied: "Forget what I wrote —yet I am glad for the sake of your kind answer. I dare say the very high value I set on your opinion made me over-sensitive. Of course you understand I don't deprecate criticism. 'I pray you pass with your best violence.' " [18] Despite these softened words, Holmes never ceased to believe that Ames was prejudiced against him.[19] "He and I were very good friends, but he always had a whack at me when he could, perhaps because there was a slight touch of irony in my sincere appreciation of his adored Langdell." [20] It is not unlikely, I think, that if the prejudice existed it was partly the result of Ames's sympathy with the feeling of James Bradley Thayer that Holmes did not treat the Harvard Law School with entire fairness when in 1882 he resigned the professorship so recently awarded him. More significant, perhaps, than the questions relating to the reality and source of Ames's prejudice, is the fact that Holmes was so sensitive to criticism that he felt injured by Ames's mild expressions of disagreement.

In the first, historical, lecture, Holmes cast up one reflection which deserves special attention, since it became a favorite among his aphorisms:

It is sometimes thought more philosophical to say that a covenant is a formal contract, which survives alongside of the ordinary consensual contract, just as happened in the Roman law. But this is not a very instructive way of putting it . . . In one sense, everything is form which the law requires in order to make a promise binding over and above the mere expression of the promisor's will. Consideration is a form as

[17] Dec. 5, 1888 (HLS). The lectures referred to by Ames were never published as a separate volume. They were included in a posthumous collection of papers, *Lectures on Legal History and Miscellaneous Legal Essays* (Cambridge, Mass., 1913).

[18] Dec. 6, 1888 (HLS).

[19] See, e.g., *HLL*, I, 200, 727.

[20] To Wesley Newcomb Hohfeld, March 21, 1914 (copy, HLS).

much as a seal. The only difference is, that one form is of modern introduction, and has a foundation in good sense, or at least falls in with
our common habits of thought, so that we do not notice it, whereas the
other is a survival from an older condition of the law, and is less manifestly sensible, or less familiar.[21]

It would be easy, I think, to overlook the full import of this
reflection, which on its face seems to say little more than that the
modern law's requirement of consideration is, like the older requirement of a seal, merely a technical or formal necessity bearing
some, but slight, relationship to practical good sense. That suggestion, of very limited significance, is, of course, contained in
Holmes's reflection. The larger, though tacit, contention related
to the prevailing will theory of contracts. When Holmes contrasted "formal" and "consensual" obligations, he spoke in the traditional language of those jurists who had analyzed the history and
structure of contract obligations in Roman and common law, language which he himself had used in the opening portions of the
lecture. Like others, he had pointed out that the liability of one
who had undertaken a sealed obligation was not historically based
on the obligor's assumption of a consensual responsibility. Neither Savigny nor other Romanists had applied their will theory to
the "formal" contracts of Roman law, and their disciples in England had followed a parallel path when they dealt with the formal
contracts of the common law—those which were executed under
seal. When Holmes, in the passage which I have quoted, asserted
that contracts validated by consideration might properly be classified as "formal" contracts along with contracts under seal, he laid
the foundation for his analytic contention that consent and will
are of far less significance in the law of simple contracts than conventional theory supposed them to be. That this thesis was implicit in the quoted passage was stated very clearly in the draft of
a letter which remains among his papers—a letter evidently sent
to Professor E. A. Harriman of the Northwestern University Law
School in 1896. In that letter he wrote as follows:

[21] *CL,* 273.

I think that in enlightened theory, which we now are ready for, all contracts are formal, and that a tacit assumption to the contrary sometimes has led Mr. Langdell astray. I had this definitely in view in what I said . . . in my Common Law . . . I will add a word of argument. I do not mean merely that the consideration of the simple contract is as much a form as a seal, but that in the nature of a sound system of law (which deals mainly with externals) the making of a contract must be a question of form, even if the details of our law should be changed. There never was a more unfortunate expression used than "meeting of minds." It does not matter in the slightest degree whether minds meet or not. If the external expression on the one side and the other coincide, the fact that one party meant one thing and the other another does not prevent the making of the contract.[22]

Holmes's second lecture on contract—that in which he analytically examined its elements—was very clearly the most controversial of the three. Holmes's analysis, sometimes misunderstood, sometimes comprehended, has been denounced and rejected by all but a very few students. The proposition most frequently challenged seems to assert that the common law does not impose upon a promisor the duty to perform his contract. Pollock, in the introduction to the third edition of his *Contracts,* with this proposition in mind, spoke of Holmes's "disposition to push analytical curiosity even to paradox"; [23] Anson, in the second edition of his treatise on contracts, was no less critical of Holmes's analysis; [24] and Holland, in the second edition of his *Elements of Jurisprudence,* spoke

[22] Corrected draft of autograph letter dated Jan. 4, 1896 (HLS). The letter was responsive to an article published by Harriman in *Northwestern Law Review,* 4:97 (December 1895).

[23] At p. xx. The bulk of the introduction to the third edition was given to comment on Holmes's lectures on contracts as published in *The Common Law.* Though Pollock disagreed with some aspects of Holmes's interpretations of history and with some elements of his analysis he described the book as a whole as "most acute and ingenious" (p. xi).

[24] Concluding his comments on Holmes's analysis, Anson made this reflection: "It is well to fix our minds on the legal consequences of conduct and thus to escape so far as may be from confusing law with ethical speculation: but we cannot afford to disregard altogether the aspect in which men view the transactions with which they have to do" (*Principles of the English Law of Contract,* 2nd ed., Oxford, 1882, 10).

disparagingly of Holmes's "ingenious inversion of the theory of contract." [25]

Understanding of the paradox is possible, I think, only if one takes into account not only the immediate context of its assertion, but, once more, two of Holmes's basic skepticisms. The immediate context was this: Holmes had found that Pollock and Anson—both disciples of Savigny—had acclaimed the provisions of the Indian Contract Act in which "promise" was defined. These were the provisions:

(a) When one person signifies to another his willingness to do or to abstain from doing anything, with a view to obtaining the assent of that other to such act or abstinence, he is said to make a proposal: (b) When the person to whom the proposal is made signifies his assent thereto, the proposal is said to be accepted. A proposal when accepted becomes a promise.[26]

As Holmes read this definition it seemed to confine the field of contract to promises relating to the conduct of the promisor. He was quite justified in protesting that such a restrictive definition eliminates assurances which the common law has recognized to be contractual:

An assurance that it shall rain tomorrow, or that a third person shall paint a picture, may as well be a promise as one that the promisee shall receive from some source one hundred bales of cotton, or that the promisor will pay the promisee one hundred dollars. What is the difference in the cases? It is only in the degree of power possessed by the promisor over the event. He has none in the first case. He has equally

[25] At p. 194. A letter from Holland to Holmes, dated March 21, 1888 (HLS), indicates that Holmes had protested that Holland's description of the risk theory in the fourth edition of the *Jurisprudence* was inaccurate. Holland had there stated that by Holmes's analysis "the promisor undertakes either to perform or to be liable in damages . . ." (4th ed., 1888, 212–213). Holland, in response to this protest, so altered the quoted passage in the fifth and subsequent editions as merely to repeat Holmes's own language in *The Common Law:* "The only universal consequence of a legally binding promise is, that the law makes the promisor pay damages if the promised event does not come to pass." A more recent and savage attack on Holmes's analysis may be found in W. W. Buckland, *Some Reflections on Jurisprudence* (Cambridge, England, 1945), 96 *et seq.*

[26] Quoted, *CL*, 297–298.

little legal authority to make a man paint a picture, although he may have larger means of persuasion. He probably will be able to make sure that the promisee has the cotton. Being a rich man, he is certain to be able to pay the one hundred dollars, except in the event of some most improbable accident.[27]

It was from the context of this criticism of the definition commended by Pollock that Holmes suggested his paradoxical analysis.

The structure of the analysis may be seen in three propositions. (1) "A promise . . . is simply an accepted assurance that a certain event or state of things shall come to pass." (2) "If the promised event does not come to pass, the [promisor's] property is sold to satisfy the damages . . . which the promisee has suffered by the failure." (3) "The only universal consequence of a legally binding promise is, that the law makes the promisor pay damages if the promised event does not come to pass." [28] In another more general phrase Holmes summarized his analysis by asserting that it treats "a contract as the taking of a risk" [29]—a risk, that is, that the promised event or conduct will not occur. On many other occasions, both in private correspondence and in public utterance, Holmes elaborated on these succinct propositions and somewhat clarified their meaning. In a letter to Pollock, for instance, he rejected the suggestion that his theory of contract made it a promise to pay damages or perform the promised act. He stated that his assertion was simply this: that a contract is "an act imposing a liability to damages *nisi*. You commit a tort and are liable. You commit a contract and are liable *unless* the event agreed upon, over which you may have no, and never have absolute control, comes to pass." [30] As judge he was able, on several occasions, to smuggle his paradox into an opinion, thus securing the satisfaction of moving a theory of jurisprudence towards an actuality of law.[31]

27 *Id.*, 298–299.

28 *Id.*, 299, 301.

29 *Id.*, 301.

30 *HPL*, I, 177.

31 E.g., *Brown* v. *Eastern Slate Co.*, 134 Mass. 590, 592 (1883); *Globe Refining Co.* v. *Landa Cotton Oil Co.*, 190 U.S. 540, 543 (1903). See also "The Path of the Law," *CLP*, 167, 174–175.

It is, I think, quite clear that Holmes's analysis of contract was derived from two of his basic skepticisms. It will be remembered, perhaps, that in the lectures on jurisprudence which he delivered at Harvard in 1872 he had questioned the Austinian analysis of "duty" and suggested that it failed to draw a line between taxes and penalties.[32] In the course of his comments Holmes had there stated that

the notion of duty involves something more than a tax on a certain course of conduct . . . The word imports the existence of an absolute wish on the part of the power imposing it to bring about a certain course of conduct, and to prevent the contrary. A legal duty cannot be said to exist if the law intends to allow the person supposed to be subject to it an option at a certain price . . . As liability to a civil action is not a penalty or sanction of itself creating a duty, so, on the other hand, it does not necessarily imply culpability, or a breach of duty, as Austin thought, who looked at the law too much as a criminal lawyer. The object of the law is to accomplish an external result.[33]

I have already suggested that if one accepts Holmes's very restrictive concept of "duty" ("the test of a legal duty is the absolute nature of the command") it is hard to refute the contention that the existence of a common-law liability to pay damages for breach of contract does not signify the existence of a duty to perform one's promise. Had Holmes, with clarity, restated his restrictive concept of legal duty in the lecture on the elements of contract, perhaps his critics would have been less shocked by his paradoxical suggestion than they were. They would in any case have been compelled to show the inadequacy of his definition of duty, a definition which he unhappily failed to make explicit in his lecture. In the lecture there was but one brief passage in which, remembering his earlier criticism of the Austinian alliance of fault and duty, one may faintly hear the echo of that criticism:

The law does not inquire, as a general thing, how far the accomplishment of an assurance touching the future is within the power of the promisor. In the moral world it may be that the obligation of a

[32] See *supra*, p. 76.   [33] *Am. L. Rev.*, 6:724–725.

promise is confined to what lies within the reach of the will of the promisor . . . But unless some consideration of public policy intervenes, I take it that a man may bind himself at law that any future event shall happen.[34]

It might be urged, with some force, that Holmes dealt with contractual obligations in the lecture not upon the basis of definitions suggested some eight years earlier, but upon quite different foundations. As I shall shortly indicate, there were, quite clearly, new foundations for his thesis—foundations which, so far as we can tell, had not been involved in his earlier discussion of the problem. It is also clear, however, that his earlier criticism of Austin's definition of duty played a not insignificant part in the paradox of 1880. In 1919, writing to Professor Walter Wheeler Cook, then at the Columbia University Law School, Holmes made some revealing comments on his risk theory of contract. "I agree," he said,

that in one sense it is not desirable to express the position of a contractor as I expressed it. Of course it is not the theory of the common law that he has an option. I dare say that it even might be proper to describe a breach as illegal, although early in my legal studies I was perplexed to discover the difference between conduct that merely was taxed or had to be paid for. I asked myself what is the difference between the mill acts and conversion, for which latter, as in the former case, you simply have to pay the value of the thing taken . . . The only legal difference that I could discover was that a contract to do the act called illegal was void and that there was no contribution between wrongdoers. The reasons that I thought and still think my mode of statement useful (though the majority of the profession no doubt would view it with repugnance) is that no contract depends for its performance solely on the will of the contractor, and that apart from special objections to wagers a man may contract for a future event that is wholly outside of his power, but the non-occurrence of which will be a breach, none the less.[35]

As we have already seen, Holmes considered that the external standards of liability in tort and crime might serve not merely to

[34] *CL*, 299.   [35] Feb. 25, 1919 (copy, HLS).

drive Kantian metaphysics from the field of jurisprudence, but to undermine the thesis of Austin that moral culpability is an essential element in legal liability. His risk theory of contract served the same anti-Austinian purpose, for it showed that there are some promisors who are liable in damages when their accepted assurances are not fulfilled though they are wholly without moral fault. If a single theory of contract obligation must embrace every type of contract which the common law recognizes, then one may be compelled to agree with Holmes that "the only universal consequence of a legally binding promise is, that the law makes the promisor pay damages if the promised event does not come to pass." [36] One may, however, feel that the longing for universality is somewhat intemperate when it demands that principle be so formulated as to make exception prescribe the rule. Though it seems clear that Holmes was right in his contention that Austin's principle of culpability is refuted whenever a contract in which the thing promised is not within the promisor's control is recognized as valid, there seems no adequate justification for denying the existence of a primary obligation to perform a contract when performance is within the control of the promisor.[37] Perhaps it was a combination of a liking for paradox and a longing for universality of principle which encouraged Holmes to formulate his risk theory of contract.[38]

However much the anti-Austinian inclinations of Holmes may have contributed to the zest of his search for a theory of contract

[36] *CL*, 301.

[37] See Harriman, *Elements of the Law of Contracts* (Boston, 1896), 302–303.

[38] In a later volume I shall consider the foundations of Holmes's "bad man" theory of law as he developed it in "The Path of the Law," *CLP*, 167, 170 *et seq*. At this point it is worth noticing, however, that the theory was intimately related to the risk theory of contract. In the Lowell Lecture on Void and Voidable Contracts, Holmes clearly revealed the relationship. "If we look at the law as it would be regarded by one who had no scruples against doing anything which he could do without incurring legal consequences, it is obvious that the main consequence attached by law to a contract is a greater or less possibility of having to pay money. The only question from the purely legal point of view is whether the promisor will be compelled to pay" (*CL*, 317).

which would discard fault as an element of liability, it seems clear
that the deeper impulse was his revulsion from the will theory of
the civilians. The alternative theory of risk offered refuge from
that Roman tyranny. If Holmes's theory were accepted, it would,
in his opinion, have "the advantage of freeing the subject from
the superfluous theory that contract is a qualified subjection of
one will to another, a kind of limited slavery." The common-law
realist was unwilling to overlook the unquestionable fact that a
promisor's relation to his promisee is not "a servitude *ad hoc*." [39]
The common law does not make its sanctions available to bend
one man's conduct to another man's will. "It never interferes until a promise has been broken, and therefore cannot possibly be
performed according to its tenor." [40] Even in the Court of Equity
when a contract is specifically enforced, it is virtually never possible for performance of all elements of the promisor's obligation
to be compelled. Would we not do better, then, in our philosophy
of law, to recognize and respect the actual limitations of public
power and cease pretending that by entering contractual relations
with another a man subjects himself to the government of that
other's will or to a new common will embodied in agreement?
Holmes's denial of that subjection and his recognition of the actual limitations on the powers of the courts of common law led
him to the radical conclusion that there is no legal duty to perform one's contracts. If the conclusion involves a somewhat per-
verse refusal to give appropriate weight to common expectation
and common parlance, one must, none the less, acknowledge that
Holmes's paradoxical thesis provided a useful reminder that legal
philosophy must bear some relation to legal fact. At the time when
he spoke, the danger was by no means inconsiderable that a subjective theory of contract, grounded in a metaphysics of will,
would become the ruling dogma. Holmes's risk theory, at the
time when he outlined it, was so paradoxical and antagonizing
that it may not have advanced the basic cause which he endeavored to serve—the substitution of objective for subjective stand-

[39] *CL*, 300.   [40] *Id.*

ards of liability—yet it did remind opposing jurists that they too had allowed logic to carry them beyond the realm of common sense.

Thoughtful students of recent legal history have suggested that there was more merit in Holmes's paradox than his contemporaries recognized. They find in an expanding collectivism, an increasing standardization of contracts, and an extension of public interest in private relations a notable tendency to make risk rather than performance the core of contractual obligation.

> To the extent that strikes, shortages of materials, or national or international policies affect the ability to perform—and they do so to an increasing extent—contract is no longer primarily directed towards performance. It is essentially the basis on which the court determines how risk of non-performance shall be distributed.[41]

Though Holmes did not, I think, see this tendency towards collectivism as a social justification for his paradoxical syllogism, he did, I take it, see a clear relationship between his risk theory of contract and the objectivity of standards of contract liability. Surely it is a demonstrable fact that the substitution of objective for subjective standards of liability in contract contributed significantly to the recent developments of doctrine described above.

The most important contributions of Holmes's analysis of contract, while related to his risk theory, were not dependent upon it. The first of these contributions was included in the lecture on Elements. It was an essentially new analysis of consideration—an analysis which effectively emphasized the element of bargain in the common law of contracts. Those jurists who preferred to look upon consideration as an Anglicized version of *causa*, and accepted Savigny's analysis, had paid little heed to the element of bargain among the ingredients of contract. They saw the intention to enter into a binding contractual relationship as the hallmark of con-

---

[41] W. Friedmann, "Changing Functions of Contract in the Common Law," *University of Toronto Law Journal*, 9:14, 39–40 (1951). See also Friedmann, *Law in a Changing Society* (London, 1959), 122–123; Llewellyn, "What Price Contract? An Essay in Perspective," *Yale Law Journal*, 40:704, 717–718, note 39.

tractual obligation and sought to cast consideration in the mold of *causa.* Holmes urged that this was a wresting of English cases from their base of common business sense. Properly understood, the doctrine of consideration is nothing more esoteric than a rule of give and take, a rule which requires of promisor and promisee that each provide something—whether it be money, promise, action, or object—as the equivalent of what he has received. "It is the essence of a consideration, that, by the terms of agreement, it is given and accepted as the motive or inducement of the promise. Conversely, the promise must be made and accepted as the conventional motive or inducement for furnishing the consideration." [42] If one deals with the cases in the terms prescribed by this test, the task of distinguishing a condition necessary for the performance of a promise and a consideration essential to make the promise binding is rendered far less perplexing. "Suppose that a man is desirous of having a cask of brandy carried from Boston to Cambridge, and that a truckman . . . says that he will carry it, and it is delivered to him accordingly." [43] Delivery of the cask might be looked upon merely as a condition which must be met before the truckman can begin to perform his gratuitous promise, or it might be seen as the bargained-for equivalent of the carrier's undertaking. In Holmes's judgment, whether delivery is to be treated as condition or as consideration depends upon how it was treated by promisor and promisee. "The same thing," he said, "may be a consideration or not, as it is dealt with by the parties." [44] Did Holmes, by making the existence or nonexistence of a contract dependent upon the reciprocal aim of the parties, allow subjectivism, in the end, to control his theory of contract? I take it that he did not. Though the lecture on elements did not

[42] *CL,* 293. Writing to John C. H. Wu in 1923, Holmes clarified the meaning of "conventional inducement." "I have called consideration the *conventional inducement* to the promise, i.e., that which by the terms of the contract as interpreted by the Court is contemplated as inducing the promise" (Harry C. Shriver, *Justice Oliver Wendell Holmes: His Book Notices and Uncollected Letters and Papers,* New York, 1936, 170).

[43] *CL,* 290.

[44] *Id.,* 292.

itself contain any very clear statement that courts should be less interested in ascertaining the actual inducing impulse behind each promise than in discovering what manifested spirit motivated the agreement, the last of the contract lectures made it quite clear that he saw the objective standard as no less controlling in the law of contract than it was in the law of torts and of crime. It may furthermore be urged, with some force, that when he said "the root of the whole matter is the relation of reciprocal conventional inducement" [45] he meant the word "conventional" to suggest that the search was not for actual, but for manifested, motivation.[46]

Before turning to the development of Holmes's argument for an objective standard of contract liability, one more word should be said of his analysis of consideration. He believed that if his analysis were accepted a much vexed question in the law would be largely if not wholly eliminated. Doubtless he referred to the views of Savigny, as restated in the Indian Contract Act and by Pollock, when he said that "it is laid down, with theoretical truth, that, besides the assurance or offer on the one side, there must be an acceptance on the other." But, he added, "I find it hard to think of a case where a simple contract fails to be made, which could not be accounted for on other grounds, generally by the want of relation between assurance or offer and consideration as reciprocal inducements each of the other." [47]

This passage has been read as the convincing assertion of a principle that "all the rules of offer and acceptance can and should be reduced to rules of consideration." [48] Though that would seem to give a somewhat broader meaning to the suggestion than Holmes intended it to have,[49] the purport of the reflection clearly favored the concentration of analytic attention upon the formal and objective aspects of obligation and a reduced concern for the subjectivities of assent. He believed that if, to the fullest extent

[45] *Id.*, 293–294.
[46] See also note 42, *supra.*
[47] *Id.*, 303.
[48] Harriman, *Contracts, supra*, note 30, 85.
[49] See Clarence D. Ashley, *The Law of Contracts* (Boston, 1911), 69–70.

possible, problems with respect to the formation of contracts could be translated into terms of consideration, much misleading talk about the necessity of a meeting of minds would be discarded from discussion. It was this emphasis on the objectivity in the law of contracts which led Holmes to favor the doctrine, condemned by Langdell, that a letter of acceptance takes effect on mailing when the use of that method of communication was contemplated by the offeror.[50]

The last of the three lectures on contract—that on void and voidable contracts—was the one in which Holmes made his most important and influential contributions to theory. It had been the assumption of previous commentators that though parties to an agreement had expressed their mutual assent, no contract was born of that assent if the expression was made under a mistake or had been induced by fraud, duress, or misrepresentation.[51] Though Thomas Erskine Holland was destined soon to change his opinion, he had spoken an orthodoxy of contemporaneous English thought when he asserted, in the first edition of the *Elements of Jurisprudence,* that a contract resulting from offer and acceptance would be vitiated by mistake, fraud, or duress.[52] The prevailing assumption, in other words, was that the assent required in all valid contracts must be "genuine." Holmes opened his third lecture on contracts with a bold challenge of traditional doctrine:

50 Holmes discussed this matter in *The Common Law,* 305–307. Cf. C. C. Langdell, *A Summary of the Law of Contracts* (2nd ed., Boston, 1880), 15–21. It was in connection with this problem that Langdell had made the startling observation: "It has been claimed that the purposes of substantial justice, and the interests of the contracting parties as understood by themselves, will be best served by holding that the contract is complete the moment the letter of acceptance is mailed; and cases have been put to show that the contrary view would produce not only unjust but absurd results. The true answer to this argument is, that it is irrelevant . . ." (*id.,* 20–21).

51 See, e.g., Pollock, *Contracts* (2nd ed., London, 1878), chapter viii. Pollock there (at 383) acknowledged his indebtedness to Savigny for clarifying the problem in his "masterful essay."

52 *Elements of Jurisprudence* (Oxford, 1880), 176–177. Though Holland repeated this statement in his second edition in 1882 (p. 199), in the third edition (1886) at page 216 he accepted Holmes's analysis.

When a contract fails to be made, although the usual forms have been gone through with, the ground of failure is commonly said to be mistake, misrepresentation, or fraud. But I shall try to show that these are merely dramatic circumstances, and that the true ground is the absence of one or more of the primary elements, which have been shown, or are seen at once, to be necessary to the existence of a contract.[53]

Holmes proceeded to deal with the problem in issue by showing that in every case in which conventional doctrine found that a contract had never been formed by reason of mistake, fraud, or misrepresentation, the true reason for its nonexistence was that either there was no second party to the contract; the parties said different things; or essential terms, seemingly consistent, were in fact inconsistent as used. The first of the three situations Holmes set forth in these terms:

If a man goes through the form of making a contract with A through B as A's agent, and B is not in fact the agent of A, there is no contract, because there is only one party. The promise offered to A has not been accepted by him, and no consideration has moved from him. In such a case, although there is generally mistake on one side and fraud on the other, it is very clear that no special doctrine need be resorted to, because the primary elements of a contract . . . are not yet present.[54]

Holmes made his second point by an analysis of the famous case of *The Peerless*—the case in which the defendant agreed to buy and the plaintiff to sell a cargo of cotton "to arrive *ex Peerless* from Bombay." [55] The plaintiff meant a vessel named the *Peerless* sailing from Bombay in December; the defendant meant another vessel of the same name, sailing from Bombay in October. Neither party was aware of the existence of the vessel meant by the other. The holding of the court—that the defendant was not bound to accept the cotton—had been explained by Pollock, as by Anson, on the ground of mutual mistake. To Holmes, this way of putting it seemed misleading:

[53] *CL*, 308.
[54] *Id.*, 308–309.
[55] *Raffles* v. *Wichelhaus*, 2 H. & C. 906 (1864).

The law has nothing to do with the actual state of the parties' minds. In contract, as elsewhere, it must go by externals, and judge parties by their conduct . . . The true ground of the decision was not that each party meant a different thing from the other, as is implied by the explanation which has been mentioned, but that each said a different thing. The plaintiff offered one thing, the defendant expressed his assent to another.[56]

The third class of cases to which Holmes referred were those in which essential terms, seemingly consistent, are in fact inconsistent. "Suppose that A agreed to buy, and B agreed to sell, 'these barrels of mackerel,' and that the barrels in question turn out to contain salt." Orthodoxy says that the contract fails "due to the fact of a difference in kind between the actual subject-matter and that to which the intention of the parties was directed." [57] Holmes once more suggested that a sounder justification for invalidity was to be found in the basic rules with respect to the essential elements of contract. "The contract is void, not because of any misrepresentation, but . . . because two of its essential terms [on the one hand, the contents of certain barrels; on the other, mackerel] are repugnant, and their union is insensible." [58]

It is not easy, perhaps, to discover issues of large philosophical moment in barrels of salt and barrels of mackerel. Yet if one goes beyond Holmes's succinct and tight analysis of particular and earthy instances to the thesis which inspired the three lectures on contract, one must recognize that he was urging a revolutionary change in legal thought. Had he seen fit to state his position in more rounded generalities—not merely to speak to the learned few who took his frame of reference for granted, but to instruct an intelligent audience in the philosophic order of battle—his lectures would, doubtless, have had a more immediate impact on professional opinion than they did. He had not yet revealed—and probably had not yet discovered—his talents as orator, and therefore spoke with the arrogance of learning, an arrogance which as-

[56] *CL*, 309. Cf. *id.*, 205–206. Of the *Raffles* case, Anson said that "the minds of the parties never really met, and there is no true consent" (*Contract*, 1879, 122).
[57] *CL*, 310.
[58] *Id.*, 311.

sumed that his audience was as much at home as he was in the world of jurisprudence. One may assume, I think, that the lectures as delivered were not as taut as they were when published, but it was through the written rather than through the spoken word that Holmes hoped to make his thought known. He did not, I feel sure, expect to convert the visible audience. He hoped, instead, that over a rather long course of time his thesis would take hold of the minds of judges and jurists and thus become a creative element in the common law.

This hope was surely realized. The second edition of Holland's influential *Elements of Jurisprudence,* published after its author had read *The Common Law,* repudiated the subjective or will theory of contract liability and urged that in the field of contracts "as elsewhere, the law books, not at the will itself, but at the will as voluntarily manifested." [59] Though Holland did not by footnote or other reference vouch Holmes in support of objectivity of standards, his letters to Holmes and his constant references to *The Common Law* in other parts of the work on Jurisprudence make it unmistakably clear that Holmes's analysis had been a significant influence behind his repudiation of the doctrine of Savigny, Pollock, and Anson. In his third edition, published in 1886, Holland, to be sure, credited Professor Rudolf Leonhard of Göttingen (later to be the translator of *The Common Law*) with the effective refutation of the will theory of contract and did not, save incidentally, seem to ascribe originating responsibility to Holmes. [60] In the long run, however, it was the argument of Holmes, rather than of the German jurists, which had the greatest influence in England and the United States. One may be thoroughly confident that it was through his reading of Holmes—both as jurist and as judge—that

[59] At 194–195. Cf. footnote 52, *supra.*

[60] At 213. Leonhard's work, *Der Irrtum bei nichtigen Vertragen* (Berlin), was published after *The Common Law.* It dealt only with the Roman law. In the draft of his letter to Harriman (*supra,* note 22) Holmes had expressed mild resentment that Holland had given others than himself credit for rejecting subjective standards in contract matters. "I had this definitely in mind in what I said about void and voidable contracts in my Common Law, although Mr. Holland at one time at least supposed it a later German device."

Samuel Williston, the father of contemporary doctrine with respect to contract in Anglo-American law, was led to an acceptance of the fundamentals of Holmes's doctrine.

In the last two of the published lectures—those on succession—Holmes dealt with complex issues of theory and of history to which he had given ingenious attention in his earliest essays and in his annotations of Kent.[61] The lectures, for all their technical brilliance, did not, like the others, bespeak a philosophy of law. They do not, accordingly, deserve that attention which I have given to the other lectures. Their central thesis was that the common law had made both reasoning and unreasoning use of fiction to allow one man to succeed to the rights of another. Succession to the rights of person deceased, whether the successor was heir or executor, was traced to the subtle fiction of the Roman law by which ancestor and heir were treated as one *persona,* thus denying, as it were, that a succession or transfer had occurred. Holmes then called attention to the willingness of Bracton to extend the fiction which justified inheritance to successions *inter vivos* by the ingenious pretension that a purchaser was a quasi heir. Thus it came about that "the mode of thought and the conceptions made possible by the doctrine of inheritance have . . . silently modified the law as to dealings between the living." [62]

This structure of fictions served to explain how a purchaser of land inherited, as it were, the rights of the seller. It did not, however, provide an answer to the perplexing question why a disseisor of land—one who possesses it wrongfully, and therefore cannot pretend to be a successor to the rightful owner—is entitled to claim the advantage of easements benefiting the land. "How comes it . . . that one who has neither title nor possession [of the easement] is so far favored? The answer is to be found, not in reasoning, but in a failure to reason." [63] The archaic tendency to personify property, not unlike that which lay behind the noxal actions, seemed

---

61 "The Arrangement of the Law—Privity," *Am. L. Rev.,* 7:46 (October 1872), *Harv. L. Rev.,* 44:738; *Commentaries,* IV, *480, note 1.

62 *CL,* 353.

63 *Id.,* 382.

to Holmes to explain the anomaly. It was natural for men in the early ages of the law to treat things as persons and to speak as if lands had rights and owed obligations:

The language of the law of easements was built up out of similes drawn from persons at a time when the *noxæ deditio* was still familiar; and then, as so often happens, language reacted upon thought, so that conclusions were drawn as to the rights themselves from the terms in which they happened to be expressed. When one estate was said to be enslaved to another, or a right of way was said to be a quality or incident of a neighboring piece of land, men's minds were not alert to see that these phrases were only so many personifying metaphors, which explained nothing unless the figure of speech was true.[64]

The central problem to which Holmes's entire study of succession was directed was to explain how it had come about that in some circumstances "a man can sue or be sued on a promise in which he had no part." [65] He was led, accordingly, to an analytical and historical consideration of so-called covenants running with estates in land. The fictions of inheritance and the metaphors of personification could not explain how it came to be that contractual rights and obligations relating to lands—undertakings which did not produce easements—could, in some circumstances, benefit and bind persons who were not parties to the contract in question. Holmes's elaborate and searching treatment of this problem need not here be considered. Neither his interpretation of history nor his analysis of the controlling concepts has been accepted by all scholars, but on this matter, as on so many others, his originating study provided a new starting point for inquiry.[66] In a later volume we shall have the opportunity to consider the extent to which Holmes the judge, when he dealt with covenants running with the land, built decisions upon foundations laid by Holmes the scholar.

[64] *Id.,* 382–383.

[65] *Id.,* 341.

[66] See in general Charles E. Clark, *Real Covenants and Other Interests which "Run with Land"* (2nd ed., Chicago, 1947). See also Henry Upson Sims, "The Law of Real Covenants: Exceptions to the Restatement of the Subject by the American Law Institute," *Cornell Law Quarterly,* 30:1 (1944). James Barr Ames was not in agreement with elements in Holmes's interpretations of history. See his lecture "Covenant," *Lectures on Legal History,* 97, 100.

In the back of his own copy of *The Common Law* Holmes listed the reviews of and comments on the book which had come to his attention. Pollock's unsigned notice in *The Saturday Review,* later supplemented by glowing praises of the volume in the dedicatory letter prefacing the first edition of his treatise on *The Law of Torts,* probably did more than any other published comment to satisfy Holmes that his years of grinding labor had been justified. Though Pollock, as we have already seen, was not convinced that all of Holmes's theses were valid—particularly those relating to contracts—he saw *The Common Law* as another proof that English lawyers were "being outrun by their American brethren in the scientific and historical criticism of English legal institutions and ideas." He called particular attention to the fact that Holmes did not "write as a member of any school of theorists or critics, and in the handling of his subjects he owes, apparently, very little to previous authors of the same kind." He further noted —perhaps to Holmes's irritation—similarities between the talents of the Holmeses, father and son. "Observers of hereditary talent may . . . note in his subtle and original following out of analogies and presentation of familiar elements in fresh lights a sufficiently plain continuance of like powers which, exercised on more popular and various topics, have for many years charmed readers of English on both sides of the Atlantic in the works of Dr. O. W. Holmes the father." [67] For the most part, American reviewers spoke with similar enthusiasm of *The Common Law,* though in *The Nation* Henry Ware Holland (in an unsigned notice) said that the book was "injured by long philosophical discussions of intent and the like, which, if they were worth preserving anywhere, would only be so in a condensed form, as a part of a complete philosophical treatment of the subject, which this volume makes no claim to be." [68]

In many ways the most critically perceptive review of the book

[67] *Saturday Review,* 51:758 (June 11, 1881).

[68] *Nation,* 32:464 (June 30, 1881). Other more favorable notices in American periodicals were: *Am. L. Rev.,* 15:331 (May 1881); *Albany Law Review,* 23:380 (May 7, 1881); *id.,* 26:484 (Dec. 16, 1882). For a very commendatory review in a Scottish periodical see *Journal of Jurisprudence,* 25:646 (1881).

was the anonymous notice in the *Spectator*. The reviewer saw Holmes's work as a brilliant and original combination of the historical methods of Maine and the analytical methods of Holland, and emphasized the degree to which Holmes's mastery of case law through his edition of Kent and his practical experience at the bar had led him to eschew "jurisprudence in the air" and "to keep his feet firmly fixed on the solid ground of reported legal decisions." The reviewer did, however, see in this extraordinary respect for the actualities of common law a somewhat unfortunate tendency, a tendency to treat its doctrines with too great respect:

> The plain truth is that our author is too much of an apologist. He hardly distinguishes, in his own mind, between the doctrines of the common law and the dictates of good sense . . . He farther seems to write sometimes as though he held that to prove that Savigny's doctrines differed from the doctrines of the common law, was necessarily the same thing as showing that the German jurist had fallen into demonstrable error. Mr. Holmes, in short, deals with the texts of the common law in the same way in which speculative but orthodox theologians deal with the texts of Scripture. They devote a great deal of ability to showing that certain doctrines are in themselves true, and at the same time labour, with great assiduity, to prove that these doctrines may be deduced from, or are consistent with, a mass of texts which, to impartial readers, seem to have but a remote bearing on the matter in hand. The textualist, whether he be a jurist or a theologian, is apt to make his readers feel that the force of a sound and sensible theory is weakened rather than strengthened by the mass of authorities cited in its support.[69]

The reviewer who thus charged Holmes with the intellectual sins of a theologian did not realize, we may assume, that the opening pages of *The Common Law,* in their initial version, had suggested that Langdell, "the greatest living legal theologian," represented those powers of darkness which the book would seek to vanquish.[70] It is the fact, of course, that the reviewer had one fault of theologians in mind, and Holmes another. It was not Langdell's

[69] *Spectator,* 55:745, 746 (Literary Supplement, June 3, 1882).
[70] See *supra,* p. 156.

respect for reported decisions of the courts of common law which led Holmes to look upon the Dean's proclivity as theological. It was rather his tendency to subordinate considerations of convenience and expediency to the rule of logic which led Holmes to label him a theologian in the law. The *Spectator's* reviewer of *The Common Law,* by contrast, saw Holmes's respect for reported decisions as well-nigh reverential. The reviewer did not explicitly say that among the sources of this reverence was a deep conviction that if the facts of English legal history were not discovered, and having been discovered were not respected, understanding of the common law might suffer those same metaphysical distortions which had warped comprehension of the Roman law. The reviewer did, however, emphasize those larger significances of the lectures which other critics seemed to overlook. He did, in particular, call attention to the light which Holmes's emphasis on the externality of legal standards cast upon the history of morals. He saw in Holmes's thesis an explanation of the apparent paradox that as civilization has advanced it has shown increasing hostility to the sense of moral responsibility. The critic denied that Holmes's insistence that for legal purposes standards must become increasingly external contained an inference that "as civilization advances, the moral judgment of mankind becomes less exacting." He found the opposite inference in Holmes's thesis. "In early ages, grown men, like children at all times, make no distinction between a hurt and a wrong; every trespasser is held to be a wrong-doer. As the moral sense develops, legislators and judges realize the fact that many acts are hurtful which, estimated simply by the feelings or intentions of the doer, are not wrong. Further reflection shows that the aim of law is to check hurtful acts. Hence the law becomes, in one sense, unmoral, just because men have learnt to distinguish between harmful and immoral conduct . . . The more wide the distinction between vengeance and the infliction of legal penalties prevailing in any given society, the higher, we may be sure, is its condition, both of civilization and of moral sensibility." [71]

[71] *Spectator,* 55:746–747.

In the lectures on *The Common Law* Holmes had revealed the texture of his mind and the structure of his jurisprudence. In that total achievement differing elements, of course, had varying import. One may see in the search for objectivity in legal standards, whether they relate to crime, tort, or contract, an awareness that the days of individualism were passing. One may find in the distrust of metaphysical abstractions, whether derived from Kant or from Hegel, a pragmatist's preference for concreteness. One may see in the distrust of the "featureless generality" [72] with respect to equality a Darwinian recognition of the brutality of nature, and of man as part of nature. In the effort to discover Teutonic rather than Roman origins for the institutions and principles of the common law, one may discover a romanticism of spirit. In any case, one can find in *The Common Law* reflections of nearly every facet of a complex mind and temperament.

[72] *CL*, 111.

I0

Professor of Law

The close attention which I have given to *The Common Law* may have seemed to place a book, rather than a living person, at the center of the stage. That placement is no accident, for it is clear that between 1875 and 1881 all of Holmes's energies which were not given to the practice of the law were committed to the essays which became the lectures, and the lectures which became the book. So far as one can see from surviving letters and other traces of Holmes's life from day to day, it was almost wholly absorbed in work. There are no indications that in this period, as in the later years of his Massachusetts judgeship, he made it a Friday evening habit to go to the theater. Dining clubs and other centers of sociability did not yet distract his attention from labor, and there is no indication that he had yet become a tea-time caller upon the ladies of Boston. One has the impression that he and Mrs. Holmes, in their apartment at the top of Beacon Street, set themselves almost wholly apart from the world around them. There were, to be sure, occasional week-ends at the house which they had bought in 1873 at Mattapoisett, supplemented by a few weeks at the end of each summer at that retreat near Mr. Shattuck's house. An occasional visitor from England appeared on the Boston and Buzzards Bay scenes, but for the most part Holmes and his wife went their isolated way.[1] While he worked on his

1 James Bryce in 1891 recalled an occasion when he and Holmes ten years before had sat together on the beach at Mattapoisett, "looking at the sweet shim-

essays and his lectures she evidently stitched her striking land-scapes in embroidery. In the spring of 1880 fourteen of her em-broidered panels were on exhibition at the Boston Art Museum. A critic in the Boston *Daily Advertiser,* speaking of her work, said:

> This is, probably, the most remarkable needlework ever done. It stands quite alone, and there is nothing in the least like it with which to compare it. Mrs. Holmes who, as Miss Dixwell, contributed embroi-dery to some of the earlier art exhibitions, is an artist; but, instead of using paints and canvas, she makes her pictures with silks and satin.[2]

That this acclaim bespoke something more serious than the paro-chial enthusiasm for the talent of Dr. Holmes's daughter-in-law is indicated by notices published a year later in the *Nation* and in the *American Architect and Building News* when the same four-teen panels were exhibited in New York at the Ladies Decorative Arts Society. The anonymous reviewer in the *Nation* described the panels as "works of fine art, of a quality, so far as we know, unique," adding

> [Mrs. Holmes's] pictures are entirely free and individual, being in noth-ing more remarkable than in their avoidance of the semblance of con-ventionality, good or bad. In fine, she is an American artist of notice-able qualities, and one speedily gets beyond thought of the materials she employs in looking at the effects she presents.[3]

A no less enthusiastic review by the sensitive and knowing art critic, Mariana Griswold Van Rensselaer, in the pages of the *American Architect,* described the works as "more like painting with threads than embroidery in the proper sense," and went on to say:

> Mrs. Holmes uses motives drawn from nature, and uses them—not in the conventionalized oriental style, faintly copied in so much home

---

mering water before we plunged joyful limbs into it, drinking our fill of our physical pleasure as to the purity of which in the eyes of the austerest Stoic, we had never any controversy" (Nov. 25, 1891; HLS) .

[2] Boston *Daily Advertiser*, Monday, April 19, 1880, p. 2, c. 3.

[3] *Nation,* 32:286 (April 21, 1881) .

work, merely to *suggest* natural effects—but to actually reproduce those effects in a kindred way to the way in which they are reproduced by pictorial art. It is a difficult enterprise, of course, and one not to be lightly undertaken by a person possessed of less exquisite taste, and less accomplished drawing, and a less pleasing sense of color than are possessed by Mrs. Holmes.[4]

Such comments as these make it easy to believe that Mrs. Holmes was blessed with an extraordinary talent, and make it particularly mystifying to comprehend the impulse which led her, when she moved to Washington, to destroy all but a very few of her landscapes in embroidery.[5]

Of Holmes's relations with his family after the move of 1875 from Dr. Holmes's house, there are few surviving records. When his sister Amelia's husband, Turner Sargent, died in 1877 Holmes became involved in the probate of his estate, but there are no indications that Holmes and his sister were close to one another, or that Holmes followed with any special sympathy the misfortunes of his younger brother, Edward, whose ill health had compelled him to withdraw from practice and seek relief from sickness in varying European and American resorts—a search which ended with his death in 1884 at the age of thirty-eight. A few letters from John Holmes, the Doctor's gentle and seclusive brother, reveal an intimate affection between nephew and uncle. Not surprisingly, in view of the slight distance between 10 and 196 Beacon Street, letters between father and son are very few and tell little of Holmes's

[4] *The American Architect and Building News*, 9:210, 211 (April 30, 1881). Oscar Wilde, after spending an evening in the Holmes's "rooms" at 10 Beacon Street, wrote to Dr. Holmes asking the Doctor to remember him "most kindly to your son, and to that Penelope of New England whose silken pictures I found so beautiful" (autograph letter, undated, Wilde to Dr. Holmes, in Houghton Library). In a letter to Baroness Moncheur, written on January 16, 1910, Holmes recalled the evening with Wilde: "I have been rediscovering Oscar Wilde. I thought he was only a witty humbug, though I remember the extraordinary vividness with which he once told us stories in our rooms. But now I am impressed with his English, his imagination even, his insight, as well as his wit." (Copy, HLS)

[5] I was told of this destructive act by Mrs. James B. Ayer of Canton, Massachusetts, a friend of Mrs. Holmes's.

relations with his parents. After the son became a member of the Saturday Club, in 1880, one may assume that the two met with something like monthly regularity, the Doctor seated, perhaps, with the illustrious survivors—Emerson, Lowell, and Longfellow —and the son with the eminent successors—President Eliot of Harvard, Horace and Asa Gray, Phillips Brooks, Senator Hoar, and William James. But such involvements with the world were not a part of Holmes's life until after he had tested and proved himself in *The Common Law*.

Did Holmes's twelve-year withdrawal and substantial isolation from the world of affairs leave marks upon his temperament? It seems to me that probably it did. In denying himself an intimate association with contemporary Boston, he cut himself off from its interests and ambitions. It is a striking fact that in his years of full maturity he had but few close friends of his own age, and of those a mere handful were Yankees like himself. This led the outer world—of which, surely, he might have been a part—to look upon him with some mistrust. When he returned to the world this mistrust of the respectable Boston which might have been his own encouraged him to seek for friendship and admiration among younger men and women and to find his most significant intimacies in associations with persons who either lived abroad or, being in Boston, were somehow not of Boston. Did the isolation of twelve years also, perhaps, add a special intensity to his later recollections of the Civil War—the reminiscence of a time when he had shared a great, if senseless, experience with others? Had Holmes throughout the 1870's given his heart to the world's contemporary affairs, might he not later have found less significance in his bloodstained years of associated commitment than in romantic fact he did? It is significant, I think, that throughout his years of isolation there is no sign that he looked back upon the experience of war with a sense of its philosophic meaning. That sense came to him later, at a time when he saw that he was somehow set apart from the world around him and sought for a view of himself and his generation which would bring them together in a common engagement far more radiant than any known to the postwar world.

One nonprofessional affiliation of Holmes, having its beginning in 1875, deserves attention. From that year until his resignation in 1882 Holmes was a member of the Harvard Board of Overseers. This association brought him into close touch with the affairs of the Harvard Law School, since he was for many years a member and for one year chairman of the Committee to Visit the Law School. With two members of the Law Faculty Holmes had already been intimately associated—with John C. Gray as close friend, with James Bradley Thayer as an employer and as "collaborator" in preparing the twelfth edition of Kent's *Commentaries*. The other two members of the faculty—the Dean, Langdell, and James Barr Ames—Holmes had not, apparently, come to know with any intimacy before he became, briefly, their associate. It is most improbable that Langdell did not realize that Holmes was the anonymous reviewer who had described him as "the greatest living legal theologian"—a description not designed to please its subject.[6] Yet Langdell, so far as we know, took no exception, when the time came for the Dean and other members of the Law Faculty to express their opinion, to the choice of Holmes as a colleague.

Perhaps it was because Holmes was an Overseer of Harvard that he was chosen—as was his father—to be a speaker at the Commencement dinner in Memorial Hall in July of 1880. It was the first occasion, in his maturity, on which Holmes tested his oratorical wings, and though he did not show in his brief address the full eloquence which he was to reveal on similar occasions in later years, he sounded both in the themes touched upon and in the manner of speech, strains which were to be heard again. It was the first occasion since the Civil War on which he had spoken publicly of its memory and of the friends who had not returned. He used an orator's images to stir his audience. "Memory spreads a floor of light from summit to summit of our experience, across which our vision moves easily and uninterrupted. Between there lie valleys wrapped in darkness, and many men wrapped in sleep." He gave glimpses of his philosophy and of his attitude towards his profession:

6 See *supra*, p. 156.

Every thing is interesting when you understand it, when you see its connection with other things, and, in the end, with all other things. And how much of all that has been accomplished to make that possible has been done within the last twenty years! To speak only of my own profession, the law, it is enough to those who are interested in its broader aspects to say that the first book of Sir Henry Maine was published the year I graduated.

There was even a chance publicly to pay a compliment to Langdell—labeled but two months ago a "legal theologian." Since *Ancient Law* was published, "great contributions have been made; and I think we may affirm with pride, that not the least important of them have come from the great lawyer who presides over our own Law School, Professor Langdell." The concluding passage was colored by the idealism—or, better perhaps, the romanticism—which was to mark so many of his later addresses. He ended his remarks with an expression of hope that the young men about to leave Harvard would

remember that the distinction of the scholar is almost our only counterpoise to the distinction of wealth. Where shall chivalrous faith rise above the cynicism of business if not in his person? Life will prove itself worth living if he puts his ambition high enough, if he remembers and believes the noble words of the President of the University,—that the duty of the scholar in this country is to make poverty respectable.[7]

These public expressions of an ambition combined with an idealism tell a good deal, I think, of the attitudes of mind with which Holmes confronted his future when *The Common Law* was published in March of 1881. At that particular juncture there was, apparently, a momentary fear that he had pushed himself too hard. He had symptoms which he "mistook for a funeral knell." [8] "Just then by accident I took up Casanova, whom I had just seen re-

[7] *OS*, 1–3.

[8] *HLL*, II, 1019. A memorandum by Felix Frankfurter, reporting a conversation with Holmes on August 10, 1932, records the incident in more detail. "He told of his own reading of Casanova just as he was finishing his *Common Law* . . . Just about this time, while brushing his teeth, he bled and said to himself, 'Well, old fellow, your box is being closed' . . . and so he wanted something to be diverted. Casanova was the thing, and he got all there was out of the strong box of the Athenaeum Library." (Copy, HLS)

ferred to by Carlyle . . . That was just what I wanted then . . . I don't like dirty books or care for indecent ones, but there sometimes goes with the freedom they imply, a temperament—a smack—a gusto, as I said, that puts life into one." [9]

Holmes's turning to the exploits of Casanova did not signify a decision to turn his back on scholarship and to enter the world. The author of *The Common Law*, who had given ten dedicated years to that brand of achievement, was not one to change his course in midstream from the pursuit of learning to the achievement of "success." Moderate wealth might well have been within Holmes's reach if, having completed *The Common Law*, he had chosen thenceforth to give all of his energies to practice. Remembering that there had, but a few years before, been a substantial chance of his being appointed to the federal district court—a chance which he looked upon with favor—it is most likely, I think, that he supposed that the publication of his book would make his selection for a state or federal judgeship not at all unlikely. The fitness of such a selection occurred to at least one of his friends shortly after the conclusion of the Lowell Lectures. On January 13, 1881, James Bradley Thayer wrote to the Republican governor of Massachusetts, John Davis Long, suggesting that to fill the vacancy on the Supreme Judicial Court resulting from the recent resignation of Justice Seth Ames, Holmes would be a suitable choice. "His recent course of lectures . . . was very remarkable and indicated the highest sort of legal capacity. You know, I dare say, the very high appreciation in which he is held by the judges and that he *inherits* legal excellence from his grandfather, Judge Jackson." [10] Governor Long did not follow this recommendation, but

9 To Lady Scott, May 27, 1910 (HLS).

10 Massachusetts Archives, Executive Department Letters, vol. 231, #9. At least one prominent citizen of Boston opposed the nomination of Holmes. A letter from James J. Storrow to Governor Long referred to the current reports that Holmes and Solomon Lincoln (1838–1907) were both being considered for the vacancy on the Court. "Both of them," Mr. Storrow acknowledged, "are good lawyers and of character above question; but I am very firmly convinced that both by nature and training Mr. Lincoln has much the soundest judgment. After all the judicial faculty, as distinguished from learning, is what measures the value of a court. Mr. Lincoln I am sure has both." *Id.*, #105.

in February nominated Walbridge Abner Field to fill the Ames vacancy. A year later, in January, 1882, when Chief Justice Gray resigned his seat on the Supreme Judicial Court to take his place on the Supreme Court of the United States "the question was again raised of appointing H[olmes] to the Supreme Court," [11] but once more another was chosen by Governor Long.

While these possibilities of judicial office were in the air another possibility began to take shape. This was, in many ways, the most natural of developments. The Harvard Law School, with some 139 students, had four professors and one visiting lecturer on its overburdened faculty. In the fall of 1881 President Eliot discussed with Holmes the possibility that he might "come out to Cambridge as professor in the Law School." [12] Eliot had taken this step on the assumption that there would be no great difficulty in raising the necessary funds for the endowment of a new professorship. On November 1, 1881, Holmes wrote the following letter to President Eliot.[13]

Boston, November 1, 1881

Dear Mr. Eliot:

Unless you take a different view I am not inclined to wait for contingencies the arising of which might not affect my determination. I am ready to accept a professorship in the Law School on the following terms if they are satisfactory as I believe from our conversations that they are.

1. I should prefer that the professorship should be entitled of Jurisprudence but the substance of the matter is not the title but the understanding thereby conveyed that I am expected to devote a reasonable proportion of my time to such investigations as are embodied in my book on the Common Law or other studies touching the history and philosophy of law. I do not mean by the above that I should not expect to teach any particular branches of the law like the other professors which would not meet either my wishes or views of expediency

---

[11] James Bradley Thayer, Memorandum Book D at 104 (HLS).

[12] *Id.*, 103.

[13] The original is in the Harvard Archives. A corrected copy, in Holmes's hand, and bearing the date "October 24, 1881," was retained by Holmes and is among his papers at the Harvard Law School.

but only that what I have indicated be regarded as an important part of my functions so that I may feel that time spent in that way is spent in the line of my duty.

2. The salary as I understand would be that of the other law professors viz. $4500, and I suppose would be the result of a special endowment. As the taking of this place will invoke a pecuniary sacrifice which so far as I can foresee the future would probably in the long run be considerable I think I should ask that as soon as any law professor's salary is raised mine should be. Without repeating I think what was understood with Prof. Thayer as to raising the salary to $5000 should be understood with me. I have to be particular on the money question as I must live on my salary. The property which I have saved being no more than a minimum fund to meet emergencies.

3. If a judgeship should be offered me I should not wish to feel bound in honor not to consider it, although I do not know that I should take it and although my present acceptance will diminish the chance of such an offer and is for that reason against the advice of many of my friends.

4. If this letter meets your views the high respect I feel for the present faculty of the school including their presiding officer as well as the personal regard which I entertain for them will make me look forward with eager anticipation to this new calling.

> With much respect
> Sincerely yours
> O W Holmes, Jr.

On November 4, Eliot acknowledged the receipt of this letter. He stated that the title of the professorship would present no difficulty, and that the salary would be $4500. He added the statement that "the understanding with Professor Thayer was only this,—that the salary of a full professor in the Law School would be raised if the resources of the School permitted." He went on to discuss Holmes's reservation of a right to consider an offer of a judgeship if it should be made. "In accepting a professorship here," said Eliot, "you do not pledge yourself to remain any definite time, & you remain free to accept a better position or more congenial employment elsewhere. On the other hand, your return to the practice of your profession simply within any period less than five years would be acceptable to the Corporation and Faculty only in the improbable case that you had not succeeded as a teacher of law." Eliot concluded his letter with the assurance that he would "set about getting an endowment at once, hoping to secure it in a few days." [14]

According to James Bradley Thayer, the President had been too sanguine with respect to the endowment. On finding that the funds could not be secured as quickly as he had assumed that they could, Eliot asked Joseph B. Warner, of the Boston bar, to take charge of the fund-raising effort. Warner first got "Judge Lowell to promise $5000 if the fund could be raised and Holmes would come, and Mr. Sidney Bartlett promised as much more." [15] When Holmes heard that these efforts were being made, he wrote another letter to President Eliot.[16]

Boston, November 18, 1881

Dear Mr. Eliot:

I have been carefully considering our conversation of yesterday and the facts of which you informed me; and I have come to the conclusion that as the money to endow the professorship is not yet provided but will have to be raised, I must withdraw my acceptance. I am unwilling that a subscription should be raised on the understanding that I am pledged to fill the place and (by implication) desire it. Such an understanding would impose on me a greater honorary obligation than I assumed in my letter of acceptance, and the contributions would certainly take the form in the mind of some of the contributors, of a favor to me. Great as is my wish to cooperate with you in anything you deem desirable for the college and much as I dislike to change the direction which my thoughts and interests had begun to take, as well as to meet the inquiries which no doubt will be made, I see no way in which the proposed plan can be made satisfactory to my feelings.

I do not mean to say that if the circumstances should not change in the meantime, I should decline the honor of the proposed professorship in case I should be told hereafter that the funds were at hand. But if you propose to raise the fund at all events, as I am not pledged, you

14 HLS.
15 Thayer Memorandum Book D, 104–105.
16 Harvard Archives.

of course are equally free and will act when the time comes according to what may then seem to you best.

> With much respect
> Sincerely yours
> O W Holmes Jr.

Eliot reported the contents of Holmes's letter to Professor Thayer who was unwilling to believe that "this block was final." He called on Holmes, accordingly, "and found, as I had expected, that he was still willing to come but wasn't willing to have his friends or any one asked to make a place for him. He intended simply to withdraw. If the College wanted to raise a fund he had no objection; and while he would not hold himself bound, it was probable so far as he now knew that he would come." Thayer went on to assure Holmes that he was confident that the sum needed— approximately $100,000—could be raised. Thayer then reported back to President Eliot and suggested that he be authorized to take charge of the solicitation, suggesting that Joseph Warner was, perhaps, too young to be wholly effective in the effort. The President was noncommittal. In the middle of the Christmas recess, however, Eliot called on Thayer and, according to Thayer's record,

said he heard that by the promotion of Gray to the Supreme Court of the United States the question was again raised of appointing Holmes to the Supreme [Judicial] Court and he thought, and I agreed, that we had better wait. The promotion of Morton and nomination of Charles Allen ended that talk. At our law faculty meeting on the 10th of January Eliot put the question to those present, viz. Langdell, Ames and me, whether the faculty were prepared to make any effort to get an endowment. There was silence and then L[angdell] expressed the opinion that it was of no use to try; he didn't see how it could be done. Ames said the same. I then said I thought it could be done and should like to try—but I should need a little time. There was no reply and no action was taken.[17]

[17] Thayer Memorandum Book D, 104. Is it possible that the apathy of Langdell and Ames reflected their lack of enthusiasm with respect to the proposed incumbent?

Within a few days Thayer, after securing presidential approval, went to work in earnest. He had already spoken to Louis D. Brandeis, who had recently formed a partnership with Samuel D. Warren, Jr. (until then an associate in the office of Shattuck, Holmes & Munroe), had been law clerk to Chief Justice Gray, and was to teach Evidence at the Law School in 1882–83. Brandeis named "a number of young fellows as likely to help and perhaps as likely to give it all." Among the names suggested by Brandeis was that of William F. Weld, Jr., a young man who, after attending the Harvard Law School and leaving without a degree, despite tutoring by Brandeis,[18] had recently inherited some three million dollars. Brandeis had spoken to Weld and found that he was distinctly interested in the possibility of endowing the professorship and giving his name to it. Thayer was reassured to learn that Weld was "glad that I had it in hand, because he liked me better than anybody. (We hadn't given him his degree at the school, and I think he failed with me, but B[randeis] said he knew it was his own fault.)" Weld had suggested one minor embarrassment. He had told Brandeis that "he thought he should like to take his degree at the school in the spring and if he did anything, it must be kept secret because neither the college nor he would wish to have it supposed that he bid for a degree." Thayer, thus briefed by Brandeis, went to Weld's office:

I explained matters to him and he asked questions. He said it seemed rather a mockery for him to pretend to a regard to learning; wouldn't it be better for him to be one of ten, say. I said he might do that, but it would be a very good thing for him to give his name to it and do it all. He said if he did he should wish nothing said about it till after the degree matter was over. "As to that," I replied, "I agree with you, but as to the degree, you may rely on our dealing with you with absolute impartiality."[19]

[18] Alpheus Thomas Mason, *Brandeis: A Free Man's Life* (New York, 1946), 65.
[19] Thayer Memorandum Book D, 104–106. Weld does not seem to have returned to the Law School. The name of the professorship was not publicly announced until 1893, though it had been filled by Thayer ever since Holmes's resignation from the faculty in December 1882.

The discussion moved smoothly through details and concluded with Thayer's suggestion that "he should do as Story did in founding the Dane professorship and request the appointment of Holmes—thus having the satisfaction not only of giving his name to the endowment but of connecting with the matter the beginning of H[olmes]'s career as professor." Thayer offered to prepare for him a paper like that which Dane had used. This suggestion was accepted and the meeting came to an end with an arrangement that on the following morning Weld would go to the office of Edward Hooper, treasurer of Harvard, to conclude the transaction. Thayer stopped at Holmes's office on the way to Cambridge and "astonished" him by saying that he thought it was all arranged and that "he had better make ready to come out." Thereafter Thayer reported his success to Eliot, prepared a letter to the corporation on the model of Dane's—"simply offering the fund, requesting that H[olmes] should be appointed the first professor if he would accept, and that the professor should be named 'The Weld Professor.' " On Thursday, January 19, Thayer noted, Weld sent in "his formal letter (in the main mine), offering his note with interest at 5% from Feb. 1 payable in a year, his name not to be known at present . . . The corporation accepted this and on Monday last the 23rd they nominated Holmes." [20] On February 11, 1882, the Overseers confirmed the nomination and Eliot wrote to Holmes informing him of the fact. "So begins happily a relation which, I trust, will prove lasting, fruitful and fortunate."

Twelve months after Eliot had written thus hopefully, Thayer made the following resentful entry in his memorandum book: [21]

Dec. 18, 1882.—at p. 103 (*ante*) and the following I have given some account of Holmes's appointment to the professorship at the beginning of the year. Alas, he has now gone, or as good as gone, and that under circumstances that were highly disagreeable. On Saturday morn-

[20] *Id.*, 106–107. In Weld's letter to the President and Fellows, after offering to make the gift he added this passage: "I request that Oliver Wendell Holmes, Jr. may be appointed as the first professor on this foundation, if he will accept the appointment" (Undated letter, Harvard Archives).

[21] At 140–144.

ing a week ago, i.e. Dec. 9, I opened my Advertiser to read that he was appointed [to] the bench of our Supreme Court and there was a long notice of him etc., etc. It was surprising; the only explanation of it was that Long must have appointed him at a venture and trusted to his accepting; but that seemed unlikely. I called at the library on my [way] into Boston. Arnold our librarian said that Thorpe, a student in Shattuck's office (where Holmes still keeps up his connection), had called on Friday afternoon and mentioned that he had been appointed; it was utterly surprising to him. In the evening Gray (who is intimate with Holmes) happened to be there and Arnold mentioned it to him; he also was surprised,—entirely. He said that it must be a very sudden thing and put on his hat and went out quickly. That morning (Saturday) Bolles, a student who writes for the paper, was in and told Arnold that he had called on Friday evening on getting wind of this, upon Langdell and the President for information. Neither of them had heard a word of it.

I at once said to Arnold, Very well, if that is so, I am relieved; I will bet $500 that the situation is this: he has told the Governor that he would consider the subject and the Governor has gone forward upon that. He never would accept without conferring with the President.

I then went in town and saw Shattuck and there to my amazement learned the exact facts which were these. Long sent for Shattuck on Friday noon or later and said that he had made up his mind to appoint Holmes to fill Lord's place if he could be assured that he would accept, and he must have his answer by 3 o'clock that afternoon. Shattuck could give no answer but said that he would find him at once; he took a carriage, got Holmes's wife, and drove to the school at Cambridge and found that Holmes was at lunch with Ames; he drove there, told him (it was then $1\frac{1}{2}$) and drove him into Boston. Whether he went at once to the Governor, whether Mrs. Holmes was in the carriage, (yes, she was) whether he saw any of his family or went at once to the State House I do not know; but he accepted the offer within the Governor's time and conferred with no one representing the college. He seems to have made no struggle for more time, not even to have conceived it *possible* that he could have more time or that it was any lowering of his own dignity or value to be pushed into a corner in this way, or that it should not have been *possible* for him to accept without a conference with Eliot. He had been on pay since Feb. 1, I think,—March 1st at any rate; the year at the school had only begun; students were here who had been mainly induced to come by his being here, and all the students had *rights*,—as the college had,—which he was bound to consider carefully. But he accepted and it was blown abroad at once.

Having done it, he did not post at once to see Eliot, he allowed him and all of us to learn it from the papers or any chance rumor. On Saturday morning indeed he called on Eliot and not finding him left his card (called twice it is said) and a verbal message that he might see him Monday morning. But not on Friday, or Saturday, or Sunday or Monday or Tuesday until Tuesday night at the Faculty meeting (coming to it late) did he have any communication whatever with Eliot or the authorities of the college. He made no other effort than the feeble one of Saturday morning after it was all published. At the meeting he made a long, excited and wholly ineffective attempt to account for his going, so Eliot tells me, but no person said a word, *not one*, except E. himself now and then, "it did not seem kind," he said, "to leave him talking all alone." To neither Langdell nor me nor any of us excepting Gray, who is an intimate friend, has he talked, unless as we have seen fit to make any approach to him. I determined to say and do nothing, but at the school on Monday,—after simply bowing to him and saying nothing, afterwards as I left the school, he was standing near as I passed and it seemed too marked to pass by him in silence so that I said, "You are going to leave us then," and he went on to talk about a little, but he seemed to have no sense of any impropriety in what he has done.

Dec. 22. Arnold our librarian says that he talked with George Arnold (the assistant) within a few days, and said he wished it understood that this was all provided for in his letter of acceptance, that he had the documents, that "the President did not blame him"—That is about as bad a symptom as any in the whole business. He says this,—as Shattuck reports to me, and Gray and others, and as Langdell tells me that he said at the faculty meeting, viz. that when he accepted he reserved the right to take such an appointment. What he did was in fact this: when he was sounded in November a year ago and accepted (the first time) in his letter of acceptance (Eliot read it to me the other day and also his own reply) "If I should receive an offer of a judgeship, I do not wish to be bound in honor not to consider it." Adding that he had no immediate expectation of it and that his friends advised him that his chances of receiving it were lessened by going to Cambridge. Eliot replied that it was always understood that a professor was at liberty to go at any time; he should only like to have it understood that as to a return to practice, it might be expected that he would not do that under five years.

Holmes, of course, is entitled to the excuse which this may furnish! And it cannot be denied that he is within the line of his legal right. But what shall be said of his sense of what is morally admissible,—of his sense of honor, of justice, of consideration for the rights of others and of their sensibilities, when he could do what he did; of his personal self-respect, indeed.

The only symptom of sensibility that he shows, to tell the truth, however, is that he says (at the faculty meeting) that he does see that he ought not to have been required to answer so soon. To be sure! Long had had Lord's resignation for a week. There were three weeks and more before Long's reign is over. If his council was not regularly to meet again for some days, yet could it not be called together in extra session? What was he going to do if H. *didn't* accept? The nomination must lie over for a week. Could he not have intimated that he *probably* would accept and had the name go in and the news not published, and so have secured a chance to sleep over it and to confer with those who had a right to be consulted? But he took it at once and seems never to have thought and not to know now that it was an unhandsome, and indecent action.

He lost his head perhaps? But my experience with him in editing Kent, which I had been willing to forget, comes all back again and assures me that this conduct is characteristic,—that he is, with all his attractive qualities and his solid merits, wanting sadly in the noblest region of human character,—selfish, vain, thoughtless of others.

Was such severity of judgment deserved? Clearly Holmes would have shown a more delicate awareness of the sensitivities of his Harvard colleagues had he made sure that they learned of his decision from him, rather than from the newspapers. Whether he did ask—or could with any hope of success have asked—the Governor for time to confer with the Harvard authorities before accepting the nomination, we do not know. The departure from Harvard was undoubtedly abrupt, and came at an unhappy time from the standpoint of those who were responsible for offering the courses announced in the catalogue. Yet the fact remains that Holmes in

268

his first written communication with President Eliot had warned him that if a judgeship should be offered to him after he had taken a teaching post at Harvard he would "not wish to feel bound in honor not to consider it." Eliot's reply had explicitly recognized that Holmes's acceptance of a Harvard professorship would not pledge him to remain "any definite time, & you remain free to accept a better position or more congenial appointment elsewhere." When Holmes withdrew his initial acceptance and indicated that if funds were raised without the use of his name as a pledged incumbent, he might well accept the post, he said nothing to suggest that that possible acceptance would be any different in its implications of finality than the first had been. It seems clear that Thayer, when he so quickly and so successfully approached Weld, had not been told by anyone of Holmes's initial and still applicable reservation of the right to consider an offer of a judgeship if it should come his way. No one, apparently, told Weld that the prospective incumbent had cautioned the president that he might resign if a judgeship were offered to him.

There is little reason to believe that President Eliot was as disturbed by Holmes's resignation as was Thayer. In 1924 Eliot wrote a somewhat rambling and reminiscent letter to Holmes—"a kind of schoolmaster's summary of myself in four pages quarto," Holmes called it— [22] in which he reflected on Holmes's associations with Harvard. "You were appointed Professor of Law in 1882," he said, "but almost immediately abandoned the professorship in favor of a judgeship. I could not be reconciled to that action on your part, until you explained to me your inheritance with regard to the function and status of judges. Langdell was never reconciled to that step on your part." [23] At the time of the resignation it seems entirely clear that Eliot raised no question of its propriety. E. W. Hooper, the treasurer of Harvard, in January 1883 wrote to Mr. Weld, the founder of the professorship, and spoke of Holmes's acceptance of a seat on the Supreme Judicial Court as "a great blow to the Law School." He went on to say,

[22] *HLL*, II, 930. The letter from Eliot was, in fact, one typed page in length.
[23] March 28, 1924 (HLS).

however, that "as he expressly reserved the right to accept a judge-ship, we cannot complain." [24] Had the Cambridge grievance been in any sense official it is hard to believe that in 1895 Harvard would have awarded Holmes its honorary degree of LL.D.

Just after taking his oath of judicial office, Holmes turned to an older lawyer for advice on one aspect of the problem. The lawyer was Francis E. Parker—"the most squaretoed seeming of angli-cized Yankees—who had a green baize door to his office with 'Mr. Parker' on it . . ." [25] Holmes evidently put to Mr. Parker the question whether or not he owed legal or moral responsibility to restore to Harvard any portion of the salary which he had received from the professorship. Parker looked at the letters which had passed between Holmes and Eliot. He also talked to Mr. Hooper, the treasurer of Harvard College with whom Mr. Weld had con-ducted the concluding phases of negotiation. Parker reported to Holmes that Mr. Hooper said

that Prest Eliot had said with entire distinctness that you were at liberty to accept the new place & that there was nothing but regret to be expressed. But I understood Mr. Hooper also to say that he had never heard of your having made this stipulation, when you accepted the place; and that the Prest did not refer to any such thing in his general remarks, though they were not inconsistent with it.

Mr. Parker also prepared a memorandum of law and morals, in which he discussed the possibility that Holmes should make resti-tution of the salary payments which he had received. The gist of the memorandum was clear: Holmes was under no legal duty to repay the sums received.

[24] The date of the letter, a copy of which is in the Harvard Archives, is illegible. On January 3, 1883, Holmes had written to the President and Fellows announcing that on December 15, 1882, he had taken the oath of office as Asso-ciate Justice. "I believe it was understood that I resigned or vacated my place as Professor in the Law School on that day. In accordance with a suggestion of the President I send this note, to express that understanding, and to request that my resignation (if one was necessary) take effect from the above mentioned date" (Autograph letter, Harvard Archives).
[25] *HLL*, II, 930.

1. The contract was expressly terminable upon Mr. Holmes's appointment as a judge. 2. The College, therefore, took the risk of the time when it would be so terminated, and this was an inducement for Mr. Holmes's accepting the place. 3. The money paid Mr. Holmes was not merely in consideration of service to be rendered, but also in consideration of his giving up, during the necessary time of preparation, a pecuniary engagement of at least equal value to the money which he received. If he returns the money to the College, he suffers to that extent a pecuniary loss, for which he is not compensated. 4. If it were equitable for Mr. Holmes to make compensation, to whom should it be made? The attraction of Mr. Holmes's name procured for the College $90,000 for a professorship. The present disappointment is to the donor. The College, in either event, is the gainer. 5. The professorship is vacated, (as the contract provided it might be vacated) by Mr. Holmes's appointment to a public office. This appointment is made, at a time, and under circumstances, when its acceptance is a duty to the Public, and to the Profession. It brings with it the same obligation, (considering the position of the Court) that a military appointment would bring to a soldier. It also entails a sacrifice of comfort, taste, and natural vocation, with no advantage in pecuniary compensation, when the increase of expense is considered. The engagement is interrupted by an event, like death, which is an undertaking of this sort, is never considered as a legal, or equitable, ground of compensation to the other party.

A letter accompanying the memorandum added a few supplementary reflections:

It remains to be considered whether you prefer to deal with the College, as a Charity, as one sometimes deals with a woman or a poor person,—that is give him, or her, both ends of the bargain. When one can afford it, this is sometimes one of the greatest of luxuries, & the most comfortable of recollections. But it must always be decided by the person himself.[26]

The records of Harvard College contain nothing to indicate that Holmes made restitution of any part of his salary. If the entire incident left resentments in the minds of some of Holmes's Harvard associates—particularly Thayer's—there is nothing to suggest that

26 Dec. 23, 1882 (HLS).

President Eliot or other administrative officers of the University held his conduct against him. Over the course of time it seems that relationships of cordiality, if not of friendship, were re-established between Thayer and Holmes.

The materials from which I have already quoted indicate that Holmes became, at least in form, a member of the Law School Faculty very shortly after his confirmation by the Board of Overseers on February 11, 1882. The minutes of the Law School Faculty indicate that he attended meetings in March and May of 1882, thus becoming a participant in the School's affairs before the beginning of his teaching in the fall of the year. It was doubtless at those meetings that arrangements of course assignments for the next year were made. The published catalogue for the academic year 1882–83 indicated that Holmes would be teaching Torts for two hours a week throughout the full academic year to first-year students, Agency and Carriers for one hour a week for the whole year, Suretyship and Mortgage for a full year, once a week, and Jurisprudence for one hour a week in the fall term—all these last being third-year offerings. The catalogue also indicated that for half the year Holmes would give a course in Admiralty, but it seems probable that it was scheduled for the spring term and that, accordingly, none of Holmes's lectures in that subject were delivered. He did not, in his "Black Book," make any reference to the preparation or delivery of lectures on maritime law, as he did with respect to all of the other announced offerings.

In assuming an academician's rather than a practitioner's responsibilities, Holmes was enabled to return to Europe in the summer of 1882. Eight years had passed since he and his wife had left New England for anything but the briefest excursions, and one may be sure that he, at least, would see one of the great advantages in a teacher's calendar of life the opportunity which it would provide for relatively frequent visits to England, the place, above all, where he felt himself to be intellectually at home. On May 20, 1882, he and his wife embarked once more for England, this time on the *Parthia*. No record equivalent to that which Mrs. Holmes made of the visit of 1874 survives. All that indicates the outline

of their travels is found in a miniature date book or diary, this
time kept by Holmes, in which various engagements and by-paths
of travel are noted. It shows that activities in England were just
what might have been expected—dinners, luncheons, and breakfasts with all the English friends: Bryce, Pollock, Anson, Maine,
Holland, Morley, Leslie Stephen, Dicey, Henry Cowper. A month
in England was followed by a short trip to the continent. The ten
days in Paris would seem, once more, to have been spent in the
isolation of travelers in public places—the Louvre, the Hippo-
drome, the Folies Bergères ("for a short time, F. not well"), and
the most renowned restaurants. After Paris came Geneva, Berne,
Interlaken, and Lucerne. Thence the journey took them—each, I
think, for the one and only time—into Germany, where they
passed through Freiberg, Heidelberg, Frankfurt, and Cologne. On
August 15 the Holmeses were back in London, remaining in England, we may assume, until their departure for home. When, precisely, they were back in Boston we do not know. Presumably it
was some little time before the opening of the Law School on September 28, 1882.

Of the substance of Holmes's Law School lectures we know
very little. A surviving student's notebook indicates that the course
on Jurisprudence consisted, almost wholly, of a redelivery of the
Lowell Lectures on *The Common Law*.[27] There is reason to believe that to the subjects covered in the Lowell Lectures he added
lectures on two other topics. One of these he had touched upon
lightly and occasionally in his early essays and in *The Common
Law* but had not examined systematically. It concerned the history
of agency and the theory of vicarious liability. A prefatory note to
the two essays on agency which appeared in the *Harvard Law Review* in 1891 explicitly stated that they "are two lectures delivered
by me when I was a professor at the Law School of Harvard College . . ."[28] The student notebook already referred to, and
Holmes's own jottings in his "Black Book," indicate that the two

---

27 Law School Note Books of Alfred Mack (HLS). The notes of the lectures
on Jurisprudence are in a book carrying on its spine the title "Gray on Conflicts."
28 *Harv. L. Rev.*, 4:345 (March 1891); reprinted without this note in *CLP*, 49.

lectures were included in the course on Jurisprudence.[29] It is not unlikely, I think, that they also were made use of in his course on Agency.[30] The other significant addition to the materials transposed from *The Common Law* would seem to have concerned the history of uses and contract in equity—materials which he published in a more systematic form in the essay on "Early English Equity" in the *Law Quarterly Review* in 1885.[31]

These lectures on agency and on equity surely could have been included in the Lowell series had Holmes been allotted more than twelve lectures. The method of discussion and analysis of the history and theory of agency is wholly characteristic of that which Holmes had used in his consideration of crime, tort, possession, and contract. His search was for the origin of vicarious liability and, as passages in *The Common Law* had already indicated, he found it in the principles and procedures of Roman law as they related to the institution of slavery. We have already seen how dissatisfied Holmes was with the conventional justification for imposing liability on a master for the injuries done to third persons by his servants—the "remote" fault of the master in selecting an incompetent employee.[32] As Law School lecturer he carried his historical inquiries much farther than he had in the earlier years. Now he documented at considerable length and with impressive learning the thesis that the master's responsibility for his servants is in fact a survival of the owner's liability for the conduct of his slaves. Though few scholars have accepted Holmes's historical explanation as sufficient,[33] it is clear, I think, that in this matter, as in

[29] The entry, at p. 154 in the "Black Book," is as follows: "Lectures written: Agency, Carriers, Suretyship. Also for Jurisprudence course on Agency (2) on Equity (incl. early hist. of Contract and Uses) (2). Delivered whole course on jurisp. also on Agency, Suretyship & Torts through Dec. 22d."

[30] Notes kept by Frederick J. Ranlett on Holmes's lectures on Agency are preserved in the Harvard Archives. They indicate that the Agency students on November 8 and 15 attended the course in Jurisprudence to hear the lectures there given on Agency.

[31] *L.Q. Rev.*, 1:162; *CLP*, 1.

[32] See *supra*, p. 163.

[33] See, e.g., Maitland in Pollock and Maitland, *History of English Law* (2d ed., Cambridge, England, 1898), II, 532; John H. Wigmore, "Responsibility for Tortious

so many others, he opened lines of inquiry which have by no means been wholly fruitless and which his predecessors had not carefully considered. Perhaps the more controversial though less frequently controverted thesis in the lectures on Agency was Holmes's very clear indication that he had the gravest doubt whether it was defensible as a matter of policy and justice to continue in the modern world a principle of vicarious liability which had its origins—and perhaps at one time an adequate justification —in the institutions of slavery:

A judge would blush to say nakedly to a defendant: "I can state no rational ground on which you should be held liable, but there is a fiction of law which I must respect and by which I am bound to say that you did the act complained of, although we both know perfectly well that it was done by somebody else whom the plaintiff could have sued if he had chosen, who was selected with the utmost care by you, who was in fact an eminently proper person for the employment in which he was engaged, and whom it was not only your right to employ, but much to the public advantage that you should employ." That would not be a satisfactory form in which to render a decision against a master, and it is not pleasant even to admit to one's self that such are the true grounds upon which one is deciding.[34]

Holmes stated quite explicitly that he found it impossible to discover an intelligible reason justifying the fiction of identity between master and servant. He admitted his "scepticism" as to the value of the traditional justifications—that it is desirable that there should be some responsible man to make good the judgment; that the master takes the risk of "such offenses as it must

---

Acts. Its History," *Select Essays in Anglo-American Legal History* (Boston, 1909) , III, 533: T. Baty, *Vicarious Liability* (Oxford, 1916) , chapter i and pages 152–154; Holdsworth, *History of English Law* (London, 1925) , 472 *et seq*. See also Glanville Williams, "Vicarious Liability and the Master's Indemnity," *Modern Law Review*, 20:220, 228 *et seq*. (May 1957) . Writing to Morris Cohen in 1921, Holmes recognized that his historical thesis with respect to agency had not been generally accepted. "The articles on agency have been most criticized—but they were honest work and I think at least followed one strand of development." "Holmes-Cohen Correspondence," *Journal of the History of Ideas*, 9:26 (January 1948) .
[34] *CLP*, 114–115.

needs be should come," but acknowledged a perfect readiness "to believe, upon evidence, that the law could be justified as it stands when applied to special cases upon special grounds." [35]

In Holmes's course on Agency—as distinguished from his two lectures on that subject in the course on Jurisprudence—the lecturer had evidently informed the class that they should consider that the law of master and servant and the law of principal and agent are founded in common principles. When Holmes resigned his professorship his closest friend on the Law Faculty, John C. Gray, took over the course in Agency for the second term. One of the students recorded in his notebook the substance of Gray's first lecture. "Prof. Gray," he reported, "cannot follow Prof. Holmes in saying there is no difference between principal and agent and master and servant. This is not the law now, and probably never was." Gray went on to put cases which seemed to him to reveal the inaccuracy of Holmes's contention and to suggest the temperamental or intellectual source of Holmes's error. "Mr. H. carries his theories of simplification too far: there is too much tendency on his part to make cases come under the principle, wh. cannot really belong there." [36] One may feel some confidence that Gray's reflections on Holmes's longing for a unifying simplicity of principle were based as much upon tendencies revealed in *The Common Law* as upon the particular thesis which he had developed in the lectures on Agency.

The student's notes on Holmes's concluding lecture in Jurisprudence indicate that he at least outlined the thesis which he was to present three years later in the *Law Quarterly Review* in the short essay "Early English Equity." [37] The paper was, in some respects, the most notable of Holmes's achievements in historical scholarship. It challenged a number of the basic assumptions with respect to the origins of equity, the history of uses, and the development of contract liability. Professor Barbour did not speak in-

[35] *Id.*, 115.

[36] Notebook of Frederick J. Ranlett on Lectures on Agency; notes for lecture of January 12, 1883 (Harvard Archives).

[37] See note 29, *supra*.

GEO O SHATTUCK
O W HOLMES Jr
WM A MUNROE

Office of

Shattuck Holmes & Munroe

Counsellors at Law

35 Court Street

Boston October 24 1881

Dear Mr Eliot,

Unless you take a different view I am not inclined to wait for contingencies the arising of which might not affect my determination. I am ready to accept a professorship in the Law School on the following terms if they are satisfactory as I believe from our conversation that they are —

1. I should draft that the professorship should be entitled of jurisprudence

First page of the corrected copy of Holmes's letter of October 24, 1881, to President Eliot—a copy which Holmes retained in his own papers.

James Barr Ames
about 1875

Christopher Columbus Langdell
about 1870

James Bradley Thayer
about 1875

accurately in 1918 when he referred to Holmes's "brilliant and daring essay" which "set on foot an inquiry which has revealed the remote beginnings of English equity." [38]

The essay challenged two principles accepted by orthodox learning. Holmes denied, in the first place, that the substantive law administered in the Court of Equity was merely the product of the Court's procedure. He also contended that "the Chancery, in its first establishment at least, did not appear as embodying the superior ethical standards of a comparatively modern state of society correcting the defects of a more archaic system." [39] He was persuaded that down to the end of the reign of Henry V the Chancery neither knew nor enforced "any substantive doctrine different from those which were recognized in the other courts except two." [40] These two peculiar doctrines related to uses and to contracts. Holmes had been led to believe that when the Chancellor imposed obligations on the feoffee to uses he was merely enforcing responsibilities which the Teutonic law had imposed upon the salman and which the courts of common law were making partially effective through the writ of covenant. Holmes also suggested that when the Chancellor, in the earliest days, provided a remedy for breach of covenants without specialty, he was "retaining some relics of ancient [Salic] customs which had been dropped by the common law, but had been kept alive by the Church." [41]

It has been said that Holmes was the first scholar to point out that "the root idea underlying the conception of the use is to be found among the Germanic tribes." [42] When he was ninety-one years old, Holmes remembered that "a hint from Henry Adams" had put him on the trail which he followed in his closing lecture on jurisprudence and the essay on Early English Equity.[43] For

[38] Barbour, "Some Aspects of Fifteenth-Century Chancery," *Harv. L. Rev.*, 31:834 (April 1918).

[39] *CLP*, 4.

[40] *Id.*, 2.

[41] *Id.*, 24.

[42] Holdsworth, *History of English Law*, IV, 410.

[43] "Egotism leads me to protest that I think I preceded Maitland on the derivation of the law of equitable trusts, after a hint from Henry Adams as to Beseler . . ." (Holmes to Dean Wigmore, March 14, 1932; HLS).

Holmes the trail had the charm of proving once more that all roads of English legal history do not lead to Rome. It was not, I think, the challenge to the prevailing assumption that the origin of uses was to be found in Roman law which led James Barr Ames to reject Holmes's contention. "The acceptance of [Holmes's] conclusions," said Ames, "would be difficult for any one who has studied his equity under the guidance of Professor Langdell." [44] Ames was willing to concede that Holmes was right in identifying the feoffee to uses as the salman's descendant, but he would not acknowledge that Holmes had sustained his thesis that equity in enforcing the obligations of the feoffee was simply providing its remedies for the enforcement of rights known and respected by the common and the canon law. Langdell and Ames were deeply committed to the thesis that equity has always sought to enforce a higher ethical standard than any recognized in the courts of common law, and they therefore rejected with something approaching indignation the thesis of Holmes that Chancery, at least in its beginnings, was not seeking to make effective a standard of ethics much higher than that of the common law. As Professor Plucknett has stated: "This [contention] has proved a very hard saying to the equity lawyers and historians; but it is nevertheless true." [45]

With respect to the second thesis in the lecture and essay—that which concerned equity's enforcement of "contractual" obligations which the Salic and the canon law had recognized—Holmes's position was somewhat less controversial, but no less fruitful than the other. Once more Ames questioned its validity,[46] but it encouraged such later studies as Barbour's *History of Contract in Early English Equity*, a book which greatly broadened historical understanding. Holmes's pride in his initiating achievement was not exaggerated when he said to a friend that Barbour's volume "showed that I had pretty well reconstructed the fish from a bone

[44] "The Origin of Uses," *Lectures on Legal History* (Cambridge, Mass., 1913), 233.

[45] "Holmes: The Historian," *Harv. L. Rev.*, 44:715.

[46] "Simple Contracts Prior to Assumpsit," *Lectures on Legal History*, 122, 125.

and a scale" [47]—a phrase which aptly characterized much of Holmes's achievement as analytical historian. He did not ever attain, or perhaps even seek to attain that wealth of detailed learning which the legal historians who came after him achieved. In the lecture and essay on Early English Equity, as in *The Common Law* itself, he formulated daring hypotheses upon the basis of an imaginative reading of selected materials. Not all of his hypotheses have been proved sound, but the suggestion of each, supported as it was by a considerable accumulation of learning, vivified the philosophic study of English legal history. It was, of course, no accident that the essay on Early English Equity included a quest for Germanic origins in English law and a denial that conventional standards of morality had been made a part of the law of England. The short essay was, in a sense, a footnote to the central themes of *The Common Law.*

The Law School catalogue indicates that there were no assigned textbooks or case books in Holmes's courses, except in his course in Torts, in which he used Ames's collection of cases. Though the publication of the two lectures on Agency as essays would suggest that Holmes was not fully a convert to the case method of legal education, introduced but a short time before by Langdell, the surviving student notebooks indicate that it was Holmes's practice at the end of each class hour in Suretyship and in Agency to assign designated cases—not passages from textbooks —for reading before the succeeding meeting of the class. One may assume that such assignments led not to analytical and expository lectures by the instructor, but to a discursive—perhaps even a Socratic—discussion between teacher and students. [48] In his Address

---

[47] To Mrs. John C. Gray, Dec. 27, 1920 (HLS) ; cf. Holmes to Morris Cohen, "Holmes-Cohen Correspondence," *supra,* note 33, at 26.

[48] In one anecdote of Holmes's classroom one may see a slight indication that question by professor and answer by student were not unknown. One who had been in his class in Torts, in 1931 recalled the incident. "I well recall your comment when a fellow-student suggested a search warrant as the appropriate method of retrieving a cap thrown on the land of a stranger. You were reminded of the man in some trouble who called aloud, 'Oh for the Horn of the Font of Bessa-

on The Use of Law Schools, delivered in 1886, Holmes referred to his experience with the case method of instruction.

During the short time that I had the honor to teach in the School, it fell to me, among other things, to instruct the first-year men in Torts. With some misgivings I plunged a class of beginners straight into Mr. Ames's collection of cases, and we began to discuss them together in Mr. Langdell's method. The result was better than I even hoped it would be . . . I at least, if no one else, gained a good deal from our daily encounters.[49]

As I have already indicated, it is not surprising that when Holmes was given the opportunity to move from the practice of law to its teaching he chose the academic life. He had made it quite clear to his friends that he hated "business and dislike[d] practice, apart from arguing cases." [50] What were the professional considerations and what were the qualities of temperament which led him, after three months as Professor of Law, to turn his back on the career of a scholar and choose that of a judge? The fullest surviving statement of the reasons which moved him are in a letter to James Bryce, written on December 31, 1882.

My motives so far as I could disentangle them in half an hour, which is all the time I had to decide the momentous question, were, in a word, that I thought the chance to gain an all round experience of the law not to be neglected, and especially that I did not think one could without moral loss decline any share in the practical struggle of life which naturally offered itself and for which he believed himself fitted. I had already realized at Cambridge that the field for generalization inside the body of the law was small and that the day would soon come when one felt that the only remaining problems were of detail and that as a philosopher he must go over into other fields—whether of ethics—theory of legislation—political economy or anthropology—history &c depending on the individual, but that somehow he must extend his range. I was however as happy as a man could desire but I felt that

rabia!' Later when asked what the horn was, he replied that he did not know, but he thought that if he had it he could have made a devil of a noise with it." Edmund A. Whitman to Holmes, March 9, 1931 (HLS).

[49] OS, 34, 43–44.

[50] Holmes to James Bryce, Aug. 17, 1879 (copy, HLS).

if I declined the struggle offered me I should never be so happy again—I should feel that I had chosen the less manly course.[51]

One strand of feeling in this tapestry of conviction deserves particular notice. At the very beginning of his legal career Holmes had hoped with passion that his study and his labor would lead him towards philosophy. His search had succeeded, for he had found that generalizations were possible—generalizations which said something of history, something of political theory, something of ethics. When he became a teacher of law he doubtless saw himself as once more confronted by the old challenge, as called upon again to deal with philosophical generalities. He came quickly to the realization, however, that further generalization, within the law, was not easy. He had already stated the fundamentals of his legal philosophy. To press beyond legal detail to more generalities would force him to travel another route than the lawyer's.

The law *stricto sensu* is a limited subject—and the choice seemed to be between applying one's theories to practice and details or going into another field—and apart from natural fear and the need of making a living I reasoned (at 40) that it would take another ten years to master a new subject and that I couldn't bargain that my mind should remain suggestive at that age. I think I was right, but there are many tempting themes on which it seems as if one could say something if one knew enough—I am glad on the whole that I stuck to actualities against philosophy (the interest of all actualities).[52]

Had Holmes, perhaps, become so accustomed to achievement under pressure that he could not easily adapt himself to the unhurried ways of scholarship? Was there also some recognition during the three months at Harvard that his greatest gifts and most ardent tastes were for clarifying *aperçus*, rather than for systematic thought? "I . . . love the *insouciance* of real intellect that just chucks down an idea, wriggling, and takes it or leaves it—instead of rigging up an image with a bogus sword and masonic jewels."[53]

[51] HLS.
[52] *HLL*, I, 281–282.
[53] To Lady Castletown, March 5, 1897 (copy, HLS).

The Common Law, of course, was something far more important than a compendium of insights, but other traits of intellect and character than those which gave that book its power would have been called upon to produce a systematic work on legal history or legal philosophy. Would not Holmes do better, and therefore find more satisfaction, in accepting the office of a judge than in assuming the role of a systematic thinker? His satisfaction might well lie in delivering perceptive judicial opinions rather than in pronouncing portentous philosophic judgments. In 1897, after fifteen years on the Supreme Judicial Court, he said that "the main excitement of life is the gradual weaving of one's contribution into the practical system of the law . . ." [54] When he made his great decision of 1882 surely the possibility of that excitement was an element which carried weight. The philosophic theses of *The Common Law* might be made working principles of the law of the Commonwealth.

In a letter written many years after the event, Holmes suggested that behind the brief and modest satisfaction which he had found in his professorship there had been some shadows of discontent:

> [A]cademic life is but half life—it is withdrawal from the fight in order to utter smart things that cost you nothing except the thinking them from a cloister. My wife thinks I unconsciously began to grow sober with an inarticulate sense of limitation in the few months of my stay at Cambridge . . . Business in the world is unhappy, often seems mean, and always challenges your power to idealize the brute fact—but it hardens the fibre and I think is more likely to make more of a man of one who turns it to success. [55]

Behind this reflection one may glimpse the spirit of the Puritan— the spirit which says that to take the easy way is to take the wrong way. "A man once wrote to me with some truth," Holmes said in 1913, "that the line of *most* resistance is the one to choose." [56] A strain of Puritanism doubtless may be found in Holmes's eagerness to accept a challenge of responsibility different from any he had

[54] *Id.*   [55] To Felix Frankfurter, July 15, 1913 (HLS).   [56] *Id.*

faced before, to deal officially with practical affairs which in themselves did not enlist his interest. Yet at least twelve years earlier Holmes had made a choice which foreshadowed that of 1882. He had determined that he would not retire wholly into the private world of learning and of thought. The Young Astronomer, still searching the heavens by evening, had by day gone into the streets among men and women. There, it seemed, he should remain, seeking, with new authority, to shape the common law.

Chronology

1841–1882

Born, March 8, 1841

Graduated, Harvard College, June 1861

Commissioned, Twentieth Regiment, Massachusetts Volunteers, July 1861

Wounded at Balls Bluff, October 21, 1861

Wounded at Antietam, September 17, 1862

Wounded near Fredericksburg, May 3, 1863

Mustered out, July 17, 1864

Graduated, Harvard Law School, June 1866

Visit to England and the Continent, May–August 1866

Admitted to the Massachusetts Bar, March 4, 1867

Begins work on 12th edition of Kent's *Commentaries*, 1869

Coeditor of American Law Review, 1870–1873

Practices law in association with his brother, 1871–1873

Lectures on Constitutional Law, Harvard College, 1870–1871

Lectures on Jurisprudence, Harvard College, 1872

Marriage to Fanny Bowditch Dixwell, June 17, 1872

Forms partnership with George Otis Shattuck and William A. Munroe, March 1873

Publication of 12th edition of Kent's *Commentaries*, December 1873

Trip to England and the Continent, summer of 1874

Delivers the Lowell Lectures on *The Common Law*, November and December 1880

Appointed Professor of Law, Harvard Law School, January 1882

Visit to England, summer of 1882
Begins his teaching at the Harvard Law School, September
1882
Appointed Associate Justice, Supreme Judicial Court, December 1882

Index

Absolute liability, 81, 185–188; of common carriers, 205 *et seq.*

Academic life, OWH's attitude towards, 280–281, 282

Acceptance, its relation to consideration, 242–243

Act, definition of, 190–192, 193

Action, OWH's respect for, 111

Adams, Brooks, 142 note

Adams, Charles Francis (1835–1915), 56–57, 58

Adams, Henry, 26–27, 31, 99, 142–148, 211, 212, 277; *Essays in Anglo-Saxon Law*, 145–148, 153, 212, 214; gives his law books to OWH, 146–147; *Education of Henry Adams*, 147

Admiralty, OWH's practice in, 108, 119, 125 *et seq.*, 131, 208–210; liability of vessels in, 160–161, 164; OWH's scheduled course in, 272

Advocacy, style of OWH's, 125–128; *see also* Briefs and arguments of OWH

Aeschylus, 112

Agency, OWH's Law School lectures and essays on, 273–274; *see also* Vicarious liability

Alden, Joseph, *Science of Government in Connection with American Institutions*, 27–28, 33

Allen, Charles, 132, 263

Alpha Delta Phi, OWH's address at in 1912, 112 note

Alpine Club, 100

Altruism, *see* Self-preference

Ambition, nature of OWH's, 5–7, 8, 14, 49–50, 101, 108–109, 132–133, 135, 153–154, 222, 253, 258, 259, 281–283

American Banana Co. v. *United Fruit Co.*, 75 note

American Law Review, 10, 93–94

Ames, James Barr, 140, 157, 229, 230, 248 note, 257, 263, 266, 280; his criticisms of OWH, 230–231, 278

Ames, Oakes A., 128–129

Ames, Oliver, 129

Ames, Seth, 259–260

Anglo-Saxon law, 145–148; *see also* Common law

Animals, liabilities for acts of, 81, 160–161; *see also* Vicarious liability

Animism, in primitive law, 162 *et seq.*, 166

Anson, Sir William R., 273; *Principles of Contract*, 157 note, 223 note, 225, 228, 233, 234, 244, 246

Anthropology, 149–150, 157

Armory v. *Delamirie*, 201

Arnold, George, 267

Arnold, John Himes, 266

"Arrangement of the Law—Privity," 9, 64 note, 69, 78 note, 79, 88, 93, 136

Askwith, Lady Ellen, 32 note

Assumpsit, 228–229, 230

Atchison, Topeka & Santa Fe Railroad, 112

Athenaeum, Boston, 106, 258 note

Austin, John, 18, 20, 47, 66–67, 68, 71–75, 93, 144, 154, 172, 174; his definition of law, 69–70, 185; his concept of duty, 76–78, 141; his theory of culpability, 80–82, 141, 161–162, 163–164, 184, 187, 236, 238; his definition of an act, 190–191; on Savigny, 203; *see also* Jurisprudence, analytical

Ayer, Mrs. James B., 255 note

Bad man theory of law, 238 note

Bailment, OWH's views concerning, 90–91, 204 *et seq.*

Balfour, Arthur, 101

Baltimore & Ohio Rd. v. *Goodman*, 250 note

Bancroft, George, 54

Barbour, W. T., 230, 276–277, 278–279

Bartlett, Sidney, 262

Index

Beaman, Charles C., 130
Becherdass Ambaidass, 10 note
Behrend, Jakob Friedrich, 153
Belper, Lord and Lady, 97
Bentham, Jeremy, 9, 20, 62–63, 65, 66, 140, 172, 177
Beven, Thomas, 188 note
Beveridge, Albert J., 34 note
Bigelow, Melville Madison, 139, 187 note, 212
Birth Control, *see* Eugenics
Bishop, Joel Prentiss, quoted, 177, 187
Blackstone, Sir William, 17, 138, 140–141, 202
Bolles, Frank, 266
Boston, OWH's feelings for, 100–101, 256; its feelings about OWH, 118, 256, 259 note
Boston Fire of 1872, 107
Bracton, 153, 166, 168, 247
Bradley, Joseph P., 129
Brahmins, New England, 1–2
Brandeis, Louis Dembitz, 110, 117 note, 264
Bridges v. *Hawkesworth*, 201
Briefs and arguments of OWH, 109 *et seq.*, 123, 208–210, 220–221; *see also* Advocacy, style of OWH's
Brooks, Phillips, 9, 256
Broughton, Rhoda, *Goodbye, Sweetheart,* 9
Brown, A., *Epitome and Analysis of Savigny,* 223 note
Brown University, address at, 3, 4
Brown v. *Collins,* 85 note
Brown v. *Eastern Slate Co.,* 235
Browning, Robert, 99
Brunner, Heinrich, 137–138, 167
Bruns, Carl Georg, *Das Recht der Besitzes,* 152, 204, 231
Bryce, James, 24, 31, 100, 102, 104, 154, 225, 273, 280–281; *Academical Study of the Civil Law,* 92
Buck v. *Bell,* 123
Burghclere, Lady, 101 note
Burt v. *Merchants' Insurance Co.,* 113
Business men, 111–112, 258
Butler, Peter, 129

Caird, Edward, *Critical Account of the Philosophy of Kant,* 152

Cambridge University, 104
Campbell, John, 98–99
Campbell, Robert, *The Law of Negligence,* 80 note, 86 note
Carlyle, Thomas, 11, 100, 259
Casanova, 258 note
Castletown, Lady, 102 note
Certainty in law, OWH's desire for, 196 *et seq.*
Chaos, common law as an index, 63
Character, Thayer's estimate of Holmes's, 13–14, 268
Chase, Salmon P., 33, 50–51
Children, 8 note, 99–100
Civil law, *see* Roman law
Civil Rights Acts, 34–37
Civil War, 1, 256, 257
Class legislation, 42–43, 47
Classification, *see* "Codes and the Arrangement of the Law"; "Arrangement of the Law—Privity"
Clifford, Nathan, 125–128, 208–210
Clifford, W. K., 104
Club, The, 142
"Codes and the Arrangement of the Law," 62 *et seq.*, 79, 83, 88–89
Codification, 62–63
Collectivism, 175–176
Colt, LeBaron Bradford, 133 note
Command, law as, 70, 80–81, 185
"Common Carriers and the Common Law," 133, 136, 204–205, 206
Common law, its Teutonic roots, 143–144, 146–148, 152–153, 205–207, 211–214, 228, 252, 277; OWH's excessive respect for, 250–251
Common Law, The, 133, 137–138, 148–149, 155, 281–282; its publication, 135; asked to produce, 136; OWH's estimate of its importance, 137; reviews of, 249–251
Commonwealth v. *Pierce,* 200 note
Commonwealth v. *Smith,* 183 note
Commonwealth v. *Sullivan,* 200 note
Communism, 47
Comte, Auguste, 67 note
Concordia, The, see *New Orleans Mutual Insurance Co.* v. *Nickerson*
Connecticut Trust Co. v. *Melendy,* 122
Consideration, its history, 226, 227, 228–230; defined, 226, 240–242; as form, 231–232

Index

Flirtatiousness of OWH, 98, 99

Force, *see* Power

Force Bill, *see* Civil Rights Acts

Forms of action, 63–64, 65–66, 189–190, 192, 193, 226

Forsyth, William, *History of Trial by Jury*, 153

Forty, achievement by, 8, 49, 135

Fourteenth amendment, 35–36

Frankfurter, Felix, 44 note, 210, 258 note

Freedom, individual, 46, 204, 216–217

Freeman, Edward A., 19, 138, 141 note, 146, 150

Friedrich, Carl J., 219 note

Froude, James Anthony, 150

Fustel de Coulanges, Numa Denis, 9, 144, 150

Gans, Edward, 152–204

Gaskell, Charles Milnes, 99

Gas-stokers strike, OWH comments on, 42 *et seq.*, 57

"Generality, featureless," 252

German, OWH's reading knowledge of, 141–142, 150–151

German historiography, 138, 141, 142–144, 214, 250; *see also* Roman law, German interpretations of

Germany, OWH visits, 273

Gibbon, Edward, 150

Giraud-Teulon, Alexis, *Les origines du mariage et de la famille*, 150

Glanville, 166

Globe Refining Co. v. *Landa Cotton Oil Co.*, 235

Grain elevators, 21; see also *Munn* v. *Illinois*

Granger Cases, see *Munn* v. *Illinois*

Gray, Asa, 256

Gray, Horace, 113, 115 *et seq.*, 130, 256, 260, 263, 264

Gray, John Chipman, 4, 18, 20, 67, 107, 130, 157–158, 257, 266, 267, 276

Gray, Russell, 20

"Great cases," OWH's attitude towards, 108

Green, John Richard, 146, 150

Green, Nicholas St. John, 18, 65, 75, 151

Gurney, Russell, 99

Güterbock, Karl Edward, *Bracton and His Relation to the Roman Law*, 153

Hall, Jerome, quoted, 181

Hammond, William G., 18

Hand, Learned, 8 note

Hannen, Sir James, 100

Hare, J. I. Clark, 230

Harriman, E. A., 232–233, 238 note

Harrison, Frederic, 123 note

Harvard College, 1886 address to students at, 4–5; lectures in, 24; methods of instruction in, 28; OWH's lectureships in, 61; *see also* Constitutional law, Harvard lectures on

Harvard Commencement dinner, OWH's address at in 1880, 257

Harvard Law Review, 140

Harvard Law School, OWH's 1872–73 lectureship in, 61; OWH as member of Committee of Overseers to visit, 257; OWH's professorship in, 231, 260 *et seq.*; OWH resigns professorship, 265 *et seq.*, 280–281; OWH's courses in, 1882, 272, 273 *et seq.*

Hayes, Rutherford B., 131, 132

Hegel, Georg Wilhelm Friedrich, OWH's hostility to, 151–152, 156–157, 169; his analysis of punishment, 169–170; on possession, 202–203

Heineccius, Johann Gottlieb, *Recitationes in elementa juris civilis*, 9

Hepburn v. *Griswold*, 50–52, 58

Heusler, Andreas, *Die Gewere*, 153, 212

Hill, James J., 112

Hill v. *Winsor*, 122, 123

Historical scholarship, 17, 19, 137–139, 144, 150, 212–213

History, the lawyer's uses of, 120–121, 144, 192, 194, 208–210, 221–222

History of law, OWH's interest in, 69, 82, 88–89, 91–92, 140–142, 211

Hoague, Isaac Taylor, 10 note

Hoar, George Frisbie, 132, 256

Hoar, Samuel, 94 note

Hobbes, Thomas, 46

Hodgson, Shadworth, 67 note

Holdsworth, Sir William, 230

Holland, Henry Ware, 249

Holland, Thomas Erskine, 63 note, 225, 233–234, 243, 246, 250, 273

Holmes, Amelia Jackson, *see* Sargent, Mrs. Turner

Holmes, Dr. Oliver Wendell, 1–2, 94,

Index

Index